A
WAY OF SEEING

Other Books by Margaret Mead

COMING OF AGE IN SAMOA

GROWING UP IN NEW GUINEA

THE CHANGING CULTURE OF AN INDIAN TRIBE

SEX AND TEMPERAMENT IN THREE PRIMITIVE SOCIETIES

FROM THE SOUTH SEAS

AND KEEP YOUR POWDER DRY

MALE AND FEMALE

THE SCHOOL IN AMERICAN CULTURE

SOVIET ATTITUDES TOWARD AUTHORITY

NEW LIVES FOR OLD: CULTURAL TRANSFORMATION—MANUS

AN ANTHROPOLOGIST AT WORK: WRITINGS OF RUTH BENEDICT

ANTHROPOLOGY: A HUMAN SCIENCE

CONTINUITIES IN CULTURAL EVOLUTION

CULTURE AND COMMITMENT

With Rhoda Metraux

THE STUDY OF CULTURE AT A DISTANCE

THEMES IN FRENCH CULTURE

A

WAY OF SEEING

MARGARET MEAD

and

RHODA METRAUX

The McCall Publishing Company

NEW YORK

Library of Congress Catalog Card Number: 71-104938

SBN 8415-0006-1

Grateful acknowledgment for permission to reproduce passages from
their work is made to Birgitta Linnér and Richard J. Litell, *Sex and
Society in Sweden* (New York, Pantheon Books, A Division of Random
House, Inc., 1967); to Konrad Lorenz, *On Aggression* (New York, Har-
court, Brace and World, Inc., 1966); and to Jan Yoors, *The Gypsies*
(New York, Simon and Schuster, Inc., 1967).
   "Margaret Mead's New Guinea Journal," directed and produced by
Craig Gilbert, 1968 (16 mm., 90 min., sound, color), is available through
National Educational Television, New York.

Printed in the United States of America
Design by Tere LoPrete

Contents

VI.   THE MEASURE OF FREEDOM: *New Guinea Revisited*

by Rhoda Metraux

Foreword

The essays gathered together in this volume were written over a period of eight years. This has been a time during which Americans have gained a new and sobering awareness of the state of the world. We have realized man's ancient dream of a journey into space. But we have also come to see more plainly some of the hazards of our dependence on an extremely complex technology. We have as yet gone only a little way toward solving the problems of which we have become aware. But we are moving, I believe, toward a deeper appreciation of the kinds of commitments we must make if we are to conserve and develop human potentialities in an emerging world civilization.

These essays are personal responses to events at different moments in time; as such, they reflect changes through which all of us have been living. However, they are grouped here not sequentially but in accordance with the standpoint from which they were written. Some have to do with the way we face the world, some with aspects of our lives as Americans and others with the changing personal relations of husbands and wives, parents and children and the situation of women at home and abroad. The last group has to do with field work in New Guinea. As we arranged these essays in clusters, we ourselves began to see more vividly the direction in which Americans have been moving than we could when the different topics were being commented upon month by month in the pages of *Redbook*.

Ten years ago interest in certain vital problems was limited to various small and specialized groups which had relatively little contact with one another. Today these same problems have become matters of urgent concern to vast numbers of people all around the world. The problems have not changed, except as they have become more acute, but we have become conscious of their impact on our lives. In the 1950's, for example, conservationists and city planners had few meeting points in their work. Saving wilderness areas and attempting to humanize urban living seemed to draw on very different interests and require very different kinds of knowledge and skill. One of the few areas of overlap was that of recreation for the millions of city dwellers whose demands for out-of-door playgrounds were increasing year by year. In the same period the small groups of responsible scientists who attempted to warn us about the transformation and possible destruction of the natural environment through the heedless misuse of modern technology gained a hearing only when they discussed the dangers of fall-out or the deadly effects of smog after a crisis in some specific city like Los Angeles. Today, however, the question of the protection of all aspects of the environment is one of worldwide concern and planning is under way for a United Nations conference on the subject in 1972.

Only a few years ago the majority of Americans thought that population control was a problem to be solved by others—the peoples of poor, backward and overpopulated countries. For ourselves, we believed that conception control was a matter of personal choice; the arguments for making information available were mainly pleas for compassion for individual overburdened mothers. Today we are coming to recognize that the protection of human beings, not only through the limitation of the number of children born anywhere in the world but also through education and new forms of social care, is a matter of concern to every individual.

Problems we were aware of earlier are now open to new interpretations. There are still students in Midwestern colleges whose activities echo the earlier mass invasions by young people of resorts such as Fort Lauderdale. But these aimless, destructive migrations look very different now in the light of serious student upheavals across the country and elsewhere in the world.

Above all, Americans are beginning to recognize how interwoven the questions are that vex our hearts and minds. No matter where one begins—whether with the students, with problems of civil rights, with the police, with the deterioration of the inner cities, with the pollution of the environment or with the development of a new ethic of responsibility—all the other problems come up also. Each is but a thread in the total fabric of our society.

The problems of smog and blight are not confined to the cities; traffic, overcrowding and air pollution are threatening even the wilderness areas of our national parks. The problems of the country-side, where there no longer is work for the poor, extend into the cities. The dissatisfactions of young people and their insistence on greater participation in decisions are challenges to customary be-havior and older values. The fact that their protests have been raised in many countries makes us aware that we are living, as never before, in an intercommunicating world.

Looking back, it seems to me that the most significant change in these years has been our growing awareness of the interconnection of problems and the interdependence of people not only in our own country but everywhere on our crowded planet. And, looking ahead, I think that anthropological perspectives on the problems we must face will become increasingly relevant. It is the anthropological view-point that gives focus and continuity to these many different essays on our contemporary life.

For anthropologists, whatever problem they may be working on, necessarily deal with a whole way of life. There is no facet of a people's existence that need not be taken into account. What their homes are like, how they classify their relatives, how they make a living, what they eat and who does the cooking, how they sing their babies to sleep, what they teach their children, how they think about illness and accidents, how they bury the dead, how they choose their leaders, how they see the past and the future, and how they think about the world and the nature of the universe—all these things enter into an interpretation of a people's way of life. However, it is not the details, as such, that matter but the relationships among them. This is why, I think, the life of a small primitive village, studied intensively, so that one comes to know every individual from the newest baby to the oldest grandparents, provides a perfect background for thinking about the problems of our own complicated world. Working on a small scale, anthropologists have learned not to fragment experience, but instead to see how each detail fits into the pattern of the whole.

Moreover, anthropologists are trained to think comparatively. No matter how different two societies are—whether both are small primitive societies that differ in their traditions, or both are modern nations that differ in their contemporary approach to political, economic and social problems, or one is a small tribe and the other a great nation—it is possible to compare their forms of organization, their ways of handling human relationships and their conceptions of man and the natural world. Anthropologists have learned not to make invidious comparisons, but to respect and attempt to understand what a people value in their culture. This does not mean that anthropologists deny the values of their own culture in an attempt to achieve a spurious objectivity. It does mean that they come to accept the values according to which they live as only one among many alternative ways of organizing human thought and emotion.

Going to the field, anthropologists expect to—hope to—struggle with new questions of how to make sense of an unfamiliar mode of living. Past experience provides a framework for thinking about what is strange; but the new experience also sheds a different light on what is already familiar.

Thinking about American culture as I meet with different audiences also has this kind of challenge for me. With every new question proposed to me by a particular audience, my memory takes me back to some experience in field work—to an early morning in Samoa forty years ago, to the market in a Balinese village twenty-five years ago, to Peri Village, in the Admiralty Islands, in 1928, when it seemed to me that only misery lay ahead for the proud Manus people, and to my visits to Peri in the past ten years, when Manus leaders have sat talking with me about their children's modern careers and the future of all the peoples of New Guinea.

These are the experiences on which I draw, and each new audience, concerned with a different problem, refocuses my thinking about the past and the present. But the vividness of field experience also enters into my awareness of an audience. I remember very vividly my first radio broadcast. It was in Australia. As I tried to focus words flung out into a void, I suddenly visualized mothers all over the country bathing and feeding their children, hustling them into their night clothes and tucking them into bed, while they half-listened to my talk. In order to speak to them, I found that I had to take into account all the other things the listening mothers must be doing at that hour.

I could see these mothers in my imagination, but I could not know how they responded to what I said. Today all this is changed. I can sit in New York and, using my own telephone, give a telelecture to students on seven different college campuses. At the end, each group of students can ask questions, so that we are all drawn together in our give and take. Or a lecture may be put on video tape. Then I can sit with the listening audience and participate in their responses. Over the years the audience has become far more a part of what is being said. The lecture and the monologue have become dialogues.

In much the same way these essays are a product of initiation and response. Readers send in questions, argue points, agree or explode in furious disagreement, and from all this we learn. There are also the occasions on which we have talked with a few of them as a group. Once on the anniversary of Hiroshima a group of young wives and mothers came together to discuss what they were doing and what they were telling their children about war and peace. On another occasion a group met with us to talk about their marriages and their hopes for their children's future. And as I go about the country giving lectures, there are very often young people in the audiences who identify themselves as readers by their comments on one or another of the *Redbook* columns. Later, when the next column is in the making, I remember what they have said. All this is what makes the material come alive for me.

Rhoda Metraux and I have worked on these essays together as part of our continuing work on American culture. Our collaboration began in Washington, during World War II, when we made studies of American attitudes toward nutrition, rationing and the problems of feeding Europe after the war. Later we worked together on studies of culture at a distance—on France, Russia, China and Germany. These, in turn, led to other American studies.

Our experiences as anthropologists are complementary. My field work has been carried out in the South Seas and with American Indians. Hers has taken her to Haiti, Mexico and Montserrat in the West Indies. Her experience in Europe has been with people in Germany, France and Switzerland; I have known best the English-speaking peoples of Great Britain, Australia and New Zealand. In 1967 we went together to Tambunam Village on the Sepik River, in

New Guinea, where I picked up the threads of my relationships to the Iatmul people with whom I had worked in 1938 and she stayed for eight months to study the life of the present generation.

We grew up a little more than a decade apart. I was a teen-ager in World War I and a college student in the early 1920's. Rhoda Metraux was born in 1914 and entered college in 1930. Though we danced to some of the same tunes, the lively melodies of the 1920's already had a nostalgic ring to those who, as they came of age, were humming the melancholy songs of the Depression years. I have a daughter and she has a son; they too are a decade apart in age. This summer I acquired a grandchild and she acquired a daughter-in-law. So our lives, differently placed in time, have complemented each other in phase.

Every topic on which we have worked together for a *Redbook* column has been a starting point for heated discussion. At different times these discussions have led to excursions into books, comparisons of our experiences in the field, the collection of a new body of materials or the review of some older study for its relevance to a new situation. Then, very often, there has been a round of discussions with the editors of *Redbook*. For sometimes things that were self-evident to us seemed odd or mysterious to them. Please spell it out, they have said. And we have tried to do so, for the editors speak in the name of the audience, to whom they are very close. Finally, there have been the responses of the readers themselves, who have contributed new ideas out of their own experience.

This complex interplay makes us feel that these essays are, in a very real sense, a co-operative venture. Their publication in this volume provides a new point of departure in a continuing dialogue. And only as we communicate with one another can we consciously shape our changing world closer to what we hope for the future.

MARGARET MEAD

I

PERSPECTIVES ON THE WORLD

And Children Shall Lead the Way

FEBRUARY, 1967

In our world, where simple and complex societies are trying together to plan a common future, what hope is there? Can countries with traditions so totally different from the technologically advanced nations participate fully in the world of today, much less the world of tomorrow? Will the people of such countries as India and China, for instance, or of Ghana and New Guinea be able to make the necessary adaptations? Can they absorb and make use of the changes that will certainly come in five, ten, twenty-five years?

Sometimes the people of a country or an area or a whole continent seem to be making tremendous progress in altering their ways of life. For instance, statistics from one country after another make clear that the adoption of modern public-health practices in protecting women and children has extended the gift of life to untold millions within one generation. But more people require more of everything necessary to keep them alive—food, above all, but also competence in the technology that goes into making life in close quarters feasible. In these changing lands, a larger population means a much more complicated social structure; it means the necessity of adapting to the continual presence of strangers; it means contact with a great variety of unfamiliar ideas.

The history of the United Nations within less than a generation records the tremendous movement of the world's peoples toward independent statehood and self-government. Even in faraway New Guinea, where men and women who are alive today were born into a Stone Age culture, adult suffrage has been introduced and children are being schooled to live in the space age. The peoples of Africa are struggling with the problems of national identity that in other forms have plagued the European community for a thousand years. The people of China are trying to transform in one generation a civilization that was ancient when our own first took shape.

Every society, simple or complex, is affected by change, and many peoples are struggling to find their way into the modern world. Can they change themselves? Can they catch up?

For that matter, we must ask whether our own people can catch up—the white children in Appalachia, the Negro children in big-city ghettos, the Indians boxed in on their reservations and all those who have been deprived, for whatever reason, of the social experiences that make new forms of adaptation easier. Can they become full participants in twentieth-century living? Can they learn the new traditions quickly enough?

Americans as a people have always been optimistic. We have built a whole civilization on our belief in progress and on our conviction that whoever came to this country could learn to accept change and adopt the way of life common to our citizens. But what grounds for optimism do we have now when we realize that all of us—even those Americans who have had the greatest advantages—wonder how we are going to cope with the changes that lie ahead? When we realize the distances that must be covered by the hundreds of millions of people whose past is very different and who have different views even about the desirability of technology?

Certainly there seem to be grounds for pessimism. The acceleration of change is such that good communication between grandparents, parents and children is becoming difficult, even among the well educated. In the scholarly fields, humanists trained in traditional forms are losing contact with scientists breaking old bounds. The few who pioneered a new technology find themselves separated from the many who are now turning the pioneering visions into practice. If the Western countries, long accustomed to coping with change, are having difficulties, won't the years ahead be infinitely more difficult for societies where change has not been part of the way of life?

These pessimistic questions, it seems to me, are based on an outmoded way of thinking about *how* change takes place. They are based on the assumption that progress is a kind of obstacle race in which everyone who runs must cover exactly the same course, step by step, meeting and overcoming exactly the same difficulties that hampered those who came before. We must examine the premise— the false premise, I should say—that the present level of the culture of a country or of deprived groups within a country is the only significant determinant of how far a people can go in the future and how fast they can move.

In the nineteenth century, when modern social science was in the making, there was a great deal of speculation about the origins of civilization and the possible "stages" of human social, as well as physical, evolution. Some theorists believed that all human institutions had evolved in a definite series of steps, the "highest" of which were represented by the institutions of the Western world. Marriage, for example, was believed to have evolved from primitive forms of "group marriage," finally bringing into being modern marriage forms and ways of counting descent.

This evolutionist hypothesis was exploded by careful studies of primitive peoples and comparisons between actual institutions in cultures that varied in style and complexity. No fixed stages were found, no necessary successions of steps in marriage forms, in ways of handling property and other economic relations or in the basic styles of social organization. "Savagery" and "barbarism" lost their specific meanings as names of stages of development toward "civilization."

The hypothesis that human institutions must evolve was exploded, but the habit of thinking this way remained with us. We did know that *individuals* make the tremendous leap from one kind of society to another when they have a chance to experience fully the ways of living and thinking in the new society. And we knew also that masses of immigrants can change their way of living if their children are welcomed into schools and the schools prepare them—and through them, their parents—for new kinds of jobs and new ways of carrying on their lives. But we never generalized from this. It was easier to assume (as we did in making our earlier immigration laws) that certain peoples were less able, that they had to accomplish too many steps in order to arrive.

But today all adults are immigrants in a changing world. And in the same measure all children, in whatever part of the world they are growing up, are native to a kind of world in which they take for granted the thinking toward which their parents can only grope. In 1957, when Sputnik was launched, American and Russian children were fully able to visualize our new relationship to space as a reality; a few years later, among the Manus of the Admiralty Islands, school children expressed almost identical ideas about space exploration. The young are able to adapt because they are not burdened or confused by out-of-date information.

We adults, on the other hand, with our heavy burden of "knowledge," can move forward with greater speed and consistency only to the extent that we can absorb and assimilate change.

It is technology that has transformed the present world, and it is technology that can help now in the creation of a shared future for all the peoples of the earth. We cannot share in the past of peoples whose traditions are very different from ours, nor can others share easily in our past. But now that the whole world, through technology, experiences events simultaneously, we can share with one another the task of making a common future. The special problem we have is not how to help anyone "catch up," but how to create a framework within this new and ever-changing world that will help all the living generations of adults, including ourselves, become citizens of the community of which our children are the true natives.

A World of Cities: Delos Symposion

FEBRUARY, 1966

Someday will the whole world be a city? We have had to coin a new word—megalopolis—for the vast areas of ungainly, fragmented urban sprawl in which hundreds of millions of people already live, and we are facing the prospect that very soon, by the year 2000, the majority of mankind will be city dwellers. This is an extraordinary transformation. Looking backward through five thousand years of history, we can see that the city has been the cradle of civilization and progress. But few of the cities of the past were very large by modern standards, and until recently only a small proportion of the world's peoples lived an urban life.

Now all this has changed. The tide of movement away from the country that began a hundred years ago has become a racing flood, and now it is the cities that support our way of life. Yet, everywhere, people also are moving out, trying to escape from crowded, noisy streets, from traffic and bad housing, from the ugliness of huge areas of our present cities. While they move out, others move in, and the city grows and spreads into the green countryside. The time has come when we must ask: How can the world of the future—a world of cities—be made a fit home for all mankind?

This was the problem that brought the members of the Delos Symposion together in Athens in the summer of 1965 for their third meeting. I was one of thirty-five men and women who came from far places to consider how cities might be planned so that people would be glad to live in them and would feel that they were living fruitfully.

The Delos Symposion is the creation of Constantinos Doxiadis, director of the Athens Technological Institute. We were his guests during the meetings. Dr. Doxiadis is a Greek builder and planner whose urban studies and projects for urban renewal and development have taken him to many parts of the world. He is also the key figure in the formation of the very new applied science of ekistics—the science of human settlement.

In our discussions we looked back to the most distant beginnings of civilization and then forward to a world of cities in an effort to grasp what is essential to ekistics, a science in the making. But the Delos Symposion was a great deal more than a meeting. It was also, figuratively and literally, a voyage. We lived on board a ship, the *Semiramis*, and cruised the windy blue Aegean Sea, and every day we gathered in the lounge for long hours of discussion. In a real sense this was a voyage into the future and into the past.

For one absorbing week we sailed among the Greek islands, sighting some only as dim shadows on the horizon and dropping anchor at others—Skíathos, Thásos, Sámos, Rhodes, Santorin, Míkonos and finally, as in other years, Delos, the ancient center of the Athenian confederacy and the place from which our symposium took its name. As we approached these islands, where long ago men had laid out towns and cities with a fine logic and sense of form, and as we went ashore to walk among the fallen columns of an ancient temple or a market place, the past fused with the present. Standing on a hilltop that commanded a harbor, listening to actors playing a classic Greek tragedy in an ancient amphitheater, gathered before the austere, archaic representation of a pagan god or walking in the footsteps of philosophers whose thinking brought us to our present state of great power and great peril, we could not but feel a sense of pride and triumph in the works of man.

In our discussions we recalled how, after a million years of living as hunters and gatherers, men invented the prerequisites of the city—reliable food resources; buildings and walls giving safe shelter; forms of organization enabling large numbers of people to live close together; scripts allowing them to keep records; and written laws making it possible for city dwellers to keep the peace, preserve their traditions, and work, paint and philosophize together. We considered how these Greeks, when they built their cities, drew on traditions of city life that were already very old, and we discussed why the Greek civilization we know represents a high point in man's achievement. We imagined how, in the ancient world, these island towns and cities must have been seen as symbols of something new and modern. And then when we came to a deserted island where the sea birds cry over the forsaken stones and only the faint outlines of tumbled walls speak of a different past, we were reminded that the Greeks, like other men of antiquity, had failed in the end to maintain the proud cities they had built and cherished.

What we saw on inhabited islands brought us back sharply to the task we faced in our daily discussions. For sometimes we came to villages peopled only by the very old and the very young, villages where the last able-bodied men were leaving their herds of sheep, their slow-yielding olive groves, and their fishing boats rocking in the harbor to go to work in factories in western Europe. In this sad present we saw what is left behind when people move away by the millions from their traditional homes into the strangled slums of great cities and the ramshackle shantytowns surrounding them. By contrast, the crumbling, half-deserted villages—and even the gay ones rebuilt for foreign visitors—gave poignant meaning to the grim statistics of the millions that somehow must be housed in cities before the year 2000—the people already on the move, and their children who will be born to city life.

At best, these lost splendors and sad failures of the past gave us a framework for looking at the splendors and the failures of the world we live in—the new buildings rising steep and high to accommodate the multitudes cramped in an island city like Hong Kong, the shacks spreading for miles around a city like Calcutta, the new buildings rising out of bombed ruins in cities like London and Hiroshima, and the vast rows of small houses in the suburbs that are eating up the once-fertile countryside around our own seaboard cities. The early navigators had sailed adventurously and perilously, as traders, travelers and conquerors, on the inland Aegean Sea. On our own voyage, the beauty of the scene, the brilliance of the light, the majesty and desolation of the ruins, kept us continually aware of what is at stake for the future.

Among the thirty-five members of the symposium many were architects, planners and engineers—men who are planning new towns, struggling with the development of whole regions, studying

the network of communications for a whole country or battling just
to get roofs over the heads of people now living in mud huts or even
on city streets. But because the building of cities and the organization
of urban living require a great orchestration of skills and vision, there
were also among us philosophers, historians, biologists, economists,
administrators, anthropologists, jurists, business executives and states-
men.

In this gathering, the sole purpose of which was to bring ways of
thinking together in a setting in which new ideas can flourish, the
experience of each contributed to the knowledge of all. We were
given estimates of population growth; world ore resources; space
requirements of each family as the standard of living rises around the
world; ratios between travel, work and leisure time as distances between homes, places of work and recreation areas increase. We were
given a picture of the waste, the destruction and the health hazards
caused by careless pollution of earth, water and air. There were accounts of how heedless travelers' feet are wearing down antiquities.

Arnold Toynbee, the British historian, sketched out the kinds of
cities known in history—the city-state, the capital city, the trading
city, the holy city, the fortress city, the port and the river cities, the
modern industrial city. I traced man's earliest and oldest needs, which
must still be met in whatever future man devises for himself. My
fellow anthropologist, Edward Hall, pointed to the complications
that arise when peoples of very different traditions are thrown into
close contact with one another. Buckminster Fuller, the visionary
engineer, talked about the new materials, the new techniques of con-
struction and the new conceptions of design that can revolutionize
building. Barbara Ward, the British economist, raised questions about
the economics of developing countries. Dinos Doxiadis, our host,
spoke of how we must maintain a human scale in designing what he
calls Ecumenopolis, the settlement that sooner or later will stretch in a
continuous network over all the habitable parts of the earth.

We considered how man shares the physical needs of all living
creatures, including the need for space—and how men have cherished, generation after generation, their particular ways of life. We
tried to think about the kind of life all human beings might have once
they were freed from hunger and want. We also saw that the city is a
trap for the millions who are fleeing from the hardship and hunger of

the countryside, only to find desolation and despair in the city that was not built to receive them.

As best we could we thought about all these things at once, because this is the kind of bringing together of problems and possibilities that must take place if we are to succeed where earlier civilizations failed. In the past, each civilization tried to keep itself intact, like people living within a walled town. Yet each civilization, even that built by Rome, was too small to impose itself everywhere; its means were too fragile to withstand the onslaught of strangers from beyond its borders; its conceptions were too limited to become the heritage of many peoples.

In the past men built for a kind of static stability. The beautiful building retained its perfection only as long as it stood unchanged. The city preserved its symmetry only as long as each structure—the cathedral or the temple, the market place, the public forum—kept its traditional relationship to all others. Such cities changed very slowly, step by step. Today we have the means to plan for long-term growth, using new materials and new techniques; but we have yet to grasp the idea of a dynamic, growing city, a city built for change, where old activities can develop in new centers and in new mosaic patterns.

Looking ahead, we realized that today the world's safety lies in cities that will flow into each other and allow for the free movement of people in every part of the world. On this point there was agreement among us. The whole world must become as one city, where all are citizens and all are willing to take responsibility for one another.

As we talked together it also became clear that if we can come to think of the whole planet as our living space, then the peopled earth can have no single center of control, no walls within which groups can close themselves in and no dangerous and endangered borders for outsiders to penetrate. Slowly, as we incorporate into our thinking the new dynamics of air transport and electronic communication, centers in the old sense will disappear. We shall have neither the walled city of the ancient world nor the disordered confusion of today's megalopolis. Instead we shall begin to create a world-wide mosaic of interests and activities that will reflect on a planetary scale the mosaic of life in each city, and we shall move toward a dynamic stability that includes all men.

Planful thinking on a world scale—not a blueprint for the future

but an appraisal of the needs and possibilities of a changing world—
this is what the Delians have been invited to attend to in each
summer's symposium. And at the end of the voyage each returns
home, enriched as an individual, to translate this thinking into the
terms of some local problem for which he has a working responsibility. In our world, unlike the world of the past, we can travel in a
few hours to any part of the earth and we can include the world's
past in our thinking, remembering and cherishing not the traditions of
one civilization but of our human heritage as we look toward a very
different future.

One World—But Which Language?

❦❦❦❦❦

APRIL, 1966

How shall we begin to talk with one another all around the globe? What language shall we use? Must we forever be dependent on interpreters? Will the speakers of a few major languages—Chinese, English, Russian, Spanish and French—dominate the earth? Must we lose the "little" languages? Or can we make a choice that will include all the world's peoples?

We are in the process of creating a new civilization in which, for the first time, people everywhere are beginning to take part in the events that are shaping our common future. The realization of the dream of world-wide communication and the growing belief that men *can* plan for change are opening new potentialities for human relationships. But there is a paradox. For although our ability to see and hear has been vastly expanded, we still cannot talk with one another easily or on an equal basis. With every door of communication opening wide, we are held back by the barrier of language.

It has been estimated that there are some three thousand "known" languages. But this does not include a very large number of living languages spoken by people whose voices are just beginning to be heard in the modern world. And looking ahead, we must think in terms of all the languages there are, not only of the few we are familiar with—even if we do not speak any but our own and perhaps one more. But we must also ask whether the idea of protecting the dignity of all languages is compatible with the hope of giving all men the chance to talk with one another.

In the past, when only a few travelers made their way to far-off places, they translated their experiences of new landscapes and new peoples, strange sights and sounds and smells, as best they could into their own tongue. Often, of course, they introduced new words along with the exotic things they brought back home. Commonplace English words like *coffee, tea, chocolate, tomato, tapioca, tobacco* and *cola* all carry distant echoes of adventurous travel, modified to fit the sound patterns of English. And when people went abroad as conquerors, traders or colonists, two things were very likely to happen. Those who were dominant imposed their own language as the high-level mode of communication; and very often they made use of a trade language or "pidgin" as a low-level mode of communication. Both practices accentuated the differences of those who came into contact with one another.

Today all this is changing, and perhaps the necessity of making a new choice presents to us a unique opportunity. We can, if we will, do away with the inevitable inequalities existing between native and foreign speakers of the major languages. It is not enough to have a few people who can converse comfortably or even many people who can address one another formally and correctly. The very rapid movement of jokes and slang, fashions and fads and slogans from one continent to another suggests that even now people, especially young people, are struggling to create a kind of common idiom in spite of language barriers. This may well be the moment, while world-wide communication is a new phenomenon, to establish a secondary world language that all the world's peoples will learn, in addition to their own, for use around the whole earth.

There are those who believe that the choice is already being made. They point to the number of people everywhere who are using one or another of the major languages for business, science and international politics. If they are right, sooner or later the languages of the most populous and powerful advanced nations will swamp the smaller languages and the world will be more strongly than ever divided into blocs. But I believe the choice is still open. If we can move fast enough, we may arrive at a decision that will bring people every-where into more meaningful contact.

It is possible that Americans may play a decisive role in what happens. We have had a very special relationship to foreign languages ever since English won out over all the languages of other colonists and, later, of immigrants who came to this country. However, the kind of choice we make will depend on our contemporary interpretation of our historic linguistic tradition.

From one point of view, the more obvious one, we have rejected every language other than our own in our developing of American English. Our insistence that every child in school must be taught in English and that adults, for the most part, must use English in their work has meant two things. Native speakers of English were freed from the necessity of ever having to learn another language and all others broke their ties to the past by giving up their native tongue. Adequate English became a symbol of full citizenship. Those who did not learn it were cut off from freedom of movement out of their own language group, and even from some kinds of intimacy with their American-educated, English-speaking children. Foreign languages became something you might study—but seldom learned to speak—in school.

Only in World War II, when we discovered that it was very inconvenient to be engaged on a world scale and ignorant on a world scale, did we recognize the wastefulness of this. Then suddenly we found that we could teach—and thousands of young men could learn—the most "difficult" languages fast and well. Fortunately, the spark of interest and the curiosity about languages is still alive.

From another point of view, the less obvious one, our insistence on the primacy of English has had as its basis the deep belief that a common language is crucial for social unity. As one result, even in the period of our greatest linguistic isolationism, a few Americans began to campaign for a world language. Out of the tradition that you could be fully American only if you spoke American English they drew the idea that the beginning of world community depended on the invention of a new, artificial language for world-wide use. Since this would be the language of no nation, it could, without offending anyone, become everyone's language.

What these pioneers did not notice, however, was that each of these invented languages, because it was basically a simplification of existing European languages, would still give tremendous advantages to those who spoke any one of them. Conversely, these artificial languages offered little to all those with a different linguistic tradition. So the various candidate languages were tried out—in vain. This, of course, did a great deal of harm, for with each failure the danger increased that more people would treat the idea and the advocates of an auxiliary universal language as silly, boring and cranky.

Why, then, are we coming back to the idea? In fact, we have not "come back" but have moved in a new direction. Recently students of the relationship between language and culture, working together with the new scientists of the cybernetic revolution, have learned a great deal about natural languages—all languages that have been molded by the speech of many people over many generations. Especially important has been the concept of redundancy that has been developed by electronic engineers.

This concept has to do with the patterning of the different aspects of speech and with what happens when the patterning is broken or distorted by some kind of interference or "noise." For example, how much can be left out and how much must be expressed in more than one way for someone to understand what is being said to him in a transatlantic telephone call? Using the concept of redundancy, linguists began to think afresh about the usefulness of all the elements, the different kinds of patterning, that give complexity and richness to natural languages. This in turn gave them the essential clue to the unworkability of artificial languages, except for very special purposes. These languages lack the resources of redundancy that make natural languages such good instruments for the most diverse users.

In the abstract, redundancy is a complicated concept, partly because it involves all the levels of speech. But every child, learning to speak, masters its uses in practice, and all of us are aware of some of the elements. Listening to a United Nations debate without seeing the speakers, anyone can tell when there is a language switch. Though we may not understand a word, our ear informs us that we are now listening to a different combination of sound patterns as well as different patterns of intonation, pitch and rhythm.

In the same way, listening to a group of English speakers whose words we do understand, we can—with a little practice—identify one as an Australian, another as a Scot and a third as a South African by consistent variations not only in sound, intonation and rhythm patterns but also in grammatical usage and the meanings given to words and expressions. As we listen, any one or all of these sets of variations may be (from our point of view) "noise"—something that interferes with our understanding of what is said—and yet, because we share what is basic to the language, usually we do get the message.

We can think of speech (spoken language) as consisting of inter-related sets of patterns, each of which, as it is used, gives us specific information. In English, for example, intonation informs us as to whether a speaker is asking a question, making a statement or issuing a command. As spoken, "Go!" sounds very different from "Go?" or "Go." Even if we do not catch the word itself, we do grasp part of the speaker's intended meaning. And when a German or a Frenchman speaks grammatically correct English but uses the intonations of his own language, we may miss a part of the message but still get the part that is communicated, in this case, by words and grammar.

Redundancy refers to the fact that the same or related or con-firming information is given by different means—at different levels, through different sets of patterns and by different elements within the same set—all interlocking in speech. A single sentence can illustrate how redundancy works. If someone said to you, "Mary had her new hat on yesterday," you would recognize this as English from the sound pattern itself. A drop in the speaker's voice at the end would tell you that this was a statement, not a question; the position of the first two words ("Mary had," not "Had Mary") would suggest the same thing. "Mary" would tell you that this was a girl; "her" would confirm your expectation. The form of the verb would tell you the event was in the past; "yesterday" would confirm this and pinpoint the time. This is, of course, a simplification and only a beginning. And if one adds that gesture and posture play a part in communication, the range within which redundancy operates is widened even further.

The important thing is that each language has its own range and regularities of patterning at all levels—on which the poet and the tone-deaf person and the little child will draw, although with a very differ-ent appreciation of the resources of the same language. Yet each can make himself understood. We are learning today that deaf children who can "hear" language rhythms only when they are magnified in special earphones can still in this way get a firm grasp of how their language operates in speech.

A language that works has been shaped by men and women, old people and little children, intelligent people and dunces, people with good memories and people with poor memories, those who pay attention to form and those who pay attention to sound, and people with all the diversity of interests present in their culture over generations. This very multiplicity of speakers creates the redundancy that makes a language flexible and intelligible to all different kinds of people who are its speakers at any time. A natural language allows for the whole range of human intelligence and responsiveness, and it is far richer and more expressive than are any individual's capacities for using it. This is why the invented languages failed—each in its form presented only a very limited set of possibilities worked out by a few people in only one period.

And this is why, if we are to have a universal language, it must be a natural language. It must have the complex resources on which all the world's people can draw. But it cannot be one of the present-day major languages now in competition. For we need to protect all the languages there are. Soon diversity of language will be the principal remaining evidence of man's extraordinary inventiveness in creating different ways of living, and language will have to carry the sense of intimacy in a way of life and the continuity of long generations. As American English expresses our deepest values and other languages give us insight into the values of other peoples, so also every language carries that which is most significant for its native speakers.

In time, this is also what a universal secondary language must carry for the peoples of the whole world—the significance of worldwide talking with one another within a shared civilization. If we chose as a secondary language the natural language of a small, politically un-important, non-European literate people, we could accomplish our several purposes.

It can be done now. It may be very difficult to do later.

Church and Society

JULY, 1967

It is the way of those who follow the Judaeo-Christian path to be troubled, to search the sky and their own hearts for signs and portents that all is not well. Such exercises of furious and exacting imagination often are followed by long periods of what some call stagnation and apathy and others call betrayal—times when the flame of religious witness burns very low, the young men who should be seeing visions turn elsewhere and the life of the church gives little light to the world.

We are just emerging from a period in which it seemed that the churches were powerless to wrestle with new forces of world-wide revolution, with new forms of warfare that threaten all mankind, and with new powers derived from science that give man incalculable capacities either to destroy the world or make it anew. With these earth-shaking changes, a new sense of helplessness, of being strangers in a world too large to love, has fallen upon many churches. But from this sense of weakness, ignorance and humility, out of this need to reach out for help, there can come the strength that will make the Christian churches of this world a mighty force to temper the storm that has been released, not by wickedness and sin, but by knowledge we do not know how to use.

Millions of people die today where hundreds died before: of hunger, of diseases that could be cured, in massacres, in wars that we have not learned to prevent. But these millions who suffer do not challenge our Christian compassion, do not brand us as sinful, more than one unanswered cry of needless suffering from a single child.

What these millions do challenge is our understanding. The Christian message has slumbered, locked in ancient and loved institutional forms; and although the residue of ages of belief has provided secular man with a conscience to question what is happening in the world, it has given him neither grace nor faith to cope effectively with the new dangers and the new possibilities.

In July, 1966, when I went to Geneva to attend the World Conference on Church and Society, which had been convened by the World Council of Churches, it seemed to me that this meeting of more than four hundred theologians and laymen was itself a recognition of the need for a new form of Christian responsibility. Christians from every continent, from old and new societies, of every race and of many faiths and practices, men and women, old and young, were gathered together to ask: What is our place in this new world?

It was the more momentous because the active participants included not only men and women who had dedicated their vocational lives to religion, but also laymen whose competence the ministries had formerly treated with tolerance at best and at worst with disdain.

The fact that many of us were asked to speak as social scientists, to discuss with churchmen what we had learned from the secular study of mankind, seemed to me a measure of the new participation by the churches in a pluralistic world. Following is my address to the conference.

In the two thousand years of Christian history we have substituted the nation for the tribe, the city-state and the empire; now we are in the process of trying to invent the structures that will contain nations safely within a world order of law, through which the love of man for man can be expressed. We learned to plant and to reap so effectively that today it is possible for one man to feed fifty or even a hundred others, and feed them well. We invented machines that dehumanized men in factories and mines; and now we have made new inventions that will make it possible to invest men with a fuller humanity than they had before. During earlier centuries of the Christian era there were many things that we could do only on a small, symbolic scale—washing the feet of a few beggars, binding up the wounds after a battle we did not have the understanding to prevent, feeding a few orphans. All these things men can now do on a world scale, thanks to the growth of human knowledge. We no longer need close our eyes to the thousands just over the mountain and sea for whom we can do nothing, for we are no longer helpless.

Science has given us ways to make the deaf hear and the lame walk, to feed the hungry and to know that all men are brothers, not only to the eye of faith and the heart of love, but also because we belong to one species among the creatures of the earth. Now in this modern, intercommunicating world we not only can see and hear one another half a world away, but we also can meet together and know one another for neighbors within the human community and brothers as the children of God.

The Conference on Church and Society is significant because it is one of an increasing number of attempts by Christians to come to grips with the results of scientific changes in the world. But such conferences will fail if they only provide sounding boards for those caught in the midst of change and opportunities for the expression of sympathy from those who look on. If these meetings are to make a difference to the world, those of us who take part in them and those of us who are in sympathy with their aims must take from them a sense of what needs to be done in the world and try to understand how to do it.

The form of sin changes through history. It is fruitless and wanton to stigmatize as sinful men who failed because they had neither the knowledge nor the opportunities we have today. And they did not wholly fail; that we today are asking what we can do testifies to this. But now it is sinful to be ignorant where knowledge is available, to neglect the search for knowledge we have the means of obtaining, to doubt that the truth can make us free.

One task of the church, the task of stewardship, is, as it has always been, to cherish and protect the lives of men and the life of the world. Today, as never before, it is possible to carry out this task.

But it is also possible for us to fail altogether, not just for a decade or a century, but forever. Our responsibility involves moral and ethical problems of new and awesome dimensions in a world in which billions of people live and which we have the power to devastate and make totally uninhabitable. If we cringe before these immense new powers, if we escape into our churches and chapels only to comfort ourselves with our own private faith, we shall indeed have betrayed the Lord who said: *Feed my lambs.*

In the past the Christian could pray for peace; he could die at the stake for his beliefs; he could sell all his goods and give to the poor. With such acts earlier Christians built a climate of opinion in which today we can organize for peace, create a world of law in which men are free to think and to choose and work toward the knowledge of how to feed all the hungry.

It is now the task of the churches to know, with precision and passion, what is known—about the organization of nations and the growth of international institutions that can ensure peace and order; about the need for and the ways of curbing the population explosion before it plunges mankind into famine; about the economics of the modern world and the limitations involved in different kinds of markets which make either poor people poorer under private capitalism or poor nations poorer under state monopolies.

It is the task of the churches to know that the forms of family life that once were appropriate for scattered agricultural and pastoral peoples, with a high infant death rate, are out of date and terribly dangerous. It is the task of the churches to know the difference between the industrial revolution, which was based on limited power and brutalizing work, and the new scientific revolution, which can free men from being slaves but involves new risks for men as individual persons. It is the task of the churches to know that our land and air and water are being polluted, wasted and irreversibly damaged, and that this need not be.

Churches have many old, incompleted tasks. We have yet fully to affirm that we are the keepers of those who live nearby—the young, the poor, the deprived at our doorstep. We still must learn not to denigrate others because their skin is dark or light. We must come to treat all women as people. But the circumstance that old tasks such as these are uncompleted is no excuse for not undertaking the new. We cannot stop at underlining our past failures—the things we could have done and did not, long ago or even a quarter of a century ago. The uncompleted business of yesterday must be absorbed into the business of today and tomorrow.

In the past we had three principal forms of Christian community. The all-embracing medieval church contained the wise and the foolish, the devout and the frivolous, the old and the young, the rich and the poor, the educated and the uneducated, the frightened and the brave. By its all-inclusiveness the church also became almost identical with the society within which it existed, sharing the virtues and vices, the prejudices and biases, the injustices and cruelties of that society, even while carrying forward the continuing message of the Christian gospel. Within this church, which became coextensive with whole communities, there were two forms of special dedication: the monastic religious order, self-selected from each generation and drawing its strength from its separation from the world, and the sect, in which a group of people originally aflame with a new vision drew apart within narrow walls in a vain attempt to keep the original vision.

These old patterns are no longer enough. The churches must shake themselves loose from their imprisonment within the archaic forms of vanishing societies. They must establish new forms of face-to-face community within which children, as they are reared, can experience faith and adults, having learned neighborliness to those close to them, can extend their sense of community to include the whole world. We need wholly new forms also in which men and women of every calling can enter into new kinds of associations within which they can strengthen one another against the temptations to use the powers given by new knowledge without responsibility or humility. Given freedom and individuality within the Christian church in an open-ended secular society, there is need also for new institutions through which to exercise the new knowledge.

There have been ages and places where Christian witness meant withdrawal from the world; there have been other ages and places where witness meant suffering and dying; there have been still other ages and places where deeds of helpfulness—caring for the orphan and the widow, the sick and the stranger—have been the principal tasks. Today churches have a threefold task: to understand what is happening, to use with wisdom and dedication all that is known, and to demand that the search for new knowledge continue unabated.

In particular, we need the support of the churches for the application of all existing knowledge to the cause of world order, international law and world-wide institutions; the establishment of food banks around the world to guard against famine; application of known methods and continued research on new methods of conception control to bring the population of the earth into balance; interim measures to bridge the gap between the richest and the poorest countries; the equalization of opportunity for racially and socially deprived peoples in all nations; the purposeful, controlled planning of our growing cities; opportunities for youth to participate responsibly in the modern world.

Only with such support from the churches can we hope to build a world in which the people of each nation are the keepers of the people of each other nation. With knowledge and no faith, we may well see a world destroyed. With faith and no knowledge, we may still see a world destroyed. With faith and knowledge bound together, we can hope to cherish and protect the lives of the men and the life of the world.

The Choice to Live

OCTOBER, 1969

We are facing one of the great crises in the history of man. There are, almost everywhere, too many people. Too many people in affluent countries stumbling over one another as they scramble for amenities. Too many in poor countries living in growing misery and dying of long-drawn-out hunger and disease. Too many old people for whom there is no place; too many children for whose future no provision is made. Too many people, even in our own society, who will never enjoy the benefits of civilization that they know exist—but not for them.

Yet within thirty years, if we do not act immediately, the world's population, already so dangerously large, will have doubled. For every person now alive there will then be two competing, literally, for light and air and space, for housing and food and water, for education and work, rest and recreation, and for intimacy and privacy—for all the most basic necessities of human existence.

Although the arithmetic is simple, the sheer numbers stagger the imagination. There are now some three and a half billion people crowding the world. It took sixteen hundred years for the world's population to grow from a quarter to a half billion and then two hundred years for the number to reach one billion, around the year 1800. At the present rate of increase, if nothing is done to reverse the trend, there will be in the year 2000 some seven billion people struggling for a share of the earth's rapidly diminishing resources. And after that . . . but who, as yet, can picture the kind of world children already born may be doomed to live in?

The evidence that we have not fully come to terms with the problems of our present population size is plain to see in small things as in large. Every time I pick up a telephone in a large city delays in the dial tone inform me that there are too many telephones in use for the existing system. Milling crowds in airports and endless delays in arrivals and departures demonstrate the fact that we do not build to meet present, let alone future, requirements.

Everywhere in our country demand exceeds what is available. There are too few homes, too few schools and teachers, too few doctors and hospital beds. Wherever we turn, the system bogs down, mainly because of the difficulty we experience in translating statistics into the needs of living people. And so I ask myself: How shall we meet the needs of the two million—and more—who will be added each year to the American population? Or the seventy million who represent, today, only one year's increase in the population of the world?

There are signs that we are becoming aware of the potential catastrophe. Twenty years ago, although there was a rumble of worry about the baby boom, many still believed, optimistically, that scientists could devise ways of feeding an almost infinitely expanding population. Many religious groups, not only Roman Catholics, but also many Protestant and Jewish groups—as well as Muslims and Hindus and other religious believers—were deeply opposed to family limitation. Research on methods of contraception was greatly stepped up, but no one could guess whether people would accept the new devices when they became available.

Even ten years ago, when many studies in progress aimed at reaching and informing nonliterate Hindu women or the women of overpopulated Caribbean islands, most people still saw family limitation as a matter of individual choice or as a social problem for some "other" group—unmarried mothers living on welfare, the people of poor countries and new countries, the shelterless people dying on the streets of a city like Calcutta.

Today, however, as we are coming to realize that we are living in a totally interconnected world, we are also discovering how grave the crisis is. Local and piecemeal solutions will not help. For the question no longer is one of the adequacy or meagerness of any one country's resources, the state of industrialization and technology, or even the size of one country compared with another.

Widespread famine in any country will breed disease; and epidemics (as we know from our experience with influenza) can spread fast and far as people travel on jet planes. Disorder, rooted in desperation and misery, can lead to wars that will affect human survival everywhere. In New York a disturbed and unhappy boy, brought to despair by the world's apparent indifference to starvation in Africa, sets himself afire in front of the United Nations. We are discovering that in exposure, in common cause and in mutual interdependence, our planet is an island in space. Whatever our differences may be, we are joined in succumbing to or meeting this danger to our humanity.

What are the chances that we will act in time? And how can we begin?

There are, as I see it, two major obstacles to be overcome. The first of these is that our perilous situation originates not in failure but in success. As long as men's hold on the means of living was precarious, population growth was negligible. The ravages of famine, war and epidemics taught men who looked at ruined cities, silent villages and landscapes turning back to wilderness that civilization might break down for lack of men to keep it going.

In the early nineteenth century, when populations were growing rapidly, the first pessimistic voices were raised. Few then dreamed of the progress of science and its applications that have made our present world civilization feasible. The tremendous expansion of knowledge through the technological revolution, the "green" revolution that has transformed agriculture, and the medical revolution have now given man virtual mastery of the earth. Population growth, in this sense, is the measure of our success.

But success has turned to menace. We must now—immediately— cease looking at burgeoning populations with the eyes of generations long dead. The pessimists feared that man's control of the natural world might be too slight for survival; the optimists hoped that man, through his inventions, could ensure a better life for all men. Both took pride in a world in which more and more children survived infancy and more people lived longer. Now, however, our pride in human accomplishment must have its source in the value we place on each human life.

The second obstacle is apparently the more difficult one to overcome. Some problems depend for their solution essentially on the responsible decisions of governments or on the actions of limited groups. In the case of atomic weapons, world security rests with the quality of the leaders we choose. But population control involves the active participation of every adult everywhere in the world. For the first time in human history the shape of the future will be determined by decisions all adults must make as individuals.

There is a kind of precedent in the way we have handled preventive medicine. Certain rules for the protection of human life have been enforced by governments through public health measures. But the assent of parents has been necessary to ensure that children are given each new treatment, each new form of immunization, that conserves life and health. The value placed on human life has spurred medical research; at the same time, medical care, especially preventive care, has fostered the belief that each individual is uniquely valuable.

We have the scientific knowledge to control population growth and the social skills to bring about a balance between the extremes of affluence and poverty on a global scale.

The many millions of women who already have chosen to use new methods of conception control indicate that much can be accomplished merely by free access to information. But I believe that we will succeed, in the end, only to the extent that we develop and implement a new shared ethic.

The new ethic must be one that will hold up everywhere—East and West, in socialist and capitalist countries, in old and new countries, in rich and poor countries and within all groups, whatever their race, their culture or their level of modern education may be. The new ethic must include people who have no belief in a future life, those for whom life on earth is the prelude to immortality, and those who see the present as one of a series of lives on earth, as men are reincarnated again and again in the same or in different forms. It must apply equally to those who still are bound by the stringencies of scarcity and those for whom abundance is the basic fact of life.

These very different viewpoints can be bound together, I believe, not so much by our will to preserve the human race for a future we cannot know as by the value we place on life itself. Central to a universal ethic must be the worth of each life as it is expressed in its fulfillment.

To begin with, we must be able to say: We shall not sacrifice living children for children yet unborn. We shall not sacrifice the needs of some children for the needs of others. Instead, we shall protect all the living *and* the unborn by assuring that every child will have the opportunity to grow up in a welcoming world in which he can reach fulfillment as a person. It is not enough that parents, privately, should welcome a child, that there should be no unwanted children and no unwilling parents. There must also be a place for each child to grow up in the world and, as part of this, trained and concerned adults who are personally and professionally devoted to the care of children.

Next we must emphasize the values that bind together, not in harsh contrast but in responsibility and hope, the very newest, poorest countries and peoples and the richest and most established. In advantaged countries we have realized how much is involved in rearing children to live well in childhood and as adults in a complex civilization. Each decade we are learning more about the number and different kinds of trained adults whose competence is crucial in rearing children and in conserving human ability and talent in maturity and into old age. In wealthy countries we are implementing, however imperfectly, this knowledge; in poor countries the task is all but unrealizable.

No two cultures are alike and no two peoples will make identical adaptations or want to rear their children in exactly the same way. But a shared concern, a shared responsibility for training and a shared interchange that will involve millions of adults the world over are first steps in bringing about a new balance among peoples.

Almost inevitably the new ethic will also lead to a new and much higher valuation of adulthood. Indeed, concern for childhood can have as its goal only a new realization of what adulthood can mean. So far, we have been extraordinarily short-sighted in our emphasis on numbers of people rather than on the quality of life open to them. As long as few could be exempted from the work that was essential for survival, most of it done by human hands, this was unavoidable. But today the situation is reversed. Those who can work *only* with their hands at laborious jobs are becoming obsolete.

Long life, beginning with a full childhood, should mean much greater diversity of life experience, a flowering of talent and an enjoyment of maturity we have only glimpsed in the past. Widely shared responsibility for children, for education at all stages of life and for the care of other adults will fill the lives of millions of people, only some of whom will be parents. It will also free millions of men and women to devote themselves to the further exploration of human maturity.

In a world in which there may be as many as five generations living simultaneously, no one, young or old, need be cut off from the experience and stimulation of people of different ages. Old men and women, who have not lived beyond their time but, instead, are part of an ongoing, changing life, and children who are just moving into that life, as they are both valued, will give new dimensions to maturity.

This is the direction in which we can move, if we will.

The choice, I think, is clear. We can move blindly into chaos and perish together, choked by disorganization and disorder and dehumanized by hunger, the loss of essential resources and our own desperate despair. It would also be possible, perhaps, to compel compliance with authoritarian restriction of reproductive functions; but this would also be a dehumanizing process.

The only humanizing choice, it appears to me, is the one that involves all human beings voluntarily. And the basis for this must be an ethic all men can share in the task of limiting the number of the living so all human beings can truly live.

Are the Natives Friendly?

❧❦❧❦❧

MARCH, 1967

I am very often asked whether Americans could feel comfortable and at home with any of the South Sea peoples with whom I have worked for over forty years.

Of course not all those who ask the question are seeking the same information. Some are curious about the actual physical conditions of everyday life. What would it be like to sleep in a native house? they wonder. Is native food edible? How bad would the insects be? Would it be possible for us to survive at all without our customary comforts?

Others are interested in the personal appearance of these South Sea peoples, not only in the ways they differ from us but also in the immense diversity between one Pacific island group and another. "Will we find them beautiful? Or will we wonder what the men see in the women and the women in the men?" Would getting to know the Samoans or the Balinese or the peoples of New Guinea increase an American's sense of himself as a member of the human race, or would their appearance, their costumes and their cosmetics be repellent? Can an American accept very different conceptions of how an attractive woman should sit and walk and talk and smell and sound?

And finally—skipping over these matters of housing, food and physical appearance—many of my questioners wonder about personal relations. "Will we like the people themselves? Will we find their way of greeting a stranger, of smiling, of treating one another, congenial or exciting? Will we find some common ground in the way families live together, the way men work together, the way women talk with one another? Or will all the details of their lives seem too exotic and incomprehensible for our comfort?"

Questions about living conditions can be answered rather simply. Wherever there is a tradition of entertaining Europeans, visitors can be comfortable. This is especially true among Samoans, who are an aristocratic and hospitable people. Long before the arrival of the *papalagi*—the skybursters, as the Samoans called the first Europeans who came in sailing ships—each Samoan chief had a special house in which to receive visitors. The *fale tali malo*, the house to meet the stranger, was always kept swept and tidy. In the rafters of the round, pagodalike dwelling, clean mats were neatly rolled up, ready to be spread for guests. When Europeans and Americans were received as visitors, most chiefs acquired some European-style dishes and cutlery, and even added sheets, stuffed pillows and mosquito nets to their stock of household goods.

The visitor's bed, made up at night, is a springy pile of mats spread on the pebble floor and covered with spotless sheets. There are certain oddities, it is true. A bark-cloth curtain separates the guest's sleeping place from that of his hosts, who come to sleep in the same house. But no enclosing house wall shuts off the view from the outside. And it is a little trying to bathe under the village shower, modestly changing from wet clothes to dry clothes under the eyes of a group of watching children. But it has been done hundreds of times.

Visitors in Samoan villages have lived comfortably and happily, well fed on fish and chicken and secure in the care of hosts who enjoy guests and consider their comfort.

The guest in Bali can live just as comfortably. The rajas have a long tradition of entertaining European visitors, mainly from the Netherlands, and honored guests are usually received in a special quasi-European house complete with beds and mosquito nets, tables and chairs, bathing rooms and lavatories. Delicious food, the result of a hundred years' experience in the combining of Indonesian and European tastes, is served with appropriate warnings: "This sauce is mild. This sauce may be a little too hot for your taste. And this one is *surely* too hot, but it is part of a complete meal." In 1936 we lived for several months in a guest house of this kind within the royal compound of a raja, safe from the importunities of vendors and attending only the ceremonies in which our aristocratic hosts took part. In recent years some guest houses have been adapted for the use of paying guests, who find them a delightful vantage point from which to enjoy a closer view of Balinese life.

Living in New Guinea presents entirely different problems as soon as one leaves the small towns and settlements where Australians and other foreigners live. Each native village is required to build a guest house for traveling government officials and for the labor recruiters, the traders, the prospectors and any others who move from one place to another. But the house-*kiap*, as this guest house is called, is usually as shoddy as the builders dare to make it. Raised on high posts, with a floor of beaten bark, a leaky thatched roof, a rickety ladder and a perilous and uncomfortable latrine, perhaps built out at the edge of a deep gorge, the house-*kiap* provides little more than a crude base for camping. Even today, travelers carry their own gear—folding beds, mosquito nets, cooking utensils—and basic supplies, since the village may have little food on hand to offer. Occasionally when a government official arrives with his interpreter, cook and any others who may be necessary for his work, he finds the house-*kiap* in a state of collapse and the villagers must temporarily empty a native house for him. Wishing the strangers well away, their hosts will neither sweep nor garnish the dwelling. Firewood and water (to wash in, not to drink, if the visitor is wise) are provided only grudgingly.

This is not surprising. The Arapesh, for instance, were reluctant hosts and guests; their own expectations of hospitality were summed up in the speeches that visitors from another village made to their hosts: "We came to your feast. We were cold. We were wet. The rain beat down upon us where we slept beneath the eaves. We were hungry."

Moreover, in the Sepik River villages the stranger—a member of a trading expedition, perhaps, or a villager's relative by marriage—used to go in fear of his life. Invited to enter a "men's house," a kind of clubhouse where the men of the clan sat on high platforms, the stranger folded his legs under him, lest some villager seize his legs from below, pull him down and do away with him.

In the lagoon villages of the Manus in 1928, land people from other villages came as trade friends, partners in the exchange of goods. Frightened in spite of their protected position, they sat on the verandas of their hosts' houses and seldom ventured out into the village. And visitors from overseas cooked and slept on the platforms of their own outrigger canoes, scantily sheltered under improvised pandanus-mat roofs. There was no tradition of easy or relaxed hospitality. Even today, when so much else has changed, Europeans on a short visit to a Manus village usually live on the boats they arrive in. There is no comfortable place for the stranger to stay, except where a European schoolteacher living in a village can supplement the meager amenities of the local house-*kiap*.

The immediate problem for the anthropologist, living temporarily in the house-*kiap*, is how to get his own house built, a project that may take many weeks full of unexpected incidents. Once there was such a tug of war between two parts of the village that not one but two houses had to be built before we could get on with life. These all are places where the New Guinea natives themselves, the Australians who work and live in the Territory, the anthropologists, surveyors, missionaries, traders and film makers—all those who come for special purposes—expect travel to be difficult. And it is.

And how about the people? Pacific islanders are part of our romantic tradition, and it is all too easy to conjure up a delightful picture out of a blend of Melville's *Typee* and Stevenson's tales and Gauguin's paintings. Or to fashion a different but perhaps even more exciting image based on recent books and films about cannibals and savages, fierce and painted, with bird-of-paradise plumes in their hair. It is fair then to ask, What are the chances of finding beautiful maidens, generous in love and song? What is the likelihood of meeting flamboyant headhunters? And of liking what one finds?

The answers are not so difficult. Where Europeans or Americans have found the people attractive, they also have found living conditions pleasant and attractive. The fact is that over long years of contact there has been a kind of matching of daydreams. The more closely a people have fitted into our older, romantic tradition of the primitive, the more easily we have accepted their version of charm. And also the people themselves, sensing that they are liked, have more easily acted and dressed, smiled and responded, in ways that have met our expectations, and have modified their forms of hospitality to meet our hopes.

In contrast, it is difficult for us to see any redeeming features in a people whose ways of treating their own bodies are repellent to us.

The idea of nose-piercing does not appeal to us. Women with shaved heads and men whose hair is dyed pink or purple do not seem attractive. The use of body paint and strange cosmetics, the pungent smells of unfamiliar ointments, put us off. A people may be tall or short, black or brown or golden, have curly or straight hair—it does not much matter. It is their mode of treating their own bodies that attracts or repels us.

In the South Seas, Americans find enjoyably exotic not those peoples with "strange" customs but those who, having learned to look like us, still walk barefoot, tuck flowers behind their ears and dress in gay and simple garments. Even the escapists among us, the ones who feel that civilization is dull and confining, are likely to choose a primitive people whose way of life includes the use of soap, cloth, starch, scissors, sewing machines, razors and modern cosmetics.

But beyond appearances there is still the question of a people's mode of life and its appeal to our understanding and conception of what is worthwhile. To this question it seems to me the answers are as various as the styles of living of the seven South Sea peoples with whom I have worked.

I found the Samoans delightful, their light, gay, moderate affection reassuring and undemanding. I have always felt that I could live for months or even years in the villages where, given a village title, I had a definite place. Yet, remembering the sound of the laughter and the singing and the dancing that goes on night after night, year after year, I realize that it is not the dancers one remembers but the dance itself. The visitor of a few days, charmed by his host and hostess, may not realize that he has fallen in love with a style rather than come to know particular individuals. It takes time to discover the bitter, covert rivalry, the intense and touchy pride, the watchfulness and lack of trust that cut through the life of a village. But these do not affect the stranger. The visitor to Samoa is always welcomed and feasted, his hosts expecting that feasting will greet their arrival on a return visit.

In Bali one learns to enjoy life as a spectator. The beauty and grace of motion, the dramatic performances of theater, opera, ballet and shadow play and the spectacle of temple feasts provide endless entertainment. And because the Balinese are an aesthetically demanding people, alert to the new dance step and the revised plot, there is

always something interesting to watch and appreciate. For the
stranger, Bali is primarily a continuing feast for the eyes and ears—a
place where the artist can photograph, film, paint, carve, write or
compose music.

But today a sense of inescapable misfortune haunts the visitor to
Bali. A large part of this most fertile land has been devastated by a
volcanic eruption. The population is outgrowing its ability to feed
itself. Political conflict has brought about disorder. The spectator in
Bali today cannot turn his back on the problems that have come in the
wake of modernization, although he may look to the past with
nostalgia. Not so the Balinese, who are caught up in the exciting
possibilities of innovation.

Much as visitors would enjoy the peoples of Bali and Samoa, it is
among the modern Manus of the Admiralty Islands that Americans
would find themselves most at home, I believe. Especially now that the
Manus have taken hold of the modern world, we can appreciate that
they are progressive and ambitious. Long ago, as traders and navigators, they sailed the local seas, buying and selling the products of
other islands. From Europeans they took the things that were really
useful—iron tools and cloth, and canvas for sails, but not canned food
or matches. And when, during World War II, they were exposed to
the hundreds of thousands of American servicemen who came
through their islands, they watched, they appraised and they selected
the parts of American culture they wanted to have as their own:
practical things—neatly planned villages, shops, a bank, a school—
and the admonition that human relations are more important than
property.

In a short twenty-five years they moved from a primary preoccupation with things—pots and wooden bowls, sago and oil, canoes and
houses—to a primary preoccupation with the kind of society they
wanted to build. And they went about their self-imposed task with
tremendous gusto and a sure sense of their own capacity to do whatever they wanted to do.

It is this enjoyment of *doing*, I believe, that would attract most
Americans to the Manus, as the Manus were attracted to Americans.
The Manus are the only primitive people I have known who would
really understand the cheerful self-confidence of that World War II
motto: "The difficult we do at once. The impossible takes a little
longer."

Neighbors vs. Neighborhoods

✗⧓✗⧓✗⧓✗

SEPTEMBER, 1962

Most Americans still carry with them, like a well-loved picture in a frame, the idea of small-town life—as a way they themselves once lived, or wish they had lived, or hope one day to live. White houses on green lawns set not too far apart, lights in windows at which shades are not pulled down, safety for one's children wherever they wander, everyone known by name and reputation. These are the values remembered by families living in city houses that stand, one just like the other, in bleak and deteriorated or jerry-built rows; in anonymous apartments; and in the vast, unbounded suburbs where the lawns must be kept green but everyone is a stranger. Older people complain and younger people wonder about the disappearance of this neighborly friendliness and trust. In modern American life each family has become, or is fast becoming, a small, self-contained unit in a world of strangers.

One reason that small-town neighborliness has almost vanished is that time and again those who grew up with it found it too confining. "No, son, I wouldn't plan to be a pilot. You Atkinsons always had weak eyes." . . . "You want to be an actress? Now, Mary, take a little advice from someone who knew you *before* you were born. . . ." However well meant, remarks like these could clip the wings of one's ambitions. A world in which the neighbors, which included most of the town, knew one's every act was restricting, limiting, confining. Each child grew up carrying the known and expected characteristics of his grandparents, his parents, his brothers and sisters, and even the marks of his own small failures as a little child. True, the neighbors often were kind, dependable people. But it was good to get away from them, to make a new life where no one knew you and where your aspirations were not treated as pretensions.

Yet, in the new life something is acutely felt to be missing. The frame of neighborly knowledge, which contained both an allowance for weakness and an unwillingness to allow for real ambition, is gone and nothing has taken its place. We have left behind (and may well lament) the familiarity and reassurance of the small, intimate neighborhood, but we have not realized the possibilities inherent in a larger, more complicated setting. In fact, in many instances we have retreated into a way of life even more limiting than the one we left.

In today's housing projects and in suburban developments, conformity—outward adjustment to the opinions and tastes of other people—has been substituted for the old closeness, longed for but also feared. People come to the neighborhood as strangers, from widely different backgrounds and influences. After they arrive, they try to become like the others in the community and hope that the others will be like them. But the difficulty is that making oneself look like other people, and even act like them, is quite different from sharing something with them.

In city neighborhoods and some suburban communities, people have a tendency to keep to themselves—often they know their neighbors only to nod to and keep self-protectively at arm's length—especially if they feel that certain elements of the neighborhood are "bad." Subtly, neighbors are associated with difficulties and times of trouble. They lend you things you have run out of unexpectedly, like butter, or extra things like party glasses and chairs. They keep one child when another is sick. They bring food at a time of death. But these contacts are limited and intermittent, and when things go well there is little give-and-take even with "good" neighbors.

So we are seldom fully aware of our neighbors as people. In fact, many of us today care far less about our neighbors than we do about our neighbor*hoods*. In speaking of "good" neighborhoods or "bad" neighborhoods, we often are not thinking about the neighbors as people at all—witty or dull, happy or sad, kind or indifferent—but as accessories to the neighborhood and their effect on our class position.

In this context, neighbors who spoil the neighborhood are people who put the wrong decorations in their windows, drive the wrong cars, neglect their lawns or come from the wrong racial or religious groups; the wrong neighbors are people whom other people—one's rich or more successful relatives and friends—might see and criticize. The right kind of neighbors are just the opposite; they are people who pull you up rather than drag you down just by living on the same street.

Either way, this is thinking of people as things. If the car stands in front of the house by the neat lawn and no one bangs in and out of the door and the right kind of tree stands in the picture window at Christmas, those who are in search of the "right" neighborhood will be content. When their friends come to visit, they won't mention neighbors at all—just what a pleasant *neighborhood* it is. If, on the other hand, the street is deteriorating, the family will deplore having to live there in the same breath with which they explain the advantages of their own house: "The children can walk to school. It's near Jim's work. We've put so much into fixing it up. But we don't really belong here." All the other people on the block are excluded. So by our particularly American form of social class—in which a class position can be invaded, diluted and lost, in which people are judged not by what they are but by how they dress, where they live and what kinds of cars they drive—the human element that comes through the sheer sharing of the vicissitudes of everyday life is crowded out. People are treated as things, as objects by which one hauls oneself up or is pushed down.

These attitudes need to be re-examined. We have the opportunity to use our new-found freedom, away from the small, familiar worlds that were safe and secure but often stultifying, to develop and diversify our lives. We are not doing this if we regard the neighbors as extensions of ourselves, or as people to be "used" or kept at arm's length, or merely as attractive or unattractive accessories to the community. The child who grows up with such attitudes grows up with a sad lack of what he will need as an American, as a person, as a dweller on this planet. He is robbed of one important dimension of living in the modern world—learning a mutual give-and-take with people of widely different tastes and backgrounds. Just as relatives are, one hopes, people one loves (but may not like) and friends are people one really likes and may come to love, so neighbors can be people whom we may like, or even come to love, or be indifferent to, or not like at all. But we can, at least, come to see them—and ourselves—for what we are as *people*—highly individual people in a very large world.

New Prospects for Old Communities

❧❧❧❧

SEPTEMBER, 1965

It is not uncommon today to hear people say that small towns and villages are disappearing. In some voices one hears regret. In others there is an unmistakable tone of satisfaction. Small towns, some people say, belong to the past.

Undeniably, in every part of the United States today old, small communities are vanishing. One after another, towns and villages are growing into cities or are being swallowed up by the suburbs that are spreading out everywhere. Some towns are actually demolished. Others survive only as impersonal shopping centers, crowded with anonymous shoppers who have recently moved into the vicinity. Still others, their old houses neglected and their gardens buried under junk, linger on as the back streets of the new, much larger communities that are crowding them out.

And yet it is hard to believe that the American small town will vanish altogether. Does the small town, which is a distinctly different kind of community from the suburb, have nothing to offer Americans today?

Europeans often ask Americans: "Where is your hometown?" Almost invariably the answer puzzles them, because the American may reply: "I was born in Winchester, Ohio, but I live in Detroit." Or he may say: "I grew up in Winchester but I have lived in Cleveland for forty years."

It is typical, in America, that a person's hometown is not the place where he is living now but is the place he left behind. And since the United States became a nation that is more urban than rural as late as the 1920's, we continue to believe that most older Americans were born and grew up in small towns and villages, and that they turned their backs on Main Street only as they became young adults.

We picture the small town in which older Americans grew up as a little community set down among farmlands. Each little town had its cluster of professional men, small businessmen and craftsmen. Less closely attached to the life of the town were the farmers, who moved into houses on the outskirts of town when they retired, where they could still keep a chicken coop or have a garden patch. Central to the life of the town was the high school, attended by children who were stirred by daydreams and often by high ambitions for success in the larger world of the city. It was here that the teachers, the tycoons and the writers who later made their mark were nurtured. Once they went away, they never returned, except perhaps to dedicate a library or to speak at a high-school commencement in a gesture of recognition of the bond to their hometown.

If this picture is the American idea of a small town before World War I, the idea of the big city was one of a metropolis populated mainly by immigrants from Europe and American newcomers to city living; by professional and businessmen and their families; by the small, wealthy group that constituted Society; and by self-selected Bohemians who had escaped from what they regarded as the drabness of hometown existence. Among these were writers like Floyd Dell, Carl Van Vechten, Willa Cather and Sinclair Lewis, who depicted their movement to the city not so much as a choice between one kind of place and another as a prevalent *way of thinking* about American life. For them the hometown (actually, sometimes, a small city of some 50,000 people) was simply where life began—the place where dreams took shape. The more sophisticated city was the place where dreams were fashioned into reality.

During the Depression years in the 1930's, many families that had long been established in cities were forced to return to farms and small towns, where the old, large houses at least provided shelter. For those fleeing unemployment, this return to the hometown represented failure in the big city. But hometowns and small cities too were experiencing a sense of failure. Factories and mills closed down. Old established businesses crumbled as customers ceased to buy. Banks failed. Those who remained felt paralyzed by the loss of the towns' old autonomy, by their own inactivity, by the failure of hope. As a result of the Depression the old way of thinking about the small town gave way to a new one. People came to believe that the only good town was an actively growing one. Only a growing town could expect to have a better school and a better library, better health services and the certainty of autonomy.

It took World War II to demonstrate the inaccuracy of the belief that growth alone meant improvement. For with the mushrooming of defense plants and the vast expansion of military installations, floods of people poured into quiet old communities. Almost overnight, tiny towns were turned into housing jungles into which, month after month, new thousands streamed from every part of the country. Every existing form of traditional organization was strained beyond the breaking point. Town governments, local commercial establishments and school systems alike were inadequate to meet the new needs. Measures intended to provide temporary relief in time of emergency became permanent fixtures, changing the faces of the old towns and creating far less desirable communities.

After the war the scramble to move in on small towns was, if anything, accelerated. New industries in search of cheap power, burgeoning industries in search of space, real-estate development companies in search of empty land and chambers of commerce that vied with one another to attract business to their communities—all have contributed to the movement of people out of large cities and into small towns. While a large plant, seeking to attract personnel, can cite pleasant community resources to tempt workers, the communities with good, but limited, resources have been helpless to stem the flood. As one result, hundreds of once-proud, independent little towns have been inundated by families requiring services that no small community can provide on a mass scale. All this has contributed heavily to the belief that times and needs have changed, that the small town is no longer what it once was and belongs to the past.

But at the same time there has been another kind of very quiet movement out of the cities into smaller communities—the movement of those who dream that in a small town they will find a kind of life for themselves and their children that they are denied by the very size and impersonal nature of big cities. Whereas in the past, stories and autobiographies focused on the difficulties of the country-bred boy and girl as they learned to live in cities, today city-bred young people are struggling to understand and respect the sensitivities, the pride and the prejudices of members of small communities that are still holding their own in spite of change. In the past, active, ambitious young people found the small towns of their youth suffocating in their intimacy and in the constant reminders that everybody knew everything about everybody. Today, in contrast, active, ambitious young people are discovering the challenge of living in small communities. A great many of them, of course, have only exchanged the anonymity and isolation of the city for the anonymity and isolation of the dismal one-class suburb. But fortunately, others have moved into real small towns and villages. They are experiencing for the first time the pleasures of knowing many people and of being known to almost everyone they meet.

In a large city it is fatuous to walk down the street ready to smile at every passer-by. To do so is to invite cold stares and suspicion. It is foolish to offer a helping hand or a lift in one's car. The most likely responses are anger or incipient fear. It spells trouble to try to help a child one does not know; city children have been taught to avoid "friendly" strangers.

The young people who are moving into small communities bring with them all these long-established rules that go with city anonymity. It is not easy to cast them off. They have no experience of being told, "But I knew you when. . . ." They do not expect anyone to be interested in the lives of their parents and grandparents. They will tell you, "I grew up in a city. It was hard to learn how to live in a town of five thousand people. But somehow I made it!"

They made it when they discovered that it is pleasant to know the people next door, when they discovered the necessary ways of relating themselves to a great many people—neighbors, members of clubs and churches, the people on Main Street and the parents of their children's friends. They made it when their eyes and ears acquired a new sensitivity. The sound of a neighbor's child crying on the doorstep tells a mother that something is wrong, and she can offer to help. The smiles that greet her as she walks down the street are signs of friendly recognition. For those who have grown up in the isolation of large cities, small-town living is an adventure in friendship and interdependence.

Historically, Americans have valued independence at all costs. In the past, the most energetic, ambitious people moved away from relatives and their childhood town to attain the greater autonomy offered by the city. This has colored all our older views of small towns. Today, many of those who have grown up in cities, with their myriad meaningless sights and noises and impersonal jostling contacts, are looking for new forms of interdependence.

If we continue to think about small towns only in terms of what they once meant to those who fled from them, they will certainly belong to the past and disappear as the past recedes. But if they mean something else—something new—in our lives, we must find out what it is.

On Friendship

❧❧❧❧

AUGUST, 1966

Few Americans stay put for a lifetime. We move from town to city to suburb, from high school to college in a different state, from a job in one region to a better job elsewhere, from the home where we raise our children to the home where we plan to live in retirement. With each move we are forever making new friends, who become part of our new life at that time.

For many of us the summer is a special time for forming new friendships. Today millions of Americans vacation abroad, and they go not only to see new sights but also—in those places where they do not feel too strange—with the hope of meeting new people. No one really expects a vacation trip to produce a close friend. But surely the beginning of a friendship is possible? Surely in every country people value friendship?

They do. The difficulty when strangers from two countries meet is not a lack of appreciation of friendship, but different expectations about what constitutes friendship and how it comes into being. In those European countries that Americans are most likely to visit, friendship is quite sharply distinguished from other, more casual relations, and is differently related to family life. For a Frenchman, a German or an Englishman friendship is usually more particularized and carries a heavier burden of commitment.

But as we use the word, "friend" can be applied to a wide range of relationships—to someone one has known for a few weeks in a new place, to a close business associate, to a childhood playmate, to a man or woman, to a trusted confidant. There are real differences among these relations for Americans—a friendship may be superficial, casual,

situational or deep and enduring. But to a European, who sees only
our surface behavior, the differences are not clear.

As they see it, people known and accepted temporarily, casually,
flow in and out of Americans' homes with little ceremony and often
with little personal commitment. They may be parents of the children's friends, house guests of neighbors, members of a committee,
business associates from another town or even another country.
Coming as a guest into an American home, the European visitor finds
no visible landmarks. The atmosphere is relaxed. Most people, old and
young, are called by first names.

Who, then, is a friend?

Even simple translation from one language to another is difficult.
"You see," a Frenchman explains, "if I were to say to you in France,
'This is my good friend,' that person would not be as close to me as
someone about whom I said only, 'This is my friend.' Anyone about
whom I have to say *more* is really less."

In France, as in many European countries, friends generally are of
the same sex, and friendship is seen as basically a relationship between
men. Frenchwomen laugh at the idea that "women can't be friends,"
but they also admit sometimes that for women "it's a different thing."
And many French people doubt the possibility of a friendship between a man and a woman. There is also the kind of relationship
within a group—men and women who have worked together for a
long time, who may be very close, sharing great loyalty and warmth
of feeling. They may call one another *copains*—a word that in
English becomes "friends" but has more the feeling of "pals" or
"buddies." In French eyes this is not friendship, although two members of such a group may well be friends.

For the French, friendship is a one-to-one relationship that demands a keen awareness of the other person's intellect, temperament
and particular interests. A friend is someone who draws out your own
best qualities, with whom you sparkle and become more of whatever
the friendship draws upon. Your political philosophy assumes more
depth, appreciation of a play becomes sharper, taste in food or wine is
accentuated, enjoyment of a sport is intensified.

And French friendships are compartmentalized. A man may play
chess with a friend for thirty years without knowing his political
opinions, or he may talk politics with him for as long a time without

knowing about his personal life. Different friends fill different niches in each person's life. These friendships are not made part of family life. A friend is not expected to spend evenings being nice to children or courteous to a deaf grandmother. These duties, also serious and enjoined, are primarily for relatives. Men who are friends may meet in a café. Intellectual friends may meet in larger groups for evenings of conversation. Working people may meet at the little *bistro* where they drink and talk, far from the family. Marriage does not affect such friendships; wives do not have to be taken into account.

In the past in France, friendships of this kind seldom were open to any but intellectual women. Since most women's lives centered on their homes, their warmest relations with other women often went back to their girlhood. The special relationship of friendship is based on what the French value most—on the mind, on compatibility of outlook, on vivid awareness of some chosen area of life.

Friendship heightens the sense of each person's individuality. Other relationships commanding as great loyalty and devotion have a different meaning. In World War II the first resistance groups formed in Paris were built on the foundation of *les copains*. But significantly, as time went on these little groups, whose lives rested in one another's hands, called themselves "families." Where each had a total responsibility for all, it was kinship ties that provided the model. And even today such ties, crossing every line of class and personal interest, remain binding on the survivors of these small, secret bands.

In Germany, in contrast with France, friendship is much more articulately a matter of feeling. Adolescents, boys and girls, form deeply sentimental attachments, walk and talk together—not so much to polish their wits as to share their hopes and fears and dreams, to form a common front against the world of school and family and to join in a kind of mutual discovery of each other's and their own inner life. Within the family, the closest relationship over a lifetime is between brothers and sisters. Outside the family, men and women find in their closest friends of the same sex the devotion of a sister, the loyalty of a brother. Appropriately, in Germany friends usually are brought into the family. Children call their father's and their mother's friends "uncle" and "aunt." Between French friends, who have chosen each other for the congeniality of their point of view, lively disagreement and sharpness of argument are the breath of life. But for

Germans, whose friendships are based on mutuality of feeling, deep disagreement on any subject that matters to both is regarded as a tragedy. Like ties of kinship, ties of friendship are meant to be irrevocably binding. Young Germans who come to the United States have great difficulty in establishing such friendships with Americans. We view friendship more tentatively, subject to changes in intensity as people move, change their jobs, marry, or discover new interests.

English friendships follow still a different pattern. Their basis is shared activity. Activities at different stages of life may be of very different kinds—discovering a common interest in school, serving together in the armed forces, taking part in a foreign mission, staying in the same country house during a crisis. In the midst of the activity, whatever it may be, people fall into step—sometimes two men or two women, sometimes two couples, sometimes three people—and find that they walk or play a game or tell stories or serve on a tiresome and exacting committee with the same easy anticipation of what each will do day by day or in some critical situation. Americans who have made English friends comment that, even years later, "you can take up just where you left off." Meeting after a long interval, friends are like a couple who begin to dance again when the orchestra strikes up after a pause. English friendships are formed outside the family circle, but they are not, as in Germany, contrapuntal to the family nor are they, as in France, separated from the family. And a break in an English friendship comes not necessarily as a result of some irreconcilable difference of viewpoint or feeling but instead as a result of misjudgment, where one friend seriously misjudges how the other will think or feel or act, so that suddenly they are out of step.

What, then, is friendship? Looking at these different styles, including our own, each of which is related to a whole way of life, are there common elements? There is the recognition that friendship, in contrast with kinship, invokes freedom of choice. A friend is someone who chooses and is chosen. Related to this is the sense each friend gives the other of being a special individual, on whatever grounds this recognition is based. And between friends there is inevitably a kind of equality of give-and-take. These similarities make the bridge between societies possible, and the American's characteristic openness to different styles of relationship makes it possible for him to find new friends abroad with whom he feels at home.

Time to Reflect, Time to Feel

※✕✕✕※

AUGUST, 1964

What are people going to do with so much leisure time—when it comes? This is a question thoughtful Americans ask as they read about the shortened workday, the shortened workweek, the shortened work year, earlier retirement. Granted, they themselves may know exactly what they would like to do with an extra ten hours a week. It is other people they are thinking about. But the question still expresses a doubt. Don't most people lack the resources to use more leisure time? Isn't it better, safer, for their hours to be filled with pressing, necessary tasks?

Most people will agree that there is little leisure now. They don't ever have time to do the things they want to do. This is particularly true of busy mothers. But it is also true of the men who spend tiring hours driving to work and home again on a crowded highway, the men who work long into the evening on a second job to support their families. It is true of high-school students who are trying to study and keep up with extracurricular activities and of married college students who are trying to combine studying with family life and, often, paid work besides. People complain about having no time. People want more leisure. But is it leisure to *do* more things that we really want?

There is a perpetual sense of crowding in our daily lives. Events involving millions of people are reported in the headlines of newspapers or they are accorded two minutes on a television roundup of news from Washington, Rome, New Delhi. And the next day they are replaced by other headlines, other news reports. And personal life is crowded. Events follow upon one another so fast that there is little time to reflect on what has just happened or to daydream about events we are waiting for—a summer vacation, the day a child returns home from college, the day when the house will hold only two because the children will be away for a whole month. Yet life is meager if it is lived only by the moment. Events caught on the fly and cast away lose their meaning. Experience becomes flat and two-dimensional—like the snapshots that catch a baby's step but not his stumbling progress across the room, or the slides fixing forever the views seen in the ten European countries visited in one six-week holiday, or the picture of the bride smiling in her wedding dress, untouched and unsoftened by the memories that retrospectively give that moment its poignancy.

There are two expressions—"Give yourself time to . . ." and "Take time to . . ."—which suggest that people have a private store of time or a fund of time, like money in a savings bank, on which they can draw if they want to, which they can use in an emergency. And these expressions, like the folk wisdom lying back of the warnings people give one another—"Take it easy," "Keep your shirt on"—point to a need in American life, to a lack we dimly feel when we complain about the lack of leisure.

For what we lack is not so much leisure to *do* as time to reflect and time to feel. What we seldom "take" is time to experience the things that have happened, the things that are happening, the things that are still ahead of us: going away from home for the first time, moving, starting the first child off to school, working into a new job, having a baby, having another baby, living through an accident or an operation, going on a long journey, getting married, helping to plan a brother's or a sister's marriage, deciding to retire, taking a foreign student to live in the house, taking in the child of a sick friend or neighbor, recovering from a fire or a flood or a bereavement, resolving a quarrel, coming into an unexpected inheritance. These are the events out of which poetry is made and fiction is written, but even in fiction and in poetry they become meaningful to us to the extent that we ourselves have experienced some of them and have had a chance to absorb what we have experienced.

There are several areas of our personal lives today in which we fail to "take time." One of these is marriage. Increasingly, young people are marrying over a weekend and returning on Monday to school or work, with the promise of a "nice long trip" sometime—next summer or next year. There are many reasons for these hurried weddings, but the central fact is that honeymoons—trips away from the familiar, where the newly married pair can be relatively alone—are going out. Yet getting married is an extraordinarily important moment in life, a time to be savored, prolonged, deeply experienced. Honeymoons are not always blissful—but then, neither is marriage. And no matter how casual or intimate the premarital relation has been, the experience of sitting down to a first meal face-to-face with the man or woman with whom one's life is to be shared, the experience of arranging one's personal belongings side by side with a husband's or a wife's, the decision as to which bed—or which side of the bed—belongs to each, is dazzlingly new. Putting all these experiences together requires time, time that can be shared fully by the two who are living through all that is new.

Another set of occasions to which we give too little time clusters around the birth of a baby. Very often today the mother prides herself on working right up to the last day, giving herself no time to live with the image of what the awaited baby will be like. Then in just a few days she comes home from the hospital to plunge into life as usual—plus the baby—instead of growing slowly into a world that now includes three people, not two. Even more important are the succeeding births, each of which is different from the one before because each involves a different family group that waits for and then discovers and begins to live with the new baby.

By taking slowly and savoring fully the days before the arrival of the newcomer, mothers—and fathers too—help the older children to absorb the whole experience. And when the newest baby is brought home, if life is not immediately bounced back to normal but instead moves a little more slowly around the new mother and the new baby—a fascinating combination for the older children—this gives the older children a chance to discover and play at their new places in the family—no longer "the baby" but the middle one, no longer "the older" but the oldest one. It gives the whole family a chance to discover how *this* baby moves, and the children time to discover the unpleasing facts that a new baby has no teeth and can't talk and to watch how its small fingers and toes curl and uncurl. Too often even the mother who has taken time to enjoy the prospect and the reality of a first baby later just fits the others into a niche that is stretched to hold them, forgetting that the experience is new to the older child, that each arrival is different and deserving of as much time for day-dreaming and feeling and reflecting.

Mourning is another area of our lives in which today we do not take time. Mourning has become unfashionable in the United States. The bereaved are supposed to pull themselves together as quickly as possible and to reweave the torn fabric of life. The reasons for this attitude are not hard to trace. We have lived through wars in which our young men went away hale and hearty and smart in their new uniforms; if they died, they died far away, and relatives and friends were cut off from the familiar, traditional rites of mourning. The age of death is constantly rising and few young children learn about death gradually, as an event that affects now one home and now another, closer at hand and farther away. And above all, with our general sense of optimism we prefer those who keep their chins up and do not burden others with their loss and grief. So we do not allow for quiet in the hours immediately following a bereavement, when time is needed to absorb the shock, free from the pressures of the world; nor do we allow for the weeks and months during which a loss is realized—a beautiful word that suggests the transmutation of the strange into something that is one's own.

The slow pace of national participation in President Kennedy's funeral rites moved and helped Americans partly because the cere-monies of parting did take time. Television viewers were taken step by step, literally, as they followed the solemn cortege to Arlington. And when that long weekend was over, people had moved in their grief as the events themselves had moved—slowly, with time on their side.

Snapshots and slides hastily made and hastily glanced at tend to overcondense experience. Home movies, like the television replication of a real event, come closer to pacing participation in life. A film of a child's first steps, rerun intermittently after the same child can walk and run and roller-skate and dance, keeps feeling alive. Parents watch-ing these first steps again with a stalwart, seven-year-old, two-wheeler rider beside them feel differently from the way they did when the baby, crowing with delight, stumbled and fell with a thud and got to his feet again. And the child himself re-experiences in tranquillity what he was too young to assimilate as he tumbled and got up again a long six years ago. In home movies we do have one device to hold old experience close and to relive it in a new setting.

But while a film can keep the past alive, it cannot help us take time to think and daydream about events that have not yet happened. Nor can film give us a way of experiencing more fully events as they happen or of stretching out moments until feeling and action match. In old Russia, when people were going on a journey those who were ready to go, cloaked and booted, and those who were remaining behind sat together for a long, precious, silent and apprehending moment before they separated. And in the days when people crossed oceans only on ships, there was the long moment when the passengers on deck and their friends ashore were still linked by bright paper streamers until at last, with a slow movement out of its dockside berth, the ship swung away and the streamers snapped.

Leisure opens the door to many things. Most often Americans think of what they would *do* with freer hours, days or weeks. If we gave ourselves and our children and our friends more time to feel and reflect, we would worry less about how people will use their leisure. For part of that leisure would be filled with anticipating, part with experiencing, part with remembering the things we have done.

Many Christmases

❧✕✖✕✖✕❧

DECEMBER, 1965

Fir trees, holly and poinsettias, bells and carols floating on the evening air, sparkling snow and prancing reindeer, a merry Santa promising presents and a bewildering assortment of Santas standing on cold street corners, stuffed stockings hung from the mantel, glittering lights on trees and a candle set in a window, shepherds and Wise Men, angels and wooly lambs, a crèche softly glowing, feasting and family gaiety, laughter mingling with children's voices—all these spell Christmas for Americans. In every region of the country and in every home there is something special—the spicy aroma of Christmas cookies, a melody, the hour of lighting the tree, dusk or cold dawn, a Nativity scene that encompasses the life of a village in miniature, a greeting in another language—that evokes the feeling, This is *our* Christmas! Yet, compounded of customs brought from a hundred lands and countless faraway homes, there is an American Christmas in which all of us share.

But what about the rest of the world? Is there one Christmas or are there many Christmases? What is Christmas like in the tropics? In the Far North? In the Antipodes? In New Zealand and Australia, summer weather and beach picnics under a blazing sun combine oddly with roast suckling pig, a carry-over from Merrie England. For almost two thousand years the Christmas story has been told and retold, and the traditions that have grown up around this festival have traveled, and in their travels have changed again and again. Around the world there are, in fact, many Christmases, old and new.

In New Guinea, where dark-skinned primitive peoples are very rapidly coming into a new, wider world, "Christmas" is one of the first English words they learn. But its meaning has no direct connection with the holiday we celebrate. In the past, New Guinea peoples depended on simple star lore and shifting winds to mark the changing seasons, but they had no concept of a year as a rhythmically repeating unit of time. For them, Christmas has been a discovery as a time-marking word that means both a year and the day that ends a year. A man will say, "I worked two Christmases to earn one box, one ax and five pounds." Or a man who is going away from his village to work among strangers on a distant plantation may say, "I will be home at Christmas"—that is, in a year. For the New Guinea native, as for the American child who is just learning about clocks and calendars, Christmas rounds out time and is a guarantee of predictability—an assurance that in some ways next year will be like last year, that day and night follow each other in orderly procession, that there are beginnings and endings and new beginnings.

In this sense Christmas resembles New Year's Day, not only in our calendar but in all the different calendars men have devised. In some countries it is this theme of the year's round and a new beginning that is the focus of Christmas. But in other countries this is the theme of the New Year, and New Year's, instead of Christmas, is the time for feasting and celebration, when visitors come and go, the occasion when gifts fall into the waiting hands of children.

Most people, however they may celebrate Christmas, think of its happening all at once everywhere in the world where people give it religious significance. But even the day of Christmas is not the same for everyone. In Bethlehem three different rites of Christmas are celebrated at different times. First comes the celebration by the churches of the Western world that follow the "new" Gregorian calendar, introduced in the sixteenth century. Then, twelve days later, just when we are celebrating Epiphany, the Christmas rites of the Eastern Orthodox churches, which still follow the old Julian calendar, begin. And finally, twelve days after that comes the celebration of the Armenian Church, whose followers still uphold the earliest tradition of the coincidence of Christmas, the day of Christ's birth, with Epiphany, the day of His baptism thirty years later. This special, rhythmic spacing of the world's Christmases is a happy accident of two calendars at this point in time; even in Bethlehem, Christmas comes and comes again, each year.

In our American Christmas we have tightly woven together the sacred and the secular strands of this festival. In many other parts of the world the feasting and the gift giving and the religious aspects of the occasion are separated. In some regions, children wait for December 5, when St. Nicholas will bring them presents. In parts of Germany this wait is filled with trepidation, for St. Nicholas may remember only their good behavior and give them presents—or he may recall their bad behavior and order his sinister assistant, Black Peter, to give them a switch. And in France, New Year's Day, not Christmas, has traditionally been the children's day. Here in the United States, where Jewish and Christian children go to school together and share each other's ways, Hanukkah, the Festival of Lights, may be the occasion for celebration.

There is a very real difference between the Christmas that is celebrated as a calendrical rite, marking the yearly round, and the Christmas that has its central meaning as a religious feast. For where the emphasis is on its secular aspects, bonfires and firecrackers and games echo still older calendrical rites; but where its religious aspects are central, Christmas marks a unique historical moment that in Christian faith meant a total break with the past and a new beginning for the whole world. Yet most often the two conceptions mingle. Christmas may be a time for lighting new fires, for blessing land and crops and water, for linking man with all living creatures—for feeding birds and wild creatures as well as man. All over the world people have brought their own most ancient hopes and fears, ceremonies and ways of thinking to bear on this festival. And if we consider which parts of the Christmas story a people have accepted and elaborated and which parts they have overlooked, we can see in their version a subtle restatement of how they understand the world and their place in it.

In Mexican villages, on the nine nights before Christmas, people commemorate in *las posadas* the journey of Mary and Joseph to Bethlehem and their vain search for a resting place among all the travelers crowded into the town. Each year nine families become, in turn, generous and giving hosts to the Child for whom, so long ago, there was no room at the inn. Soon after dark the villagers gather and walk in a long, winding procession through the streets, carrying candles and accompanied by music, to bring the sacred figures to the home of the host for that night. They knock at the door and ask for shelter, and now a peasant family proudly makes reparation for the old refusal by welcoming the Child. Each night the host also entertains the villagers, especially the children, who play a kind of blindman's buff, trying to knock down a *piñata*, a gaily decorated pottery container filled with sweets.

The theme of "no room at the inn," of the generosity of the very poor despite their deprivations, has its smaller counterpart around the world in the candle that is set in a window to guide the homeless child to a safe haven and in the welcome that may be given the stranger who asks for food.

Elsewhere the theme of the traveling gift-givers, the Wise Men, has caught men's imagination, and a great many traditions have grown up around the stories of their journey. An old Russian version, which has echoes in Italian tradition, reflects the close relationship of grandmother and grandchild in those societies. It tells how the Wise Men asked an old woman, Babushka, to accompany them. But she was too slow or she had no present to give and they left her behind. Ever since, Babushka has wandered around the world looking for the Child, and every year she leaves presents for the world's children, who remind her of what she missed.

But this is only one way of imagining the Wise Men. In Haiti they are the familiar Three Kings, proudly crowned and richly robed, and it is they who usher in Christmas with a gaily solemn dance on Christmas Eve. Here the theme of magnificence is central, and it matters greatly to Haitians that one of the kings has a dark skin like their own. In modern Haiti, Santa Claus, there sometimes called *Tonton Noël*—Uncle Christmas—in a joking tone, is replacing the older figures. They still come, but they are losing their old glory, and with it the simple ecumenical structure built around the idea of the kings as representatives of all mankind is disappearing too.

Around the world there are many Christmases, and the customs of this festival are part of a tradition that lives and grows and changes and still carries with it very old ideas. In the contemporary world the Christmas tree, with its lights and shining balls, is almost ubiquitous. But some scholars think it represents a mingling of two quite different conceptions. In the Middle Ages some peoples of western Europe celebrated the feast of Adam and Eve on December 24, and for this occasion decorated fir trees with "apples" to represent the tree in the Garden. At the same time, in celebration of Christmas, they set a candle at the top of a tall staff, or built up pyramids of lights on tall wooden candelabra. The eventual combining of the two was something that may easily have happened, but the play of imagination around the tree with its lights and decorations has wiped out all memory of one of the older themes. For contemporary Americans the gay tree has its own significance, and for many people around the world it is now an essential part of an American Christmas.

There are many Christmases, but none is static. Nowadays more and more children picture Santa Claus not with a sled and reindeer but coming down from a starry sky onto the snow in his own airplane laden with new kinds of toys. It may not be long now before St. Nicholas, once a bishop, later the patron saint of children and sailors and still later turning into Santa Claus, may become an astronaut who circles the globe and carries Christmas into space. Americans have created a new kind of Christmas out of old traditions, religious and secular, in which all Americans, whatever their faith, can take part. Now, in turn, our version is spreading around the earth, reaching remote valleys where people are just coming into the modern world. Our version of Christmas is far removed from many the world has known, but it carries the ancient conception of the brotherhood of man.

New Year's—A Universal Birthday

❦❦❦❦❦

DECEMBER, 1968

Just before midnight an expectant hush falls on the party gaiety. Someone throws open a window. In the moment of waiting silence the thoughts of some turn to the past, while others, making a half-serious wish or resolution, look to the future. And some only wait impatiently. Then suddenly the spell is broken as bells ring out, whistles and sirens blow and the holiday-makers join in the din with their horns and shouts of "Happy New Year!"

New Year's is a festival of transition, the point where end meets beginning. It is a celebration of the idea of time, an idea that has captured man's imagination for millenniums. Traditional celebrations, however they varied over the centuries and in different cultures, gave formal and public expression to feelings of awe and wonder, mourning and rejoicing, repentance and hope and purpose, the sense of men's relations to one another and to the whole universe.

But New Year's today has become for most people the mere shell of a celebration, without content or focus. Everywhere there are parties: office parties, parties in homes, country-club dances, crowds in hotels and night spots, pushing and raucous crowds in the streets, moody crowds in bars—and the lonely feel doubly alone. There is incessant talking and noise and almost everywhere there is too much to drink—too often the prelude to louder noise, accidents on the road and hangover headaches on New Year's Day.

We treat the New Year casually. In our time it has become a wholly secular holiday. Only a few tag ends remain of old beliefs. There is the modern Mummers Parade in Philadelphia, but no one now connects this with the old idea that at New Year the world is turned topsy-turvy. We attribute no magical power to our resolutions and no one treats the events of the day as omens for the year. No one waits to see who will be the first to step over the doorsill (a dark man, good luck; a fair man, bad luck; a woman, death).

Few of us remember that the decrepit Old Year, whom we picture in cartoons as a bowed and bald Father Time with his sickle, is also a figure of death; or that the baby New Year, chubby and smiling as a cupid, is also a symbol of love and light. These two figures survive, often as figures of fun, but we barely acknowledge their older meaning. And almost no one now realizes that in our own tradition the pealing of bells, not only at the New Year but also at births and weddings and on other occasions marking a transition, once was intended to drive out evil and all that might endanger what was so newly begun. Instead, our noisemaking has become a very slightly ritualized salute to the future.

But noise is only one way of marking a transition.

In Bali, once every four hundred days quiet descends. On this day nothing stirs on the whole densely populated island. People speak of it as "the Silence," the Balinese New Year. On every other day the roads are crowded with hawkers, people going to and from market, small boys driving oxen or water buffalo and people hurrying lightly under heavy loads. On feast days there also are gaudy processions with their orchestras and theatrical troupes traveling to the villages where they will perform.

The air on every other day is loud with the sound of voices, the shouts of vendors, laughter at jokes, the squalling of babies carried on the hips of their child nurses, the yapping of dogs and the music of practicing orchestras. Even in the deepest night the quiet is broken by shrill cockcrowing, dogs barking and lonely peasants out in the fields playing bamboo xylophones softly to themselves. But on New Year no one moves about and every sound is hushed. Each family, its fires out and offerings arranged in the house temple, stays at home to observe the Silence.

Looking the world over, one very striking thing is the limited number of ways in which men have regarded the progress of time. Many peoples treat time as we do, as a stream that flows forever onward, never passing the same point twice. What is passed cannot come again.

Other peoples, such as the Balinese, think of time as a cyclical process, as if time were a wheel that periodically turned on itself. And some peoples have regarded man's life as part of a cycle—the individual is born and dies and eventually is born again. Very often, just at the turning point—at the end of each year or of a set of years—people have believed that this was potentially a period of great danger when the sun might never rise again or the earth might cease to be fertile or all human life might be destroyed in some great disaster. To avert the danger many peoples have ritually fasted and organized their affairs—paying their debts, ending their quarrels, cleaning their houses, rebuilding their temples and in other ways straightening out their own and the world's affairs. Then, when the new time has come, they have celebrated its arrival with other rituals, some expressing joy at danger overcome, some interpreting omens for the future and others designed to make the new time safe and fruitful.

Our own feeling that the turn of the century has a special quality carries with it something of this sense of precarious balance at the transition from an old to a new cycle. Already, at the end of the 1960's, we are engaged in predicting what life will be like for our children in the year 2000, and we are concerned with preparing the world for the millennial shift to a new thousand-year cycle. But we have no rituals to focus our activities, only a diffuse sense of concern that shapes our discussions of the year 2000, as deeper emotions once gave meaning to ceremonies of transition.

To a certain extent the heightened sense of the meaning of time at New Year is related to the invention of calendars, and peoples who have no script and no calendar for measuring regular intervals over a very long span have a more limited conception of time. For them time stretches back only as far as memory does and forward into the lives of their grandchildren, and it is only the seasons that come and come again. Very indefinitely, also, time goes back to the beginning, when they as a people came into being.

The belief may be that this beginning was only four or five generations ago, just beyond the reach of the memory of living men, as it was for some of the peoples of New Guinea. Or it may have been long, long ago, its extent unmeasured and unmeasurable, as the Iatmul people of the Sepik River in New Guinea believed. And memory can be extraordinarily stretched out, as it was among Polynesian islanders who kept track of the names and adventures of important ancestors in strings of genealogies that went back sometimes to mythological beginnings.

Even so, without the idea of a calendar it is impossible to conceptualize great spans of time. In the past hundred years we have stretched out time over millions of years in reading the history of the earth. Today we also have the means of dividing time into milliseconds for fine measurements. All this has depended on complex inventions.

But for primitive peoples, day and night, the shifting patterns of the night sky, seasonal changes in winds and weather, seedtime and harvesttime, the waxing and waning of the moon, the changing position of the sun and, of course, the birth, maturation and death of human beings—all these changing and recurrent aspects of the natural world have given men ways of punctuating time and marking transitions.

Some peoples have made very little even of these ways of marking time. When I was working among the Arapesh of New Guinea, I myself began to wonder what the date was. They had names for moons, such as "the moon when we get bananas from the deserted yam gardens." But as each family planted its garden with yams and bananas at a different time, they called the same moon by different terms. They said to me: "You count the moons, but we just know their names." All they really knew was some names that could be appropriately used, and no two families followed the same calendar. They even thought it was odd that anyone should expect a moon to have only one fixed name.

Other peoples had a much more definite sense of cycles. In the past the Manus of the Admiralty Islands spoke of days and nights (measuring the length of journeys, for example) and moons and then of time expressed in terms of the life span. They would place an event in terms of other significant events, saying "when my father was a child" or "when I made the last marriage payment for my daughter." But they had no way of measuring, as we do, the months that become a year and the years that become a decade or a century.

When the Manus moved into the modern world they seized upon the European calendar, learned every detail about how it works and now talk endlessly in calendar time.

"Today is Sunday, the thirteenth of November, 1966," they would say to me. "It is just six weeks before Christmas."

The Manus write down not only the year and day of the month but even the hour on which a baby is born or a quarrel is ended. At home or away from home they know exactly the date on which their children will be taking final examinations and they plan for the future, setting their goals as we do by dates. With one leap they have taken over the conception of time that moves onward and its modern handling.

Heirs as we are to so many traditions, we have relegated all the solemn beliefs and celebrations connected with the turning of the seasons and the year to our different religious calendars. For a time in western Europe, this meant that people lived by different calendars and celebrated the New Year at different seasons. In 1582, when Pope Gregory XIII modified the old Julian calendar and decided that the secular New Year should come (as it had for the Romans) on January 1, Catholic countries made the change quickly; but Protestant countries continued to use Old Style dates for a long time and to celebrate the New Year as a spring festival, on March 25, as medieval Christians had. England (and so England's colonies) made the change only in 1752. Few people today think of this, though there is an echo in a New Year's song we have assimilated into Christmas carols:

> "Here we come a-wassailing
> Among the leaves so green."

The Jewish religious calendar, by contrast, has been stable for a much longer period, and the ceremonies ushered in by Rosh Hashana, which comes at the beginning of the first month of the year (the autumn of the secular year), still carry the symbolism of beginning and ending, repentance and rejoicing, death and life, darkness and light, that is the central expression of our human sense of transition.

In spite of our heritage, we make very little of the turn of the year. All that remains is the vague feeling that it is an occasion to be remarked, the sense that it is a time when people should come together, as families do to celebrate a birthday. And perhaps, just because it is a holiday that once focused men's deep emotions about the past and the future and the continuity of time, the New Year may again become infused with meaning. A world society that must take into account the lingering traditions of all peoples may come to observe it as a day in which humanity can celebrate a common birthday in time.

Man on the Moon

❧❧❧

JULY, 1969

The day a man steps onto the surface of the moon, human beings will be taking a decisive step out of the past into a new reality.

Long ago our ancestors lived on very small islands of the known, scattered on an unknown planet. The whole of a universe could be encompassed in a hilltop and a valley, the steady stars, the wandering Pleiades and the waxing and waning moon. Mountain walls, vast plains, dark forests and the fringing seas cut off little groups of men from knowledge of what lay beyond their own familiar patch of earth, and the arching sky was accessible to them only in fantasy.

Today the deeply important thing is that the same set of inventions that is opening the universe to exploration also has made our world one, a bounded unit within which all human beings share the same hazards and have access to the same hopes. This is why I think the moon landing is a momentous event.

But as we wait for the astronaut to take that first step onto a part of the solar system that is not our earth, it seems to me that our vision is faltering. We have followed each stage of this venture into space. Through the camera's eye we have already looked down at barren stretches of moonscape and we have seen our own world, a small, shining globe in space. But as the first climax approaches, wonder at the unknown and a sense of the magnificence of the achievement are dimmed and tarnished by doubt and the feeling on the part of many people that "all this is meaningless to me."

The same questions have been asked for a decade. Why go to the moon? Why spend all that money on a space program that will change no one's daily life and solve none of the problems of human misery on earth? Can't we put the same money to much better use here? Why not put the earth in order before we take off into space? Who cares whether we or the Russians win this "race"? With the danger of nuclear warfare and the menace of uncontrolled population growth—both the outcome of modern science—confronting us, why should anyone get excited about one more technological success, the landing of a man on the moon?

These are the wrong questions to be asking, I think. They are evidence, it seems to me, that we are suffering from a failure of the imagination, a failure of nerve, that psychiatrists are beginning to recognize as *future shock*. It is well known that people who go to live in a strange place among strangers whose language and manners are incomprehensible often suffer from culture shock, a state of mind in which, alienated and homesick, they temporarily lose their ability to take in new experience. In somewhat the same way many people are shrinking from the future and from participation in the movement toward a new, expanded reality. And like homesick travelers abroad, they are focusing their anxieties on home.

The reasons are not far to seek. We are at a turning point in human history. What is required of us is not merely a change in our conceptions, but also in our sense of scale. The only parallel to the situation with which we are confronted lies five hundred years in our past, just before the great era of world exploration.

Then, in the 1420's, Prince Henry—an extraordinary technologist whom we only vaguely remember as "Henry the Navigator," brother of the king of Portugal—gathered around him a great company of scholars, astronomers, map makers, pilots, instrument makers and craftsmen in Sagres, on a lonely promontory reaching out into the unexplored Atlantic. They created a new science of navigation and invented a new kind of ship, the lateen-rigged caravel, which could make headway against the winds and was designed for long sea voyages. Up to that time ships navigated from island to island or from point to point, close to shore; where this was impossible, few men sailed intentionally.

For forty years Prince Henry sent ship after ship into the Atlantic and down the coast of Africa, hoping to solve the "impossible" problem of circling the continent. His were not the first craft to reach the nearer islands or to attempt the African voyage or even to rove the open Atlantic. But the men who sailed the caravels were the first to study and plot systematically the winds and currents off the African coast and, eventually, on the open seas from the North to the South Atlantic. And it was from seamen trained in Sagres, only a few years after Prince Henry's death, that Columbus learned his seamanship.

Prince Henry and his company of scientists and technicians formed one of the small clusters of men whose work began the transformation of the world. They solved no immediate problems. The Moors, against whom Henry fought as a young man, still were a threat to Mediterranean Europe when he died. The Portuguese inventions made feasible long voyages of discovery, but no one knew what lay ahead. And certainly no one could foresee that the greatest innovation was the new approach to problem solution, which combined theory and the deliberate creation of a technology to carry out practical experiments. Only today do we fully realize that this linkage of science and technology in the thinking of Prince Henry and others of his time made possible a world in which people could believe in and work toward progress.

The parallel, of course, is an imperfect one. Where it breaks down most seriously is in the number of people involved. In the fifteenth century only a handful of men were aware of the tremendous breakthrough in knowledge. Today in an intercommunicating world, millions of people enter into the debate and are part of the decision-making process that will determine how we shall deal with the knowledge, the anxieties and the hopes that are part of this contemporary expansion of reality. And it is extraordinarily difficult for vast numbers of people to move simultaneously toward change.

We could slow down and wait. We could turn our attention to the problems that going to the moon certainly will not solve. We could hope that, given time, more men would become aware of new possibilities. But I think this would be fatal to our future.

As I see it, this new exploration—this work at the edge of human knowledge—is what will keep us human. It will keep us from turning backward toward ways of thinking and acting that have separated men from their full humanity. For humanity is not to be found by going back to some Golden Age when communities were small and the people living in them knew and trusted (but also, in reality, often bitterly hated and despised) one another. Humanity is not to be found in any kind of romantic retreat, in any denial of present reality, in any decision to rest within the known.

Humanity lies in man's urge to explore the world. It lies in man's unique drive to understand the nature of the universe within which he lives. It lies in man's capacity to question the known and imagine the unknown.

Step by difficult step men expanded the world they knew to include the whole of the planet and all men living on it. In the seventeenth century, men's conception of the universe was transformed by the telescope, which brought the moon and the stars nearer, and by the microscope, through which the once-indecipherable nature of matter was made intelligible. Once men could count only the smallest collections of objects, and until our own generation the organization of vast assemblages of facts was an infinitely laborious task. Today the use of computers allows men to think about organized complexity on a scale entirely new. And now, finally, we are moving out from the earth as living beings, in the persons of the astronauts, to experience space with all our capacities, our wonder and thirst for understanding. For the first time we are exercising in full reality what has been truly called man's cosmic sense.

Each stage of discovery has enlarged not only men's understanding of the world, but also their awareness of human potentialities. So I believe we cannot stop now on the threshold of new experience. We must put our knowledge to the test. Human potentialities, unexercised, can wither and fester, can become malignant and dangerous. A society that no longer moves forward does not merely stagnate; it begins to die.

The exploration of space does not mean neglect of the tremendously difficult problems of our immediate environment. It will mean, I think, the development of a new context within which we can look for viable solutions. Up to now, our ideas about what can be done have been either utopian or essentially parochial, while the problems themselves affect the well-being of human beings everywhere.

It is no accident that the Soviet Union and the United States, the two largest organized modern states, have built and launched the first successful spacecraft, while the governments of the 180 million people in the Common Market countries of western Europe have continued to bicker divisively and ineffectually over which stage of a shared rocket should be built by whom and have been unable to find ways of co-ordinating their efforts. Nor is it an accident that these two countries are moving ahead so fast in changing and raising the level of education—though in this we still, by far, lead the world.

In part the success of the Soviet Union and the United States has resulted from the fact that these two countries have—and have been willing to commit—the resources in money and men and organization necessary for so large-scale an enterprise. In part it is owing to their orientation to the future. Soviet and American men and women have no monopoly on talent. But each of us, as a country, has been able to attain the precise and magnificent large-scale co-ordination of effort necessary for building spacecraft and for becoming pioneers in the space age.

The very thing that has made the space program successful, but also in the eyes of many people boring, is awareness of the crucial importance of detail. The rehearsals, the repetitiveness, the careful steps, the determination on absolute precautions and the participation of the citizenry in something that might, but must not, go wrong—all these things also are essential to the success of an enterprise on a new, unprecedented scale.

No country, as yet, has fully recognized the fact that the scale of our major human problems is not local or national but regional or world-wide. No country has realized that we must simultaneously include both extremes—the individual and all men—in working toward social solutions. Individual human dignity can be assured only when all men everywhere are accorded and accord to others their full humanity. National solutions are inadequate as they are based on past conceptions of human differences, uneconomic uses of resources and barriers to communication that no longer exist.

We have yet to discover how to co-ordinate effort to solve social problems on the scale that will be necessary. This will mean, as it has in the space program, work with small models, new kinds of simulations and trials and intensive learning before we move into large new systems of organization with planetary repercussions. No more than the fifteenth-century men who opened the seas to exploration can we see what lies ahead. But unlike the early explorers, we have learned how to direct our efforts.

The lunar landing will be a triumph in its own right. But at the same time nothing can demonstrate more cogently, I feel, that there is an intimate and inescapable connection between man's pursuit of his destiny and his attainment of his own humanity than the intricate technological co-ordination combined with individual human courage that characterizes both the American and the Soviet space programs. There is no reason for alienation from experience that will enhance our common humanity. Voyages to the moon—and beyond the moon—are one assurance of our ability to live on the earth.

II

THE
PUBLIC GOOD

The Egalitarian Error

❧❧❧❧❧

AUGUST, 1962

Almost all Americans want to be democratic, but many Americans are confused about what, exactly, democracy means. How do you know when someone is acting in a democratic—or an undemocratic—way? Recently several groups have spoken out with particular bitterness against the kind of democracy that means equal opportunity for all, regardless of race or national origin. They act as if all human beings did not belong to one species, as if some races of mankind were inferior to others in their capacity to learn what members of other races know and have invented. Other extremists attack religious groups—Jews or Catholics—or deny the right of an individual to be an agnostic. One reason that these extremists, who explicitly do not want to be democratic, can get a hearing even though their views run counter to the Constitution and our traditional values is that the people who *do* want to be democratic are frequently so muddled.

For many Americans, democratic behavior necessitates an outright denial of any significant differences among human beings. In their eyes it is undemocratic for anyone to refer, in the presence of any other person, to differences in skin color, manners or religious beliefs. Whatever one's private thoughts may be, it is necessary always to act as if everyone were exactly alike.

Behavior of this kind developed partly as a reaction to those who discriminated against or actively abused members of other groups. But it is artificial, often hypocritical behavior, nonetheless, and it dulls and flattens human relationships. If two people can't talk easily and comfortably but must forever guard against some slip of the tongue, some admission of what is in both persons' minds, they are likely to talk as little as possible. This embarrassment about differences reaches a final absurdity when a Methodist feels that he cannot take a guest on a tour of his garden because he might have to identify a wild plant with a blue flower, called the wandering Jew, or when a white lecturer feels he ought not to mention the name of Conrad's beautiful story *The Nigger of the "Narcissus."* But it is no less absurd when well-meaning people, speaking of the physically handicapped, tell prospective employers: "They don't want special consideration. Ask as much of them as you do of everyone else, and fire them if they don't give satisfaction!"

Another version of false democracy is the need to deny the existence of personal advantages. Inherited wealth, famous parents, a first-class mind, a rare voice, a beautiful face, an exceptional physical skill—any advantage has to be minimized or denied. Continually watched and measured, the man or woman who is rich or talented or well educated is likely to be called "undemocratic" whenever he does anything out of the ordinary—more or less of something than others do. If he wants acceptance, the person with a "superior" attribute, like the person with an "inferior" attribute, often feels obliged to take on a protective disguise, to act as if he were just like everybody else. One denies difference; the other minimizes it. And both believe, as they conform to these false standards, that they act in the name of democracy.

For many Americans, a related source of confusion is success. As a people we Americans greatly prize success. And in our eyes success all too often means simply outdoing other people by virtue of achievement judged by some single scale—income or honors or headlines or trophies—and coming out at "the top." Only one person, as we see it, can be the best—can get the highest grades, be voted the most attractive girl or the boy most likely to succeed. Though we often rejoice in the success of people far removed from ourselves—in another profession, another community, or endowed with a talent that we do not covet—we tend to regard the success of people close at hand, within our own small group, as a threat. We fail to realize that there are many kinds of success, including the kind of success that lies within a person. We do not realize, for example, that there could be in the same class one hundred boys and girls—each of them a "success" in a different kind of way. Individuality is again lost in a refusal to recognize and cherish the differences among people.

The attitude that measures success by a single yardstick and isolates the *one* winner and the kind of "democracy" that denies or minimizes differences among people are both deeply destructive. Imagine for a moment a family with two sons, one of whom is brilliant, attractive and athletic while the other is dull, unattractive and clumsy. Both boys attend the same high school. In the interest of the slower boy, the parents would want the school to set equally low standards for everyone. Lessons should be easy; no one should be forced to study dead languages or advanced mathematics in order to graduate. Athletics should be noncompetitive; every boy should have a chance to enjoy playing games. Everyone should be invited to all the parties. As for special attention to gifted children, this is not fair to the other children. An all-round education should be geared to the average, normal child.

But in the interest of the other boy, these same parents would have quite opposite goals. After all, we need highly trained people; the school should do the most it can for its best students. Funds should be made available for advanced classes and special teachers, for the best possible coach, the best athletic equipment. Young people should be allowed to choose friends on their own level. The aim of education should be to produce topflight students.

This is an extreme example, but it illustrates the completely incompatible aims that can arise in this kind of "democracy." Must our country shut its eyes to the needs of either its gifted or its less gifted sons? It would be a good deal more sensible to admit, as some schools do today, that children differ widely from one another, that all successes cannot be ranged on one single scale, that there is room in a real democracy to help each child find his own level and develop to his fullest potential.

Moving now to a wider scene, before World War I Americans thought of themselves as occupying a unique place in the world—and there was no question in most minds that this country was a "success." True, Europeans might look down on us for our lack of culture, but with a few notable, local exceptions, we simply refused to compete on European terms. There was no country in the world remotely like the one we were building. But since World War II we have felt the impact of a country whose size and strength and emphasis on national achievement more closely parallel our own. Today we are ahead of Russia, or Russia is ahead of us. Nothing else matters. Instead of valuing and developing the extraordinary assets and potential of our country for their own sake, we are involved in a simple set of competitions for wealth and power and dominance.

These are expensive and dangerous attitudes. When democracy ceases to be a cherished way of life and becomes instead the name of one team, we are using the word democracy to describe behavior that places us and all other men in jeopardy.

Individually, nationally and, today, internationally, the misreading of the phrase "all men are created equal" exacts a heavy price. The attitudes that follow from our misconceptions may be compatible with life in a country where land and rank and prestige are severely limited and the roads to success are few. But they are inappropriate in a land as rich, as open, as filled with opportunities as our own. They are the price we pay for being *less* democratic than we claim to be.

"All men are created equal" does not mean that all men are the same. What it does mean is that each should be accorded full respect and full rights as a unique human being—full respect for his humanity *and* for his differences from other people.

The Police and the Community

Who is a policeman?

Superficially, the answer is obvious. Anyone can recognize the uniformed policeman walking his beat, directing traffic, stopping a street fight, driving a patrol car, arresting a pickpocket, keeping a crowd in order or answering a frantic call for help. But if you were to ask the question of any group of one hundred Americans you would discover that no two answers were exactly alike.

Our images of policemen contain many contradictory elements. The policeman is the big, smiling Irish cop beloved by the entire city—on St. Patrick's Day. He is the children's friend. ("If you get lost, ask the *policeman!*") He is also the bogy-man who threatens small delinquents. ("If you do that again, the *policeman* will take you away!")

He is the frontier sheriff with a ready gun, administering rough justice inside or outside the law, or he is the tobacco-chewing Southern sheriff conniving with a lynch mob. He is the link between respectability and corruption—the man who has to be paid off. He is the man in disguise who traps the narcotics pusher. He is outside authority, the stranger who uses brute force to keep order. He is the rescuing hero who talks the would-be suicide back from the edge of the roof and who, singlehandedly, disarms the homicide.

And today, on millions of television screens, the policeman appears not as an identifiable individual but as one of an impersonal mass of men, helmeted and armed, charging a mass of demonstrators who are yelling derisive obscenities. He is the good guy and the bad guy, honest and venal, barbarous and humane.

The police as they are presented to Americans—and so, of course, to themselves as well—have many faces, real and imaginary, whose outlines conflict with one another, blend and change with time and place and circumstance.

In the United States we do not have any centralized policy-making and standard-setting system, as most European countries do, for selecting, training and directing the activities of the thousands of men and the handful of women who carry out all the complicated operations necessary for keeping the peace, enforcing the law and meeting emergencies. Most of us would be hard-pressed to name many of the various kinds of police organizations that function at different levels, representing the Federal Government (the FBI, for example), the state, the county, the city, the village.

The extreme diversity of our system—and the different sources of our traditions—becomes apparent when one realizes that in different parts of the country, police activities are carried out locally by sheriffs and their deputies in 3,000 counties and in some places by county police as well; by constables in some 20,000 townships and county districts; by small, sometimes part-time, forces in about 15,000 villages, boroughs and incorporated towns; and finally, by large-scale, bureaucratized forces in more than 1,000 cities. And in each community, relations with the police are shaped by the people who live there.

So every American, building on his own experience, on the mythology of law enforcement at different times in our history, on fictional accounts and, most important of all, on the slanted presentations of crime in the daily news, creates his own picture of what policemen should be and what they are.

Our police, especially the urban police, have to meet the demands made on them by some of the most complex communities the world has ever known. They do not make the laws and they cannot, by themselves, establish community standards. Ideally, they are the community conscience, firm and evenhanded. In fact, it is their job to provide whatever the community will support or tolerate in the way of law and order, including order that is outside the law.

They are expected to keep the city running smoothly in spite of holiday crowds, storms, strikes and power blackouts. They are expected to establish quiet, safety and respectability, particularly in middle-class and well-to-do sections of the city, where this means watching over the safety of people and buildings and cars, keeping the children in hand unobtrusively and removing the drunken, the disorderly, the inappropriately dressed, the rowdy and all those who arouse suspicion. It means keeping crowds in good humor or facing the threat of mob violence. It means investigating homicides. It means working with insurance companies to reduce the number of large-scale robberies; yet it also means implementing the policy of many insurance companies that, in the case of minor thefts, simply pay off the insured rather than require investigation. Police work means enforcing traffic rules, giving tickets or not giving tickets or fixing some of the tickets given. It means keeping addicts, prostitutes and gamblers off streets or confined to certain streets. It means racket-busting or collaborating with racketeers or containing rackets within "safe" limits.

For the police, in fact, law enforcement means meeting the different, often incompatible demands that are made on them: by the respectable and the moral (including those whose standards were formed long ago or in a different country), by the poor and the desperate, the wealthy who want their fun kept under cover, the vice lords who commercialize "sin" to make it more attractive, the legitimate businessman and the racketeer, each of whom expects protection. Police work means meeting the demands of the political radical and the political conservative, the timid and the touchy, the sick and the disoriented and the stranger.

Today Americans are faced with the hard facts of spreading lawlessness. Anonymous crime, a great deal of it committed by juveniles, is on the increase everywhere. In cities the informal arrangements that once helped to keep violence under control have broken down as newcomers to old neighborhoods treat the police as the enemy—along with slum landlords and profit-gouging businessmen. And everywhere, older boundaries are vanishing or are made meaningless by changed patterns of living, the speed of transport, the wide coverage of television. Americans living in small towns still believe that theirs is a world where "you can leave the doors unlocked"—and then find they are wrong. Crime and the very contrasting methods of dealing with it, which once were confined within narrower limits, meet unaccustomed eyes; and the police, who are held responsible for safety and order, are put on the spot.

So the police everywhere have become the focus of confused controversy over what they do and do not do and what the remedy is. They are photographed and televised. They are attacked, defended, vilified and all too seldom praised. The police themselves, who are Americans like other Americans, are not sitting quietly by. They too stand embattled. They who once kept picketers on the move and protected scabs in union battles, who presided grimly over May Day parades, now join other municipal workers—firemen, sanitation men, teachers and welfare workers—in strikes against the cities in which their positions have become so ambiguous.

We hear about members of a police force who are "enforcing the letter of the law" to produce a slowdown during contract negotiations. We hear about their rebellion against civilian review boards and their complaints that Supreme Court decisions have tied their hands in dealing with suspected criminals. We have witnessed the fury with which they attack students who force them into unwanted confrontations.

The general public impression is that somehow our present police system has failed and we are facing a crisis in the maintenance of public order.

I think this is a mistake.

It is true that we are facing a crisis. It is our American style to define as a crisis any situation that calls for large-scale, organized change. We treat the situation as almost irremediably bad, brand the outmoded institution as a dismal failure and castigate those responsible for keeping it going. Finally, when we have roused ourselves to fever pitch, we try for some immediate—and, too often, short-term—solution.

At present we are in a turmoil of change. We are looking with new intensity at our unmanageable cities, at the awakened and accelerating demands of black Americans for changes that will wipe out three hundred years of insult and neglect, at the restlessness of our students and the inappropriateness of much of our education, at the wasteful use of our irreplaceable resources, at the unresolved inequities of opportunity for the rich and the poor. And looking at the lawlessness that is one symptom of transition, we are also asking: What is law and order? What part are the police playing?

At this moment when we are reassessing who and what we are, it is not astonishing that we should become aware in new ways of the incongruities inherent in our existing police methods. But concentrating on the present, we overlook the fact that we have been a country of multiple and contrasting standards from our earliest beginnings. We teach our children, as a first lesson concerning freedom of thought, about Roger Williams and Anne Hutchinson, who broke away from the Massachusetts Bay Colony to found freer settlements in Providence and Portsmouth. But we do not emphasize the fact that we began as a people whose freedoms would seem impossibly unfree to us today.

We celebrate our high moments of progress, but we lay less emphasis on the conflicts of belief and attitude underlying all our struggles to extend the vote, expand education, raise standards of living, curb corruption, make labor secure in its negotiations with management and give wider opportunities to more Americans. Some members of each generation, reared to accept the same ideals, have found shortcomings in the life around them. Newly horrified, they have created a crisis and have achieved some change. Nevertheless we remain a people with multiple standards.

I think we are fully justified in asking how we can improve the safety and the security of everyone in our complex communities. But I do not think we shall succeed in doing this simply by reforming the police system and certainly not by making new, unworkable demands on the men who carry the day-to-day burden of police work.

The compromises made by the police, the corruption they participate in, their sense of alienation from parts of the community, the anger they vent on rioters and their own rebellion against being treated as men undeserving of just reward for difficult, often dangerous work—all these are responses both to the kinds of community in which they operate and to the unease and dissension from which no one is exempt in a time of change.

We are struggling toward a new conception of interpersonal relations in our open society, one that will enlarge men's freedom through their concern for one another. What we are working toward is not merely order, but a new kind of order.

A necessary part of this, in our public life, is a police system that is genuinely integrated into the community. The present situation, symbolized by review boards in which the beleaguered police are on one side and all complaining citizens on the other, is what we do not want. Nor do we want a federally controlled police. The national government can help communities raise and unify technical standards and meet their obligations, but the police should be responsive specifically to local needs in all their complexity.

The police can become the police of all the people in a community only if their tasks of preventing crime, of stepping in when breakdowns occur and of meeting human emergencies are much more fully shared by other arms of the local government. The larger and more diversified any community is, the more difficult it is for any one agency to know who lives in a neighborhood, what their problems are and how to meet those problems realistically. For a long time we have encouraged specialization; what we lack now are meeting points for the caretaking specialists who are concerned with the safety and welfare of children, the aged, the destitute, the addict, the newly discharged mental patient, the potentially dangerous. In each community we need meeting points among such agencies and the police, so that they can work with one another.

The new concept of community mental health, in which all the people of an area become the concern of a center that co-ordinates many kinds of service, can provide the basis for planning how independent, specialized agencies can become mutually supportive. Simply by establishing liaison across professional boundaries, such a center can increase the chances of speeding appropriate action. In the long run, however, it will lead to something much more important— new ideas for preventive care based on wider experience, new forms of training and new careers to carry the knowledge into practice.

This is, I think, the way to work toward a redefinition of police organization. When the police force becomes part of a network of care for public welfare, we shall begin to draw on more diverse talents in the men who choose this career and we shall be able to develop new standards of education and training. We cannot form a model police force following some blueprint, but we can aim to build one in which shared responsibility for a city's well-being reflects and furthers that city's sense of community. Now we have many images of who policemen are. Then they will be our other selves.

Privacy and the Public Good, I

APRIL, 1965

Privacy—the right to live part of one's life out of the public eye, according to one's own choice, and free from interference by others —is taken for granted by Americans. The right to privacy is closely bound up with our sense of individuality and our belief in the value of personal choice. It includes the freedom to come and go and to speak wherever one may be without the feeling of being under observation. The desire for a personal life of one's own choosing is part of the American dream of the open frontier; today the expectation of greater freedom of choice keeps a stream of people moving from small towns into our larger towns and cities. Yet the very strength of our commitment has created a dilemma in which both personal privacy and public safety are in jeopardy.

We are faced by two kinds of danger. The first has to do with the invasion of privacy by the new technology—the devices that enable an outsider, often an anonymous outsider, to break in on a person's life without his consent and even without his knowledge. Wire tapping and the use of hidden microphones to overhear confidential conversations are perhaps the most familiar. But there are many other such devices—cameras with telephoto lenses, film that can be used to take pictures in the dark, listening devices that can be beamed from a distance and the so-called lie detectors—all of which vastly enlarge customary spheres of observation. Generally speaking, people connect their use with crime detection, but the inference is that they can be used against anyone almost anywhere.

The second danger arises out of an apparent indifference on the part of ordinary citizens to crimes that are committed in public, sometimes before their very eyes. There are the crimes that take place on dark, lonely streets or in empty corridors and elevators of huge buildings. There are also the holdups and muggings and murders that take place in broad daylight in full view of passers-by. A national outcry has arisen against such crimes as these and against the apathy of those who do not lift a hand to help the victim of an attack. There has also been an outcry against the activities of private citizens' groups organized to protect their home neighborhoods. The result is bafflement and a sense of outrage.

Although these two dangers appear to be quite different in their effect upon personal security, they are actually only two parts of one picture the components of which have become disassociated in our minds. How has this happened?

In the first place, we have somehow ceased to recognize that responsible knowledge of who someone is, where he is and what he is doing is as much a protection of innocence as it is a deterrent to crime. In the public view the policeman, the immigration and the customs official, the fire inspector and many others with legal investigatory powers have come to be regarded as enemies of privacy. We have lost sight of their protective role and have confused personal privacy with privacy from the law.

Still another source of confusion exists that goes back to a rejection of the viewpoint of the small community where everyone is known and no sharp distinction can be drawn between neighbors' sanctions and public opinion. In a small community common knowledge, based on watching and listening, on memories of past events witnessed or surmised and on shared gossip, is a form of protection, but it can also be turned against any person or group whose standards the community neither understands nor accepts. People in a small community may protect only too well the eccentricities of those who "belong"; their accumulated knowledge, however, leaves little room for privacy.

In contrast, life in a large city offers extraordinary possibilities for anonymity. In the accepted sense there are virtually no neighbors. People living on the same street seldom know one another's names; even those who have lived in the same building for many years may have little idea of how any individual among them spends his time. In a city the women who spend long hours watching the street from their windows may go entirely unnoticed, and their efforts to pry seldom affect anyone's feeling of privacy. In a city it is possible to move in ten different circles of friends whose several paths never cross. There is no one to listen in on a party line, no one to make officious comments, no one to spread insinuating rumors in an ever-widening circle.

By the same token there may be no one to lend a helping hand. A desperate cry for help may go unheeded. Indeed, no one may recognize it for what it is. Experience of city living among strangers of many different backgrounds has the effect of lowering most people's alertness; their assumptions about what is happening so often turn out to be incorrect. If a man is lying in the street, who knows whether or not help is already on the way? A street chase may be real or it may turn out to be part of a scenario enacted in a natural setting. A cry in the night might mean that someone is in trouble but it might not. Who can tell? Let the police or other people handle the trouble—if it is real. It is safer not to become involved. Lending a hand to a stranger may be dangerous; summoning help may lead only to a string of infuriating questions about oneself.

So we have come full circle. However, one new thing emerges—the confusion of anonymity with privacy. The anonymity of city life does, of course, offer a person privacy from the prying eyes of neighbors and aging relatives and from the long memories of people who "knew him when"; it offers freedom from petty sanctions; it relieves the individual of the necessity of continually asking himself, "What will people say if . . . ?" Compared to life in a small town, it allows each individual much greater latitude. But it also encourages a kind of blindness and deafness to the well-being of others. And this, in the long run, results in harm to everyone.

The confusion, the failure to distinguish between anonymity and privacy, suggests that many people have stopped at a halfway point in their adaptation to city living. They have welcomed its privileges without asking what responsibilities these entail. They have welcomed its freedom without asking what safeguards are necessary. The anonymity that is an inevitable aspect of urban life rules out many forms of behavior and knowledge that serve to protect people living in a small town. Having left these behind, people do not ask what the urban alternatives may be. Instead, they tend to attribute to impersonal watching and listening all the motives of personal curiosity and prying.

Yet if we are to reap the benefits of urban freedom and privileges, we must overcome the hazards of not knowing and not being known. Recognizing the nature of the hazards is a necessary first step. Finding new means of protection is the second. This brings us back to the new technology—but in a different context. For the devices we have rejected because they can be (and have been) used to invade individual privacy can also be used to ensure public safety, without which privacy itself becomes a nightmare isolation.

Public safety and individual privacy are, in fact, inseparable. The question we face is not whether one must be sacrificed to the other but, rather, whether we prefer to risk the loss of both or are willing to work toward the development of a new sense of responsibility and trust consonant with urban living. Above all, we need to rethink the uses of modern devices for watching, listening and recording, and to recognize their safeguarding functions in protecting the potential victim from attack, the potential thug and murderer from carrying out a crime, and the bystander as well, whose feeling of helplessness in a situation of danger has been unfairly branded as apathy.

As steps on the way, we need to go over every point at which the anonymity of the individual may cease to exist or at which the investigatory powers of public officials may be brought into play and to analyze what really is involved. We need to ask why the police patrol the streets, why fire inspectors must have free entry into buildings. We also need to ask what changes we have already accepted—why we are willing to be fingerprinted at our schools or jobs and why it is important for everyone to carry means of identification—and what hindrances stand in the way of other new forms of behavior.

In the past we accepted the policeman walking his beat as an insurance of the safety of people and homes and shops. More recently we have come to take for granted the roaming radio patrol car—the same police officers, but only occasionally present on any one street and less personally related to a neighborhood, at a greater remove. Would not a device by which the sights and sounds of a street could be continually monitored be a safer one? Like the familiar policeman on his beat, the man watching and listening in a nearby police station would be attuned chiefly to a break in the ordinary pattern. He would not, any more than the patrolman, look at or listen to each passer-by, children on the way to school or workers on their way to their offices. Like the patrolman, his eyes and ears would be attuned to the unusual—the cry of someone who fell, the scream of someone afraid—and help could be dispatched where and when it was needed. So, also, the witness to an accident or a crime would know that he could, with a gesture or a shout, summon help.

In smaller, old-fashioned apartment buildings we accepted the presence of the doorman and the elevator man, who between them could keep entrances and corridors under surveillance and look after the needs of tenants. But in great modern apartment blocks, even a dozen guards could not provide full protection in the long, empty corridors and the elevators. Tenant groups have discovered this for themselves, and have discovered as well the difficulty of summoning aid when trouble occurs. Here again, the presence of listening and watching devices—and the knowledge that one watching person, trained for emergencies, was paying attention—would allow people to come and go with security.

These are only two examples of the conditions under which our new technology could be put to constructive use, expanding and transforming older forms of urban protection to meet the needs of modern living and actually widening the areas within which individuals know that they can live their own lives safely. The new devices would return to the ordinary wayfarer the protection he once had on the street, and would assure his personal security on train and subway platforms, in the corridors and on the elevators of huge buildings, and on lonely freeways (where no one will offer help to a stopped car) at night. But their full adoption would mean more than this. It would signify a new stage of responsible acceptance of an urban style of living.

Privacy and the Public Good, II

APRIL, 1967

The furor roused by the prepublication controversy over William Manchester's book *The Death of a President* throws into sharp relief our conflicting beliefs about the individual's right to privacy and the public's right—and need—to be informed. How much privacy and for whom? How much information and of what kind? Do different rules apply to different people? Or at different times?

Striking a balance of some kind on these issues is a problem that must be solved daily in the press and over television, by journalists and writers, and above all, by those on whom the searchlight of publicity is trained. When does disclosure become invasion? When does omission become a kind of censorship? If people do not agree on what the rules are and when they apply, open conflict is always a possibility. That conflict is especially likely to occur when the central event evokes deep emotions, public and private. In the case of Manchester's book, confusion was added to conflict by a variety of contending appeals to "history."

It was claimed by some that history would be distorted, robbed or betrayed if the book was published as Manchester wrote it; others claimed that history would be distorted if it was *not* published in this form. At the same time various mystical statements were made, such as that history once recorded cannot be suppressed. But what is history? Certainly it is not the events themselves, though they are the subject matter of history. In the simplest sense, history is what historians write afterward about events that have occurred well in the past. And contemporary discussions of recent events are not history, but only part of the whole body of materials, meager or full, on which the interpretations we call history later will be based.

Manchester's book concerns a tragic event with implications for the whole world. But the issues behind the controversy have a much wider application than to this one particular book.

It is important, first, to differentiate between the reasons for preserving a record and publishing it. Documents and papers are preserved so that future historians will have at their disposal as much source material as possible on which to base their assessments of the past. A book or an article is usually published, however, because it is timely, and because its author and publisher are concerned not with history but with influencing events still in the making. The press and other communications media want to catch and hold the attention of large audiences by presenting news vividly and vitally—sometimes sensationally. Moreover, in a democracy the public *needs* to know, for example, how a president or prime minister actually proceeds with a task, how he is carrying the burden of responsibility and making use of the immense power of his office, what his expectations are, whether or not he is engaged in entangling and unacknowledged political or social alliances and whether his actions, public and private, are consistent with his words.

In the world in which we live, this kind of knowledge about every important political figure is an essential part of our insurance against being duped and misled. In our own country, attempts to manage the news or shape opinion through use of official handouts to the mass media, however carefully prepared, are likely to be discredited. Moreover, the sense of having free access to as much information as possible about men and the events they take part in is the only assurance that the American people will be able to make wise and realistic political choices.

For a public figure this results in an almost total lack of personal privacy, since we make no clear distinction between what is personal and what is public in his life. Although we often make heroes of public men, we also have a continuing interest in every, possibly shabby, detail of their lives. In fact, the mud that attaches to the public image of the politician helps us feel that there is a real person behind the larger-than-life pictures on the billboards, the ghost-written speeches and the eulogistic descriptions. And intimate views of a public man on a holiday or relaxing with his family or recuperating from an illness reassure us that we have a three-dimensional picture of him.

In this sense, what goes on behind the scenes but is not hidden from view is very relevant to public policy. The feeling of knowing the man is an important aspect of knowing what he stands for. This extreme vulnerability to immediate publication of any and all details, however trivial, shameful, amusing or merely ridiculous, is part of the burden that public figures must accept. Though the public may sympathize with this lack of privacy, people still want—and need—to know.

Once the searchlight is turned on, no one is shielded from its glare. So the lives of those related to the principals also become public property. We learn how wives run their households, how courtships are progressing and how the escapades of children are treated. This was not always so, but today the families of public men, largely by their own choice, have entered the arena. When mothers and wives and sisters-in-law campaign for candidates and when children are present on every occasion from a political rally to the reception of foreign dignitaries or the take-off for a trip into space, can they still be treated as private individuals? Of course, wives who have assumed responsible public roles inevitably share the same fate as their husbands. The same rules—or lack of rules—apply to their activities, public and private.

But the whole question of publicity and publication takes on a different meaning after the death of a public figure. For then whatever is published about him, especially when those close to him are involved, has relevance, not only to the past, but also to the present in which others have become the central figures. In the handling of these matters, we do have workable conventions. The survivors may seal their private papers or tape-recorded documents for any period they wish to designate, securing the information for posterity but removing it from contemporary discussion. In the same way, public men and women can take the steps necessary to protect those close to them by setting their seal on their private papers, just as they make their wills on any other subject. These are conventions on which there is, or has been, common agreement.

Therefore, in theory, reticence is feasible. Publication is not necessary to protect the record. For this purpose it is necessary only that documents should be protected from physical destruction, that they should be kept safe from mice and cockroaches and white ants, from fire and storm, from mildew and mold. It is not even necessary to gather them in archives or make public their existence.

Viewed from a distance in time, events are seen to have interrelationships indiscernible to those living through them. Historians reach out far beyond the formal record in their search for information. Their training leads them to depend not only on organized contemporary accounts, but also on the evidence that can be derived from records that were made for other purposes, such as letters, diaries, ledgers, pictures and all the apparently trivial materials in which men and women express themselves without special concern for the public or the future. The discovery of new documents gives zest and variety to the historian's task of interpretation, and indirect, unintentional records are precious sources on which he can work undisturbed by the passions and conflicts of living witnesses.

But in the modern world it is becoming increasingly difficult to take the long view, the historian's view, of events. The glare of publicity during a man's lifetime and the spate of words published about his every activity and utterance stimulate our desire to know what there is to know almost instantly.

But this is not all. The immense possibilities of modern communications tempt us to believe that we can in some manner control history. During a man's active career he—and his associates—naturally wish to forestall and combat criticism. Since books will be written, why not seek out friendly writers to write friendly books; and if intimate pictures of family life must be part of the public record, isn't it desirable to set the stage and bring in the chosen photographer? But today this desire to show a man from the best vantage point extends also into the future. Far from waiting for the judgment of history— once thought to be beyond control, as God's judgment was beyond human control—men attempt to shape not only the present but also the future's view of the present.

Manchester's book and the controversies it aroused can be seen within all these contexts. The desire of the Kennedy family to have the book written may be interpreted as a way of getting a great deal of research done, for obviously the author would not have done the work without the goal of writing and publishing a book. The documents he assembled so painstakingly, especially the interviews with living witnesses, the tapes of which are to be deposited in the Kennedy archives, may well be invaluable.

The desire to have the published account *now* must also be seen as part of our complex attitude toward public men. The very fact that the book's publication caused an uproar indicates its relevance to events now taking place and the men involved in them, not merely its relevance to the past or to the necessity of preserving information for the future. For it is not only members of the Kennedy family and those close to them whose feelings and stature may be damaged by the statements made in a published account. Like every President, John F. Kennedy had successors, rivals, competitors and enemies, and it is they—like others in similar situations—who are most likely to be damaged by the early publication of books in which, without their consent, their earlier actions and views are exposed and judged in relation to the central figure. And we may well ask, should these men be exposed to the kind of emotional calumny, characteristic of a partisan book, to which in the nature of the case they cannot reply? Is this not an invasion of their still-ongoing public lives?

But beyond all these issues, there is the question of contemporary attitudes toward history and of contemporary writers as the makers of history. Certainly this book and the controversies about it will provide an immense amount of documentary material for the eventual use of historians, mainly about the climate of opinion in 1967. That is, the conflict over the Manchester book is in itself now part of the material of history. How future historians will interpret this conflict, no one today can predict. What is clear, however, is that the book and the conflict reveal how we are attempting to extend to the future the methods we use to portray, to know about, and in so doing to control, contemporary public figures. But such an attempt to shape the record is in fact an invasion of the future.

When attention is focused on a major public figure, a President of the United States in whom tremendous power and responsibility are centered, it is inevitable that the need to know, the fear of knowing, the intolerance of weakness, the resentment of succession, the desperate desire to preserve a hero figure and the corresponding impulse to scale the lost hero or his successor down to far less than human size, will create immense difficulties in the handling of public communications.

What we must work toward is a set of practices that will assure us of sufficient day-to-day knowledge of the public figures to whom we entrust our political and economic fate. What we need are the facts to help us deal with the present; what we also need is a record that is open to the insights of future generations.

The Two-Party System

❧❧❧

At the time of the 1968 election Americans were disturbed as they had not previously been during my lifetime by the fear that we might be facing a constitutional crisis. During the campaign, when it seemed possible that George Wallace might build up a strong-enough following in various parts of the country to deny a majority of electoral votes to any one candidate, there was a rising clamor for reform in our election system. Many urged that in the future the President and Vice-President be elected separately and by direct popular vote. Even the more sober and cautious argued for reform of the electoral college so that electors would be bound by the people's vote; and in a situation in which an election went to Congress, they argued for reforms that would ensure that the newly elected congressmen made the decision, not those who were defeated or retiring.

At the same time there were the ongoing arguments about the weakness of our present system of nominating candidates and debating the issues on which a party was to take a stand. Anger and frustration left many Americans with the feeling that campaign speeches were empty of meaning and that they had no real choice of candidates.

This lack of enthusiasm lay like a pall over thoughtful voters who were a little older than the students and young people who had worked so ardently for Eugene McCarthy and Robert Kennedy and who were plunged from high hope into sorrow and deep despair. But in the end, in spite of their doubts and because of their anxiety that by staying home they might precipitate the crisis they feared, people turned out, and for the most part voted along party lines. However disillusioned, most Democrats voted for Hubert Humphrey; however unenthusiastic, most Republicans voted for Richard Nixon; and independents, as they always do, distributed their votes according to strong personal choices, antipathies and attitudes toward particular issues.

What actually happened was that the great majority of the people of the United States, irrespective of the candidate for whom they cast their ballot, voted in favor of the two-party system. I believe that the vote expressed the deep American faith that the interaction of two fairly symmetrical, complexly organized parties still provides the best way we know of to work out our problems and make our national contribution to keeping this imperiled world safe.

But I think we had no special consciousness of what we were doing. Americans in general are not aware that the two-party system, which we share with other English-speaking nations, is a very special political invention, in which each party depends on the strength and challenge of the other and both must be capable of taking initiative and leading the country. Historically we have had hundreds of minute parties made up of groups who have rallied around a particular cause, from vegetarianism to the single tax. Occasionally one of these has snowballed into a "third" party strong enough to elect a governor, a congressman or a senator, or even to gain prominence on the national scene with a candidate for the Presidency. Some third parties have spoken for voters, like the Progressives in the 1920's, who were ahead of their time and many of whose ideas were eventually incorporated into accepted liberal thinking. Others have represented voters who felt left out because in their social thinking they had been left behind.

It is significant that in the 1968 election many Americans vastly exaggerated the number of those who were likely to vote for George Wallace out of such a feeling of exclusion. Third parties often come into prominence because in the major parties there is no room for fanaticism—for a candidate who is convinced of his infallibility or for voters who believe that their candidate, and their candidate alone, is fit to lead the country. Only in the most exceptional circumstances have we made a place in a major party for a charismatic leader, and then only when, like Theodore Roosevelt, Franklin Roosevelt or

John F. Kennedy, he was a man who enjoyed challenge and strong
opponents.

In this expectation of mutually respected strength our kind of two-
party system contrasts strongly with the single-party dictatorships of
Communist countries, the single-party governments of some newly
emerging countries and the multi-party systems of western Europe or
a country like India. The two-party system was caricatured in Indonesia, where a belief in party politics was combined with a sense of
obligation to massacre opponents before they could take over and
massacre those they had displaced. In both single- and multi-party
systems there is a deep-seated assent to the belief that there is only one
good party, which should have supreme power. Parties other than
one's own are feared and hated when they are strong, and when they
are weak they are valued to the extent that, as temporary allies, they
make possible a government that can beat down the strongest single
opponent. Multi-party systems (such as we have seen in France and
Germany, Spain and Italy), which now succeed and now fail in attempts to turn themselves into a one-party system, build on the
weakness of small, particularistic parties, each of which would prefer
to control all of them.

The two-party system is grounded, I believe, in the kind of family
that is characteristic of the English-speaking countries—Great Britain, Canada, the United States, New Zealand and Australia. We
expect that in a family both parents will have integrity, conscience
and independence of mind, and that children will grow up best
realizing that their mother and father have differences of opinion and
separate as well as shared interests. Marriage as we see it accords
women, as wives and mothers, certain forms of dignity, including the
right to dissent on matters of religion, politics, community welfare
and intellectual interest as well as on the details of homemaking
within a lasting and devoted partnership.

Ideally in German and French families, parents settle their differences and decide on courses of action in private, so as to present a
united front to their children. In contrast, in American families the
idea that there are two sides to every question is learned daily at home
in the interplay between parents and children. One day Mother is the
ally who says that Johnny may have a bicycle if Father agrees—and
in the end Father does. Later Father is the ally when Mother thinks

that Johnny is too young to set out on a bicycle trip alone. And as the child learns that sometimes one parent and sometimes the other supports his immediate wishes, he also learns that both have his good at heart, even when this is not at all apparent. He learns that his happiness depends on their both being there, face-to-face, expressing different views and reconciling their differences. He discovers that it is not good when one parent always wins and that many victories are *pro forma* and many defeats no more than the concession that it is the other person's turn to win—a salutary kind of learning that will be a protection against political cynicism in later years.

This kind of experience in childhood lays the foundation for understanding that both sides—or both political parties—even when they oppose each other most forcefully, can be related to an overarching good—in the home, the child's and the family's well-being; in the country, the nation's well-being. "His Majesty's loyal opposition" is not an idle phrase but a magnificent conception. And in the United States the idea that the President is not only the leader of his own party but also the President of all the people is crucial to the American sense of freedom to challenge, oppose and change positions.

Normally this sound common sense, as we understand it, has the effect of modifying the belligerent feelings brought into play in a political campaign. Once the election is over, we tend to move, though perhaps only temporarily, toward acceptance of the voters' choice. A college student who had worked hard and enthusiastically for Senator McCarthy and later for Vice-President Humphrey expressed very well this postelection mood:

"My first reaction was to hope that Nixon would have a miserable time and as a consequence would be defeated in 1972. But I realized later that 1972 is far away, and that really much more important than plotting to defeat Nixon is trying to work *with* him to solve the problems of the country. With competent, liberal and able people working with him, he may be able to accomplish a lot. If I were in a position to help him, I would. As it is, I will give him the best chance to succeed before I begin to criticize him. . . ."

That is it in a nutshell.

Our feeling of crisis is past and we are ready to see what the two parties, watching each other, attacking each other, fighting for the majority position and admitting only temporary defeats, can do—not just to keep the country going, not just to make patchwork repairs or changes by reversals of policy, but to work out the problems we face. For the election in no way solved the political problems that led to the crisis: the problems of the war in Vietnam, the divisions at home caused by the war or the urgent problems of domestic policy. The campaign gave Americans of all shades of opinion an opportunity to voice dissent, but the election failed to translate dissent into new political direction.

So there are great difficulties. The young who are reaching voting age, all those who have been treated as wards—or, more exactly, stepchildren—of the state and denied the rights of full citizenship, the disgruntled liberals who voted mainly out of a sense of duty and not because they felt any candidate reflected their views and all those who followed George Wallace's dissident, reactionary leadership—any or all of these may break the present truce at any time.

Especially deep, real and in one sense unbridgeable is the gap between the young, all those who have grown up since World War II, and those of us who grew up earlier. We of the older generation can never in any way acquire the experience of those who are now coming to maturity in a new age. Young people can, if they will, learn how we became what we are, because we have lived the experience and express in adult form the result of our upbringing. They can, if they will, learn to understand the actions of those in power. We of the older generation can, at best, facilitate the development of new ways into a wide world for those who, succeeding us, will come into their inheritance. And we must do so, for only by including the questions of this generation can we begin to look for answers that will be meaningful to all of us. Only by reshaping our major political parties so that their working is comprehensible to this generation can we hope that young people will cherish the political system their early life has prepared them to work with ably and responsibly.

Must Women Be Bored with Politics?

OCTOBER, 1964

An election year leaves many American women with mixed feelings in which disgust and repudiation often predominate. Phrases like "juvenile antics," "cheap tricks" and "public show" crop up in their minds as they watch behavior in which their dearest hopes for better schools or better care for the aged or reduced danger of war appear to have been turned into political footballs to be kicked up and down the field by scuffling rival candidates, and many women turn their backs on this apparently irresponsible game. Fifty years ago, when women's suffrage was a burning issue, neither those who looked with high hopes toward the prospect of women's voting nor those who predicted disaster could have foretold that the major response of so many women would be what it is today—abysmal boredom.

Boredom is an odd emotion about which psychologists know very little. One of the more useful definitions is that it is a state of unresponsiveness, when one suffers because there is nothing one can do or say or feel about a given situation. But why is it that so many women are bored by politics? Is politics a male art for which women have no talent?

There are two aspects of American campaign politics that have little appeal for most women. One is the element of play—an interest in the game for its own sake, regardless of the stakes. The other is the sense of personal involvement in a struggle for power—the thrill of taking part in a contest. When we treat politics as, among other things, a gladiatorial combat, these two elements merge in the mounting excitement and tension of a campaign.

Women in general are less interested in games than most men are. Even though they may sometimes become fascinated by bridge or canasta, they are usually too involved with real things to be deeply attracted by games.

But women are not bored by contests when they feel that they are fighting *for* something—a local fight over a school issue, for example. When they feel that the future of their children may be at stake, they can fight with grim and single-minded determination. Like the females of other species, women can and will fight furiously *against* anything that appears to endanger their young. And involved in any battle, women usually want to win at any cost—an extension of their tendency always to take life seriously. Nor are they bored when a candidate for political office appeals to them as a knight-errant. For his sake they will fold reams of paper, stuff mountains of envelopes, trudge strange streets, accost strangers and ring strange doorbells, energetic and tireless in the cause they have espoused. Once their devotion is won, women can accept politics as a fight.

They have a very hard time, however, in those elections in which one candidate is basing his whole campaign on the weaknesses of the other side and on the hope of playing upon the hostilities, the fears and the angry inferiorities of his countrymen. Such a campaign is an invitation to kill for the fun of killing. At its best it can be compared to a fox hunt in which the hounds are following close at the heels of the running fox. At its worst it takes on the hot fury of an appeal to a lynch mob. Women enter such battles at great danger to their commitment against meaningless destruction. For men there is still the game, the joys of the contest and the possibility of stressing the fight instead of the fighters. But the women who gather around a really destructive candidate can have a glitter in their eyes that chills the spines of the men on both sides. To the extent that politics is also a real fight, most women's participation in politics is bound to be different from men's. To the extent that men can forget what they are fighting about in the sheer exhilaration of shouting slogans and downing opponents, most women are likely to become alienated. Men, trained to the use of weapons for long thousands of years, have learned some circumspection in handling and using them. Women, on the contrary, whose experience in fighting is more limited, can too easily lose their sense of what the limits are in a fight.

Perhaps if women remember that in general they fight well only when they are fighting for something they take seriously, and that they are more dangerous than men when they are caught up in destruction, they can develop a better sense for the aspects of a political campaign in which they can take a genuine interest. For in spite of the shouting and the catcalls and the spitballs left over from the schoolroom and the playground, it is, of course, an extremely serious business to choose the men who will lead the country.

Women's stake in the orderly conduct of the affairs of the country and the world is as clear as men's, and because they do not enjoy the game of politics as much, it is less complicated. This means that they can more readily keep their eyes on the real issues.

In every campaign many efforts are made to blur the issues and to substitute personal appeal or righteous pronouncements for clear statements on policy. Especially at the state and local levels, many attempts will be made to appeal to party loyalty as a way of electing doubtful candidates. In their home communities women can keep their feet on the ground and their heads clear by paying attention to the smaller issues that will be settled in the course of the campaign. In a national election year we count on the presidential candidates to carry with them congressmen and senators who may have lost touch with their constituents as well as the new men who are just beginning to be heard. Similarly, at the state level, governors and members of the state legislature may be swept in and out of office with the presidential vote. Here are the points of political conflict where women, by keeping their attention on the issues that matter to them particularly, can make a good fight for things that must be tackled at the local level: medical care; schools; parks and playgrounds for children; beaches on which to bathe safely; wildernesses where we can catch glimpses of the earth as it was before man occupied it completely; effective and humane institutions to help the mentally ill; care of neglected children that will turn them into people, not simply the parents of other neglected children; city planning for human living; and attacks on poverty that are thorough, imaginative and compassionate.

Nor need women limit their attention to the problems closest at hand. They can give their attention to the widest issues that affect people around the world—food and medicine for the three-fifths of the world's population that today is deprived of the most basic care, planning that will help move all men toward an ordered world and away from the danger of a nuclear explosion.

All candidates—presidential and vice-presidential candidates, candidates for the House and the Senate, as well as candidates for state and local offices—will tell you that they are in favor of these things. But women who have learned not to take things at their face value can make the campaign make better sense, in their own terms, if they keep looking at the record. What did these candidates do when they were in office? And if they belong to organizations that are interested in particular issues, they can keep on confronting all the candidates. Granted that campaign promises often are broken, the more forcefully they are made, the harder it will be to break them. As the League of Women Voters has demonstrated, issues matter. And ballots can be split to keep the issues sharper.

Politics need not be boring—for women who are aiming at getting something done.

Mrs. Roosevelt

She was handing round homemade cookies and lemonade herself. Her guests that summer afternoon in 1940 were a little group of women who had come to Hyde Park to ask her help in making a film about women in the community. It was the first time I spoke with Mrs. Roosevelt, and her grave, attentive listening to our talk gave me my first and most vivid impression of her personality.

Anyone who ever saw her on a public platform knew her ability to catch and hold the attention of a great crowd. But in spite of her striking height and unmistakable presence, she had the ability to move without the least obtrusiveness. Time and again during the war years, I saw how she could enter a committee meeting and slip into her seat without once disturbing the even tenor of the discussion.

On the night of Franklin Roosevelt's election to his fourth term as President I met her in the Poughkeepsie railroad station, sitting alone in a badly lighted coach, unnoticed and unnoticing, while she tried to get on with reading a great pile of letters and papers, part of the unending stream that came to her from all over the world.

For very young Americans her life had already taken on some of the qualities of a myth, and of all the people I talked with about her shortly after her death, an eight-year-old girl described her most succinctly: "She was the wife of a very important person who lived a long time ago. She was married when she was twenty-three. She helped a great many people in a great many ways."

But for each generation who knew her, she represented something different. She reminded me of my pioneer great-grandmothers who crossed the plains and helped bring order to the chaotic frontier towns—one of the long line of determined wives and mothers who saw to the schools and set up the libraries, who saw a wrong and set about righting it. For the women who grew up in the 1930's, the daughters of mothers who had only dreamed of accomplishment, she represented the fulfillment of hope. And for the youngest generation of wives and mothers, struggling with babies and housework, her life held the promise of later years of wider activity. Yet her life is unique. She had no actual predecessors and she can have no single successor.

Mrs. Roosevelt's imagination had extraordinary scope, but it always was related to the things she herself saw and heard, to the people she knew. By traveling to the Antipodes or talking with people in New Zealand and Australia, she learned to include them in her thinking. Each step she took farther away from home enlarged the areas in which she took on responsibility. In her later years she belonged to the whole world, her personal contacts linked by thousands of miles of air travel and thousands of letters received and answered.

Nevertheless, her world-wide activities, her untiring efforts on behalf of children and all those who were comfortless—all these things were based in her home. Because she was her husband's wife and the mother of his children, she took on the tasks that were there to be done. As her husband assumed more and more important roles she patiently, laboriously learned whatever was necessary so that she might stand beside him, complement his interests, support him in the state, the country, the world. With each step, as her own name became more widely known and she was recognized as a person in her own right, she widened her responsibilities. Yet she was essentially without personal ambition. When she acted, it was in response to someone else's need. Five children of her own had accustomed her to a kind of life in which there were never enough free hands and still there had to be enough time for everyone. She had the qualities of a busy mother, trying to get through the day and yet ready to stop in the middle of anything to answer some immediate question, to meet some immediate need.

She had the lack of vanity that was the only safe cloak for an awkward, too-tall girl who felt herself gawky and strange among others who were both beautiful and brilliant. It was a long time before she would submit to the bother of dressmakers and vocal training that others urged upon her. But in later years her relaxed presence and her voice, which had acquired a depth and warmth that could move millions, bore witness to the rigorous self-discipline with which she undertook the tasks she meant to do.

As no other one American woman has done, she epitomized the women who have made the United States a society in which the rights and needs of the young, the weak, the poor, the tired, the aspiring, must be met. And she always spoke, not as a fanatical crusader, but as the mother of children who wanted a better world for all children. It is significant that those who opposed her politically tried to break this continuity by criticizing her relations with her own children, and that those who tried to strip her of her dignity vented their hostility against her by calling her "Eleanor." It was her opponents and enemies who addressed her with familiarity; those who loved and trusted her called her "Mrs. Roosevelt."

Probably no one in our time has been asked and has expressed an opinion on so many different subjects. Yet each opinion, always given frankly, honestly and competently, had value not because of any expertise she had, but because she consulted her own feelings and spoke out of her own experience. She had seen a forlorn and desolate house. She had personally carried food to young women prostrated by influenza in World War I. She had visited with children in some earth-floored schoolroom in a village on the other side of the world. She had read an article or a book, or she had received a letter. She had seen something with her own eyes; she had listened. The world in all its immanence kept flooding in on her, and she was never too tired to attend. I used to welcome every opportunity to speak in her presence, because I knew that if I could say something that mattered, she would take it in and make it part of something that she, better than anyone else alive, could say to the conscience of the world.

For long years her life was essentially a public life. Yet she never learned to think of people as anonymous members of some group or audience or panel or as part of an unidentified mass. Each person was an individual to her. Entering a great hall, holding the orchid which she preferred to lay quietly on the table while she spoke, she would often pause halfway down the aisle to the speaker's platform to greet

someone she had once met somewhere else. Nor did she react with
surprise when someone would come through a crowd to ask: "Mrs.
Roosevelt, do you remember me? I wrote you a letter five years
ago. . . ."

Each of us who knew Mrs. Roosevelt, however slightly, will carry
a different set of vivid, warm, breath-taking memories of her
strength, her sympathy, her wisdom. What will abide with me will be
her gentle, omniscient warning to all of us when she was working at
the United Nations. Then, thinking into the future and the difficult
years before us, she said: "I know the American people have the
necessary courage, but will we have the patience it will take?"

Peacekeeping

DECEMBER, 1962

During the past years, the issues of nuclear testing and fallout roused to action that part of the adult population which generally is least likely to take public responsibility—women with babies in baby carriages. With immediacy and determination these young mothers emerged temporarily from their homes—some with and some without their young children—to protest, to march, to demonstrate against actions they believed might hasten a nuclear holocaust. Then as time passed and nothing further happened, many of the young mothers went back to their yards and their kitchens, to their never-ending woman's work, with the feeling, perhaps, that their efforts had been in vain.

But while the bomb tests and the missile rattling have gone on and we have again become accustomed to a succession of indecisive international incidents, it is my belief that the appearance of these women has a special and hopeful significance in our approach to the questions of war and peace.

What these young mothers were trying to do, and what women the world over can hope to do once they realize their unique potential, is best expressed, I think, by a word that is becoming increasingly popular in this country. That word is *peacekeeping*. And with the idea of peacekeeping, so simple and obvious an echo of woman's work of housekeeping, a new role for women in the political processes of the nation and the world has come into being.

Peacekeeping emphasizes several things that women know more about than most men do. Men speak more naturally and easily about *making peace* or, in a valiant and military vein, about *waging a peace offensive* or *winning the peace*. These are all masculine phrases. Each emphasizes the effect of a single great burst of effort—to win a peace as one wins a war, to make peace as one makes war. And the two kinds of phrase—peace winning and peacekeeping—emphasize a difference between men and women that, while it does not apply to all men and women or to all societies at all times, is generally true of the world as we know it. Men are usually best at the kinds of activity that demand an intense pull of hard work—and then are completed. Just as man has hunted big game, built houses and bridges and composed symphonies, so it has been his prerogative to wage war and win peace.

In recent years, however, we have come to realize that peace cannot be won by a single burst of energy and effort in the traditional masculine sense. We can, in fact, no longer "win" peace or "wage" peace or even "make" peace. Today, with the threat of nuclear extinction facing us, men can no more protect their countries by fighting and dying than private citizens can prevent and correct crime by going about heavily armed. Peace is a state of society that has to be worked at every day. Up to the present we have had real peace only within a particular society or within a country where all people have recognized one another as part of the necessary ordering of life. And what once applied to small societies applies now, with the threat of global extinction, to the entire world.

Our hope today rests not on peace *winning* but on peace*keeping*. And peacekeeping demands the patience, the fortitude and the endless, unremitting efforts that are so much more characteristic of a woman's than a man's role in society.

Through the ages it is women who have carried out the smaller, endlessly repetitive tasks—preparing meals that are no sooner cleared away than work on the next one must begin; sweeping away the dirt from the floor of the cabin or the split-level house moments before muddy feet lay down new damp tracks; making beds that are tumbled and must be made again day after day, week after week, year after year. This is housekeeping. This is the continuity of living in which children are born and reared and human character is formed. A home is not built once and for all time. A house can be built, yes, but the work that makes and keeps it a home is continuous and unremitting. So also with peace.

The new awareness implicit in this word peacekeeping, which has been so striking whether it has been expressed in the President's warning of a long pull or in the phrasing of representations to the United Nations, will not, of course, be easy to maintain. For most men and some women the temptation to get out and do something big and daring and immediate to solve a problem, to settle an issue, is very real. Even the young mothers about whom we have been speaking chose temporary, dramatic expedients like marching and picketing to express their initial reactions.

It is for a much bigger task, however, that their gifts are really needed. For it is they who can best keep alive the sense of what peacekeeping is and the belief that it is possible and bearable. More important than marching groups inspired by an apparent dramatic emergency is an expressed willingness on the part of women to take over a fair amount of the monotonous, exacting, repetitive, never-finished task of peacekeeping.

This means establishing and maintaining in every community in the United States, and ultimately in the world, groups of women who can incorporate the need for peace into the expectations of children, and can make the meaning of peacekeeping clearer to people everywhere.

The world over, boys as they grow up will have to learn new forms of heroism—more like the heroism of the farmer and the gardener and the stockman than the heroism of the lion hunter. They will have to learn that they can protect their families, their fellow citizens, their country, the whole human race; only by watchfulness, endurance, patience and imaginative innovation.

By conveying their particular talent for these qualities to their children, to their men and to the world, women may well become one of our most important resources in the cause of peace.

Unwitting Partners to Youthful Violence

❧❧❧❧

MAY, 1965

Nowadays youthful violence knows no seasons. Not many decades ago spring, from May Day to Midsummer's Eve, was the time when college deans and presidents were alert, watching for the restlessness and listening for the well-known signals that might easily set loose pandemonium. Annual student riots were traditional, seasonal and catching. News of one was likely to touch off another in a nearby college. But the epidemic usually was mild and short-lived.

Today we are witnessing something very different. All through the year, accounts appear in newspapers and on television, describing scenes of youthful disorder that have occurred in the recent past, are highlighted news of the day or are forecast for the near future. Nothing in such accounts suggests that these disorders are wholly spontaneous or essentially prankish. On the contrary, whether the outbreaks take place on the streets after a high-school football game or during a college holiday or in some home where a party is in progress, descriptions of them suggest that as long as the madness lasts the rioters are overcome by impulses which they, their elders and the representatives of public law and order are powerless to bring under control. Outdoor television cameras are located at strategic spots, and hourly newscasts play up the intensity of the excitement, the numbers of police and firemen who have failed to quell the fury, and the casualties in broken heads and wrecked property. Figuratively the riot is a storm that cannot be contained.

Heavy blame for public youthful violence has been placed on the

mass media. And it is true that all around the world, days or even
weeks before a provocative film opens, before the Beatles arrive,
before a jazz festival takes place, before the date of a holiday—Easter,
Labor Day or a bank holiday in England—the news media raise the
alarm. How many young people will take to the roads? How many
will crowd into the airport? How many will pile up on a beach? How
many, depending on whether they are vacationers or have come to
protest, will gather to dance or chant in some place that is unprepared
to accommodate their activities? The publication of road maps and
routes helps the crowd find the way. The early arrival of newsmen
spurs the crowd to excitement. But the alerted police and citizenry
also play their parts in providing an appropriate mood and setting for
the drama for which everyone is prepared and which may involve not
only the one community but also the whole nation—and, in a matter
of hours, the whole world—as audience.

Actually, not the mass media alone but the forces of law and order,
the businessmen who gamble on the possibilities of profit, the heads of
schools and colleges, the clergy who spread the word through their
sermons and the parents and other guardians of the young all play
some part in rousing the storm—in provoking these periodic invasions, mass outbursts and demonstrations. Large-scale youthful rioting cannot succeed without adult provocation and connivance. And
just as an American mother, speaking of her two-year-old son with an
undertone of pride, will say, "I couldn't do a thing with him," so also
the head of a school or a police chief will report that he is helpless in
his efforts to halt a student strike or youthful rioting—and attentive
audiences will respond to the tone of voice that gives away his half-
conscious collaboration. Mass violence occurs chiefly when those
who are its audience sympathize, openly or in secret.

This is something we cannot long avoid recognizing when we ask
what kinds of mob behavior will break out next. Nor can we long fail
to realize how frequently those who are forecasting trouble—those
who ask these questions—are either gleefully anticipating the excitement of the event or balefully anticipating the excitement of restoring
order.

For adults can play two quite different roles in provoking youthful
outbursts. They can egg on young people to do exactly what they

wish they were young enough, foolish enough or brave enough to do—turning youthful violence into an expression of their own still-youthful wishes or their adult exasperation at constraint. Or they can drive the young into staging an unsuccessful outburst of exuberance or demonstration of rebellion through which their own weak sense of control is reinforced as policemen swing nightsticks at the rioters, pummel them with jets of water, turn aerosol sprays on them and herd them into patrol wagons.

Where the spirit of connivance is strong the youthful riot succeeds. No one could stem the onrushing crowd, divert the honking cars, stop the dancing in the streets, separate the raging opponents, halt the marching youngsters, silence the rhythmic chanting, get the students back indoors. And if you investigate carefully, no one tried—hard enough.

It is not sufficient, then, to ask why there is so much youthful violence and why it is spreading. In addition it is necessary to ask what is happening in the world that makes these dramatic outbursts—youth breaking through bounds safely or youth breaking through bounds and suffering for it—so congenial on a world-wide scale.

In part the answer is related to contemporary attitudes toward power and attempts to counter feelings of helplessness. When mothers report that seventh-grade children have smashed the furniture at a birthday party, they are reporting that children can seize power and do not have to behave. When the young people rushing into a town break into taverns and empty beer barrels into the streets, what the rest of the world sees is that for a visitor to a strange place, restraint may not be necessary. When citizens of Saigon watch their children burn the American library, they notify the world that the United States is not invincible.

In part the answer lies in the increasing tensions of living in an overcrowded world. There is a continual questioning: What does the individual matter in this mass? What is the meaning of a single vote? How can a single voice be heard? What channel can carry a single protest effectively? What has happened when the world becomes aware of an individual only as a demonstrator who is willing to turn himself into a living torch, or as a murderer whose face, if he succeeds in killing a world statesman, becomes known everywhere? Whether people live in small towns or large cities, whether they can still hear their neighbors' voices or use air conditioners and television to wrap themselves in a cocoon of meaningless sound, they are increasingly conscious of the presence of too many people cramped in too small a space.

Spurred by these feelings, the urge to reassert one's individual will, the insistence that one is not a mere particle (one three-billionth of the world's population), but instead an individual who matters, can be a potent force. Joined to the wish to escape confinement by breaking something—smashing the furniture, wrecking shops, shoving people and bloodying their noses—it becomes a violently destructive force.

So far, however, most youthful rioting in the United States and Britain has been confined to destroying objects, not people. Serious injuries and fatalities, when they have occurred, have been almost entirely accidental. This is in sharp contrast to situations in which the battle is real and opposing forces are genuinely joined in a struggle for political or ideological power. For then there are instead of riots the serious, carefully organized activities of men, young and old, who go out with deadly intent to destroy and kill until they win.

Thus it becomes clear that present-day youthful rioting is essentially a drama, a dramatic expression of the tensions within the individual who, wherever he may be, feels hemmed in and powerless to move or to get his hand on the reins. And the larger drama we are engaged in, all of us, is one in which with one voice we urge young people to assert themselves, however meaninglessly, while with another voice we tell them—and ourselves—that the performance is carried out in vain.

This is an expensive form of ceremonial, and a dangerous one. And we shall not lessen the danger or alter the pattern of violent drama by merely strengthening the external forces of law and order. Doing this only raises the stakes and, in the end, the level of violence. What we need to do is to understand and think through our own individual and group involvements as adults. For every time an adult pretends to be unable to control the outburst of a child less than half his size, every time parents plan parties for school children and leave them unchaperoned to turn off the lights, break the furniture and toss glasses out the windows, every time a resort community begins by inviting crowds of young people without preparing for their orderly accommodation, everyone becomes an abettor of violence with all its dangers. As individuals and as members of our communities we need to develop greater responsibility toward those who react to our own unspoken wishes and fears.

Universal National Service

❦❧❦❧❦

SEPTEMBER, 1966

Young Americans in every part of the land are finding their voices. Whatever the issue, more and more of them—girls as well as boys— are declaring themselves. When they speak up it is most often to protest: "It isn't fair!"

This is a generation that does not readily accept things as they are. There are some young people, of course, who are merely restive—the black-helmeted boys who race into a town on their motorcycles and the boys and girls who converge in masses on holiday resorts. And some, like the students at an eastern college who marched all day out of "general discontent," seem to be protesting mainly for the sake of protest.

But others, an ever-growing number, are concerning themselves seriously and vigorously with public issues. Through sit-ins, stand-ins, teach-ins, marches and demonstrations, on campus and off, they are debating and taking positions—a wide variety of positions—on civil rights, academic freedom and responsibility, the forms of voluntary service young people should be allowed to give, the kind of war they are willing or unwilling to support, whether those who are called upon to bear arms should not also have the right to vote, and above all, the inequities of the draft. Faced with adult responsibilities, they are protesting their status as nonadults. Confronted by problems of policy, they are demanding their right to take part in decisions that affect their lives and the lives of others, as students, as wage earners (or as uneducated and unemployable young people) and as parents and citizens. In short, they want a voice in the affairs of the country.

Especially they want to be heard when, on any issue, they protest: "It isn't fair."

Today the focus of protest is the draft. The sense that what is happening in the draft isn't fair has made it the central issue on which a great many dissatisfactions converge. And the inequities of the draft may make it a stumbling block for a whole generation. The most obvious inequities are those that affect the lives of young men—not only the relatively small number who are called to military service but also those who are deferred, perhaps indefinitely, and those who are rejected permanently. But there are other inequities, less obvious but equally serious. For this system, because it concentrates on young men, sets girls and young women apart as if they did not exist. And because it concentrates only on military service, it is a threat to this generation's growing sense that what happens to any of them will affect the future of all of them.

It is significant that the strongest protests among young people against the present system do not come from those who have the least hope of preferment—the dropouts, the unskilled and those who have the brains but not the means to go to college or professional schools. Rather it is the students in our colleges and universities, those whom the present system most favors, who are most loudly protesting the essential unfairness of making their less-privileged age mates carry the heaviest burdens of hardship and danger. What we are seeing is not a widening rift between those who have some possibility of choice and those who have none. Instead, we are witnessing an upsurge of discontent among those most favored.

It is significant also that girls see the draft as an issue on which they too should take a stand, as they have on other contemporary issues. Together with boys, they have worked for civil rights, they have served in the Peace Corps and other voluntary organizations that allow them to give practical expression to idealism and they have joined actively in the dialogue on the issues of war and peace. All this has placed them in a different relationship to the young men of their generation even where, as in the draft, their interests and their very existence are disregarded.

The system of the draft thus brings to a head, as young people themselves see it, the question of whether it is fair to ask only some members of a generation to give involuntary service to their country;

whether it is equitable to exclude all the rest of that generation—all the girls, all the boys who lack the qualifications necessary to meet military requirements and all the boys who are exempted for reasons beyond their control.

And so a new question is raised, a question that many people are asking today: Would a universal national service be more equitable?

There are those who will object to any innovation. But for those who are sensitive to the long history of our American struggle to reconcile responsibility, privilege and freedom and for those who are tuned to the protesting voices of contemporary young Americans, the idea of universal national service will have a special appeal. By setting aside older ideas and instead shaping a program to our own expectations, we may transform a service asked of and given by all young people into something that is peculiarly American—a worthy sequel to our conception of universal free education for every child in the United States, regardless of race and color, creed and class.

Universal national service is still only an idea. But for a moment I should like to suppose . . .

Suppose *all* young people were required to register at the age of eighteen. Each one, girl and boy, would be given a series of educational and medical examinations that would place all young people within the whole group of their generation in the country. Each also would be given an opportunity to state the kind of service to the country he or she could in good conscience give. No one would be exempt—or disregarded—in the old sense. No one would be relieved of the obligation to give two years, let us say, to the country, working under direction and living on the same subsistence allowance as everyone else. But equally, no one would be excluded from the privilege of being individually and carefully assessed, helped and brought as close as possible to our best standards for education, skill, health, civic knowledge and responsibility. No one would be excluded from an opportunity to know and work with young people like and different from himself or herself. No one would be excluded from the experience of leaving home and the home neighborhood and discovering a new environment and a different set of demands and possibilities. No one would be excluded from the opportunity to develop a special talent merely because he or she lacked the expected foundation of knowledge or skill or even the awareness of how such a talent could be developed.

Those who did not know how to plan a trip or read a map or make up a budget or talk to a stranger or fill out a form or follow written directions would have a chance to learn. Those who had been over-protected, who had been in "good" schools since nursery-school days, associating only with other children exactly like themselves, studying until they felt that book knowledge was running out of their ears, would have a chance to discover new directions and work in new settings. By the time they are eighteen, many of our most privileged children have had fifteen years of schooling without any chance to put their learning to work, while a very large proportion of our least privileged children have had to survive ten or more years of utterly unrewarding sitting in dreary classrooms, learning less and less, falling further and further behind, suffering defeat of hope and denigration of individuality. Both would profit by living and working within a new group of peers in an unfamiliar place, by the discovery that they had recognized rights and obligations and by the experience of finding out that they were neither exempt nor excluded from responsibility.

Universal national service would not mean that every boy and every girl would be set the same task. On the contrary, it would mean the mobilization on a national scale of a great variety of activities to meet the needs of our country and of our young people. It would fulfill our most basic obligations to our young men and women and provide them with appropriate means of giving service. It would open new doors for a great many. But it would not provide individual freedom of choice in any simple sense. At eighteen, young people are moving toward adult life; they themselves are asking for adult status. Combining all this would mean the development of a new sense of what is fair and equitable—for everyone.

Looking to the future, it would be necessary for some—boys and girls—to learn the skills essential to our industrial world and for some to begin the training required to produce the next generation of scientists, engineers, physicians, nurses, teachers and technicians. What we hoped to accomplish by deferring certain students from the draft—that is, to provide for the necessary quota of trained and qualified men—would still be important. But now we could include young women as well, setting goals for their achievement that few girls have had in the recent past. And those, boys and girls, who are excluded today from the exercise of their talents would be given a chance to find themselves. We would still need to meet the requirements, different at different times, of our armed services. The difference would be that those who were selected to carry this responsibility would not be the *only* ones who were called on for service. Nor would we be faced by the all-but-insoluble dilemma of finding special ways of showing appreciation for those who volunteer and of compensating adequately those who are serving involuntarily.

However it was organized in detail, universal national service would not absolve young men and young women from responsibility. All of them, whatever they were doing, would be committed for a certain time to some form of activity as citizens, full citizens, with a voice in what they were doing and responsibility for what they had in hand. Eighteen-year-olds, both the privileged and underprivileged, are unready for parenthood in a complex world. But they are ready for many forms of adult activity that involve the companionship of girls and boys as equals, as individuals, all of whom have a stake in what they are accomplishing. And all of them would benefit by the experience of a kind of life, for a limited period, in which obligation, privilege and responsibility were combined, in which no distinction was made between rights and duties as they took part in the very varied and necessary tasks of protecting, conserving and developing the country in which they expected to live as self-sustaining adults, free to make their own choices and decisions.

The current protest, "It isn't fair," has grown out of the uncertainties and inequities of segregating one ill-defined group in a whole generation. A universal national service may be the one equitable answer.

Student Power, I

Ten years ago it would have been very hard for anyone in the educational world to prophesy that within a short time our college and university campuses would become arenas for students shouting defiance at authority. Change was in the air, but it seemed to be taking a very different direction. Old universities were expanding, low-level institutions were upgrading themselves and new colleges were opening as fast as buildings could be thrown together and a faculty of sorts assembled to accommodate the swarms of students demanding entrance.

The pattern of teaching and learning remained the same as in the past. The one alteration was that study appeared to have been domesticated. Students wanted married quarters, deans argued whether young wives should be allowed to give up their chance for an education in order to support their husbands, and student-parents struggled with the difficulties of combining babies and books.

There were some signs even then that all was not well. There were the students who were smoking pot and experimenting with LSD and other drugs. There were the students who were dropping out—not the poor students, who couldn't make the grade, but the best students, who complained that life was passing them by outside while they sat in classrooms listening to lectures. There were the students who ridiculed their elders' hope that "something" could be done, once and for all, to rid the world of the danger of the bomb. The students realized that the possibility of total destruction is here to stay. But these seemed comparatively small worries to harassed ad-

ministrators who had to find new sources of funds and who wondered whether they were running institutions of learning or some
new form of nursery.

Today, instead, administrators have to deal with militant student
groups in rebellion who believe in direct action, legal or illegal, because (they say) "it works"—as strikes and riots and demonstrations
by other groups also get results. And the administrators must deal
with trustees and regents and legislators, who tend to believe that
the students are the new barbarians who want to destroy in a day
what it has taken hundreds of years to build up, and with a faculty
many of whose members, covertly or openly, support the students'
aims.

There are others, wishful thinkers, who say that student power is
only a catch phrase, a fiction invented by mass media in search of
sensational events and likely to exaggerate what they find. It is true
that modern channels of communication—linking the peoples of the
world and the student populations everywhere—help to make tem-
pestuous responses models for spreading discontent. But student
power is a reality.

The extraordinary thing is the time it has taken us to grasp that an
irreversible change is taking place in the relations of students and
educational institutions. We have tended to treat each outbreak—
each demonstration, sit-in, talk-in, teach-in, march, angry scuffle or
riot that results in bloodied heads, arrests and outcries against bru-
tality—as if it were unique. It is less surprising that the students themselves know and care little about the history of their activities.
Student generations are short and each new group entering a college
or university makes its own beginnings. Frequently the majority of
students has been a more or less passive or even mildly hostile
audience to the early stages of conflict; but in moments of crisis these
onlookers (often to their own amazement) have been caught up in
the need to demonstrate their solidarity of feeling with more vocal,
activist and endangered classmates. Then, for better or worse, they
too have become part of a movement.

A few people with longer memories look back to the days of the
Freedom Riders who went to the South, to the summers when students went to Mississippi with SNCC groups to register voters, to the
early civil rights demonstrations in northern ghettos. Some look back

to the Cuban revolution and the heady excitement of belief that a handful of rebels could bring down corrupt regimes. Others think of the students who organized protests for peace, stirred up feeling against the war in Vietnam and agitated against the draft in this war, which seemed to them so meaningless and immoral.

These have been some of the themes that have activated students all over the country. But there have been others—the demand that students have the right to set their own standards of dress and sex and living; and finally, as at Columbia University in the spring of 1968 (and elsewhere, though less spectacularly), the demand of students for a real voice in academic decisions about what shall be taught and by whom, what the composition of the student body, black and white, should be and what the university's relations with the larger community should be.

Looking back, it would be easy to conclude that the student movement got under way mainly in response to the public issues that at different times have stirred the imagination and the conscience of student—and faculty—idealists. But I think this would be as mistaken as the view that student power is no more than a new version of traditional student restlessness or that it is a creation of the mass media.

We have to remember that student power is not parochial, made in America and confined to this country. Its dimensions are world-wide. National boundaries and the invisible ideological barriers dividing the world have not limited or contained student activism. Each country has its own sore spots. Students in England, France, Germany, Italy, Pakistan, Czechoslovakia, Yugoslavia, Indonesia, Japan, Mexico and elsewhere, even Red China, have found significant causes to give focus to their protests. Sometimes student action has had wide repercussions. In Japan several universities have been closed for long periods. In Czechoslovakia young people added their strength to the protest against the Soviet exercise of power in Prague. In France the student revolt precipitated nationwide strikes, a national election and a major economic crisis. Any explanation of student power has to include the world and the restlessness of young people everywhere.

An explanation has to include also, I believe, a whole generation, of which students are the most visible. They are congregated in very conspicuous numbers, and it is the students who have the means and the training to be articulate. In a real sense they are the spokesmen for their generation: they have an institution, the college or the university, which they attend and which serves as the focus of their criticisms and demands. In the eyes of many of them it has come to stand for the whole Establishment, for the enemy of an emergent new world.

How have they come to this view?

First there is our obvious inability to cope with the sheer numbers of young people in and out of school. Twenty years ago we talked glibly about the "baby boom" and then about the dire effects of the population explosion. But in spite of all our talking, what we did to prepare for masses of young people was on too small a scale, shoddy and too late—and this at a time when we were also demanding "excellence" in education and much greater intensity of effort on the part of those going to school.

The result has been crowding, poor facilities, schools in antiquated or unsuitable temporary buildings, poorly trained teachers (and far too few of them), inadequate supplies and—inevitably—irritability, impatience and strained relations between students and teachers and between students and the administrators who have to keep things going. The result also has been a deep sense of frustration for students whose basic education was too poor to prepare them for the next stage of schooling and for whom there were neither jobs waiting nor opportunities for training in the technical skills we know are needed.

All this has been the outcome of our inability and our unwillingness (as when communities have voted down the increased taxes or bond issues needed to support adequate programs) to plan for the increase that was laid out fair and clear in the census books twenty years ago. Our failure is, I think, a grievous reproach to a society that regards its children as its most precious possession. And it is evidence of a discrepancy between aspiration and actuality that students—and young people who did not even have the opportunity to be students—have not failed to recognize.

Then there is the tremendous leap ahead in the proportion of students who are seeking further education and training. In 1939 only 14 per cent of the eighteen-to-twenty-two age group in our country was in college. Today the proportion has risen to 46 per cent of the same age group, and there is no reason to believe we are approaching the saturation point. In our kind of civilization, in which education is not only the passport to personal success but also the basis of successful ongoing life, specialized training of many kinds is no longer the privilege of the few but the responsibility of the many.

This means that we now have—and we shall have for a long time to come—new kinds of students entering our colleges, our professional schools and our centers for specialized training. Some come with the expectation that now they will be treated as young adults; some hope that this new stage of education will make up for the blight of their childhood. What they find instead is that they are treated as irresponsible minors subject to the most arbitrary decisions. Many of them hope that now, when they are learning to think as individuals, they will be treated as individuals. What they find instead is that they are treated like packaged goods—so many to be processed, pushed through the educational maze, examined and granted degrees at the end of a standard course.

Under these circumstances, who can be surprised that one of the principal demands students are making is for "participatory democracy"—for the right to have a real voice in the decisions that affect their lives?

Focusing attention on the young as style setters and consumers (roles attributed to them by adults) does not make up to them for the lack of a real place in contemporary life or for the discrepancies between what they are taught to aspire to and expect and what they experience. But these things are not sufficient to account for the student revolt and the restlessness of the whole generation around the world. The hostile attacks by the young on the old and the established, the bizarre forms their rejections of convention take and their use of meaningless destruction as a weapon—these I attribute to a profound distrust of all those in power.

We speak of the generation gap, but I believe this distrust is the mirror image of the distrust members of the older generation, living in a world they feel has got out of hand, have for themselves and one another. For one thing is certain: no power like this—no voice for the voiceless—has ever emerged without many sympathizers in the strongholds of existing power structures. So strong is custom that the very right to dissent must be supported by those who ostensibly have no need to dissent.

What has happened, I believe, is that we have displaced onto the young our own sense of malaise, our distrust of our ability to cope with the deep changes we have brought about in the world; and the young are acting on our communication to them. Our distrust is clear, I think, from the emphasis we have put on the manifestations of student power rather than on the actual causes of disturbance. The danger is that as long as we continue to distrust ourselves, as long as we continue to respond with alarm instead of conceding with honesty that our world is not as we would wish it to be, our and their distrust can only grow and spread to include new and still younger groups.

The problem posed by student power is not how to contain it or simply how to meet the immediate demands of the activists, for efforts to do this and no more will lead only to the formulation of new demands. The problem now is how to bridge the ever-widening generation gap and find a new basis for trust that both generations can share.

Student Power, II

MAY, 1969

Militant students are purposefully disrupting part of society—the college and the university—by refusing to accept the role that has been traditionally assigned to them as submissive and dependent members of the academic community. They have become passionate and sometimes violent critics of society. They do not like the world as they are coming to know it and they want to see change—now. They want the academic world, in which they are—however subordinately—participants, to be at the center of change. The most active dissidents are using the tactics of disruption to force confrontation and to gain their ends. This, in essence, is the meaning of student power.

Their rebellion is commonly attributed—mistakenly, I think—to the existence of an ordinary generation gap. Such a generation gap is, in fact, something we try to bring about through education. Americans expect the young generation to be different from their elders, and we have been willing to work very hard to make this possible. The belief that our children will think differently from their parents and others of the older generation, and be better off, know more and do better, is intrinsic to our conception of progress. For this reason we never have taken adolescent rebellion and the dissident views of young adults as seriously as others do in countries where the attempts of young people to break away from the past are treated as the first steps toward revolution. But while we have expected our children to question the past and make new beginnings, we have not expected them to rise up in revolt against the educational process itself.

The students' deliberate use of the tactics of provocation and disruption is, as I see it, a symptom of a serious breakdown in communication. The immediate danger lies in the temptation on the part of the larger community to meet force with force. The only possible result of repression is that students, even those who are not dissidents, are confirmed in the belief that established authorities are their enemy and are not to be trusted. So violence spreads from one campus to another and from one age group to the next younger. By concentrating our efforts on restoring order, we entirely miss the point of what the disturbance is about.

I believe that students are playing an important role in alerting us to the vastness of the contradictions in our social life, in convicting us of continuing to act on outworn beliefs and holding back from social change because of meaningless fears. In contrast to earlier generations, these students are idealists with no Golden Age in the past or future. They are intensely concentrated upon the present, and their attempts at confrontation are alarm signals to which we must respond.

To this generation, which lacks a sense of history and has grown up in an affluent society, misery and want make no sense. These young people have been taught that it is technologically feasible for every individual to have enough food, for every family to have decent shelter and access to the basic necessities. It makes little difference whether they are the children of comfortable, suburban middle-class families or the children of deprived minority groups—the black, the Puerto Rican and the Mexican-American children of city slums, white children from isolated parts of Appalachia or children from communities whose means of livelihood have vanished. The meagerness of our efforts to overcome want and misery are inexplicable to them.

So also it seems to them a kind of madness to go to war against the people of a small and miserable country, to kill and get killed, when there are so many other, far more promising ways of using our tremendous resources and prestige to influence the state of world politics.

Though they want change, it is significant that these student rebels have no blueprints of what change should be. They raise questions and they want answers. Above all they want answers to the question: What is relevant?

It is the question they ask not only as they look at our political and social life, but also as they consider their position as students. They object to the conditions under which they are permitted to become and remain students, to the arbitrary control of their personal lives and to the lack of response to their demands for changes in the rules about what they must learn, how and when and from whom.

These young people—or at least those of the middle class—were brought up with a certain respect for their autonomy as individuals and their freedom, even as children, to make choices about their own lives. I believe they are challenging what is still, at the college and university level, an essentially medieval conception of the relationship of teacher and pupil and a conception of knowledge as absolute (as far as students are concerned) that is wholly inappropriate to our present view of organized thought. Here again, their rebellion against discrepancy is an alarm signal we cannot avoid.

The problem of meeting social criticism and that of restructuring the role of students are joined. Any attempt at solution must take both into account. As a first step we must re-establish communication. Essentially this means *listening* and getting across to students that they are being heard. We must convey to them that no one, as yet, knows the answers, and that working toward them requires not confrontation, but partnership. Then, on a long-term basis, we must reorganize the whole relationship of teaching and learning in such a way that the interpretation of experience will deepen and expand communication among all those concerned with the educational process. Only in this way can we re-create and strengthen the trust on which the survival of a society depends—our own or any other.

The first steps are already being taken, hesitantly and pessimistically, in colleges and universities. In some cases, unfortunately, student demands are being met by a kind of supine agreement. In others a real effort is being made to work toward partnership within the existing university structure. Here one can hope that joint action will bring about a situation within which students will have a voice in decisions. This will mean also that they will take responsibilities commensurate with greater freedom. For the present, success in quieting turbulence and reaching agreement depends on the development, however slowly and painfully, of some ability—on both sides—to hear as well as to speak.

But it will depend also on how we look to the future and think about student power in a different context. It has been estimated that within a few decades, one-third of the population, adults of all ages and children, will be actively involved in getting some form of education or specialized training at any one time. Education is certain to become our greatest social and economic enterprise. Even today education is not the exclusive occupation of the young and the particular responsibility of a limited number of adults concerned with teaching, counseling and administration.

To an ever-increasing extent men go on or come back to educational institutions for further or new training long after they have established themselves as skilled and competent adults. To a lesser extent, but in growing numbers, young mothers, once their children are launched in school, are returning to school to explore new ways of relating themselves to the community outside their homes. Very large numbers of adults take part in training programs that, by whatever name they are called, are educational in purpose. And finally there are the much older adults for whom retirement opens doors to new horizons through seminars and courses designed especially for them. Yet all this is only the beginning. Clearly student power, in a sense we have scarcely begun to think of it, can become a ferment working through our whole society.

Of course, expanded communication depends only in part on formal study. Not long ago a study of how Americans conceptualize time brought out a generation difference. Younger Americans use the idea of time relatively. What is a "long" or a "short" time depends on the context: a long time in the development of human civilization is a short time in the evolution of human life. In contrast, older Americans treat time absolutely: one hundred years is a long time; ten years is a short time. But there were exceptions. Grandparents who were close to their grandchildren had taken over the newer way of thinking, and for them, certain other aspects of contemporary life were easily accessible.

We can, if we will, work toward an organization of education in the future in which the young will be the teachers of their elders as often as they will be students and in which men and women of all

ages, as students and teachers, will have continuing access to one
another's ways of framing experience. The openness of the system,
the freedom with which people will feel they can move in and out of
it and their enjoyment of periods of learning throughout a lifetime
will depend, I believe, on the extent to which we build in both
autonomy and responsibility from the earliest years as a unifying
principle.

As long as most students were young and education was a prelude
to work or marriage or—for a privileged few—a professional career,
parents and teachers could demand that for the short years in which
students were in school they should be subordinate, submissive and
totally subject to supervision. The rebellion of today's students forces
us to realize that nothing of this kind is possible now.

Beginning with these students and looking ahead, we shall have to
design a wholly new kind of studentship in new kinds of institutional
settings. As long as institutions of learning are only partly supported
by students' fees and parents must continue to contribute financially
to their children's education, students will remain subordinate to the
dictates of others. Men and women of any age, as soon as they become students again, will lose their adult status. And education will
continue to be fragmented, as it is now, into age-graded institutions in
which people of the wrong age are intruders.

I believe we must treat everyone at eighteen as a young adult who
has economic, political and educational control over his—and her—
own life. It means the vote for eighteen-year-olds and positive provisions for students to vote wherever they are. It means draft reform
that will take into account essential stages of study and work experience. Above all it means economic independence, so that each student, equipped with his own funds, will be able to make his personal
choice and will be free to decide when and in what setting he will get
his training.

Various methods of underwriting the economic independence of all
students have been discussed. For example, we can provide adequate
salaries for students out of public funds, through taxes, exactly as we
pay for other essential services. I believe, however, that private funds
from foundations and individuals still will be needed to underwrite
new, experimental educational programs and the salaries of individually innovative students. Young men and women who are earning

the right to study by making responsible use of opportunities are likely to be serious and hard-working. And older men and women will feel justified in returning to school or entering programs of training because of the dignity and security of the student's position.

We should not ask a man to choose between dependency on his parents, dependency on his wife or the assumption of a heavy burden of debt in order to attend school. Nor should we expect wives to forego education for financial reasons. Only when education is fully available to all those at any time who are ready to make a choice will we begin to have a free flow of knowledge and a balance between responsible learning and action.

Inevitably this will mean drastic changes in educational institutions also. Instead of places set apart, schools at all levels will become settings where students and teachers can work in partnership, but they will also be integral parts of communities through the in-and-out flow of people and ideas. We need a society in which the continual asking and answering of questions keeps communications open. And for this we need students who are people like other people.

Twenty years ago we made no real provision for the educational situation that exists today. It was a failure of foresight and imagination. Today's students are attempting to gain by disruptive force what should have been in the making during all these years. It is a very poor—and may yet be a tragic—use of student power. But their mutiny against an inadequate system can have one unexpected benefit. It can alert parents to the needs of the future for their own children. It is not enough to bring up children to become individuals with high expectations and confidence. It is also necessary to work toward a way of living in which confidence is not misplaced and expectations can become reality.

Race and Intelligence

❧❀❧

SEPTEMBER, 1969

In the sharply accelerating struggle of black Americans finally to achieve full, unequivocal membership in our national society, the schools are storm centers, as they have been so often in the past. Americans believe education is the key to opportunity for the individual and to progress for the nation. Inevitably, schools and the kind of education at all levels open to disadvantaged groups, especially young black Americans, are a focal point in the struggle for the recognition of diversity that is shaking the country.

The present conflict is not unique. It has its counterparts elsewhere in the world; in our own country it marks the culmination of a long series of struggles to make our ancestral diversity a source of national strength. It is the mixture of hope and despair, the bitter intransigence and the new assertiveness of young militants, that gives us a sense of uniqueness at this stage. In spite of the sound and fury, however, I think we are moving toward new, viable solutions.

But the outcome is by no means assured. We still can stumble and fail to reach the goal of creating a truly open society. The principal stumbling block is the belief, shared by many people, that Negro Americans constitute a race.

Recently an attempt has been made—one of many, past and present —to establish the claim that Negro Americans, as a race, are less intelligent than white (or other) Americans. This latest effort is set forth in a long technical article by Arthur H. Jensen, "How Much Can We Boost IQ and Scholastic Achievement?" published in the *Harvard Educational Review*. Although nominally the discussion concerns the question of the heritability of intelligence within whole groups, the fact that Negro Americans are the focus of the discussion of race differences indicates just what is at issue. The contention is that the consistently lower scores achieved by Negro Americans on tests designed to measure IQ and the impermanent effects of very short-term educational "enrichment" programs (for example, the recent Head Start projects) indicate that, as a race, they are less intelligent than other Americans.

If the conclusions were correct, it would mean that Negroes were genetically less well equipped than others to benefit from the kinds of education and training, developed in Western civilization, that open the full range of occupations to members of our own or any other contemporary society. It would mean also that the barriers of ancient prejudice that are being broken down, and not only in our country, would be replaced by new barriers apparently supported by science, and the key to opportunity would be snatched away.

But the arguments are specious. They are based on the false premise that Negro Americans represent a "race."

There are new facets to the arguments as they are presented now. But the *kind* of argument, based on the false premise of race, is an old, familiar one in the struggle to incorporate in our society (or to close the doors to) many different ethnic groups. It is illuminating to recall what happened in the past.

In the decades between 1870 and 1920, millions of immigrants surged across the country and crowded into the ghettos of our growing cities, displacing earlier comers—the Irish, the Germans and others—who were already making their way. These immigrants differed from most older Americans (as well as from one another) in appearance, language, traditions and customary behavior. Those who came, for example, from southern Europe—Italians, Greeks, Spaniards, Portuguese—and from eastern and central Europe—Poles, Russians, Ukrainians—were popularly believed to belong to different, unassimilable "races."

Faced with the presence of these masses of newcomers, so many of whom were poor, illiterate and unskilled, pessimists in this country declared that with few exceptions they would always remain at the bottom of the economic and social ladder and that they would soon drag the whole country down to their low level. When intelligence tests were invented, early in the twentieth century, these provided the pessimists with new arguments. Test results showed that, comparatively, the school-age children of many immigrant groups obtained lower IQ scores than other American children. These results were interpreted as proof of the inferior intelligence of these "racial" groups.

But there were also the optimists—educators, classroom teachers, settlement workers and others, including leaders within the immigrant groups. They got down to the hard, practical task of turning the children of immigrants into Americans through education. Less directly, the adults also were transformed as children brought the new language and new ways into their homes. Some forged ahead rapidly in the schools; these belonged to ethnic groups, such as eastern European Jews, in whose traditions learning and scholarship were honored. Others, whose older way of life had cut them off from learning, gained far less from schools and tried other routes.

There were also, among the optimists, some who thought that knowledge of the backgrounds of the newer ethnic groups and of the adaptations they were making could advance the process of integration. This was my mother's hope, for example, when she made the first field study of an Italian community, in Hammonton, New Jersey.

Later, in the 1920's, when I was a student, I returned to the same community to study the relationship of speaking Italian or English in the home to children's test achievement. What I found was that the home language was related to the IQ levels attained; the scores of those speaking Italian were lower. Though all the children came from a similar background, such factors as lack of knowledge of English, lack of experience with the settings of American life and lack of motivation to do well on the tests depressed the IQ scores of the Italian-speaking group; in the English-speaking group better knowledge of the language, more familiarity with American ways of living and a greater expectation that test-taking was rewarding tended to remove inhibitions, so that these children could more readily draw on their actual, individual potential.

Insights based on more accurate knowledge played a part, over a period of time, in breaking down the prejudices incorporated in popular, mistaken beliefs about ethnic groups as "races." The integra-

tion into American life of the children and grandchildren of immigrants and their achievements have made us realize how ridiculous the
predictions of the pessimists were. Today we take pride in the multiplicity of ethnic traditions on which we have drawn in our culture.

Yet many Americans still hold unyieldingly to unscientific folk
beliefs about race. The only thing that changes is their application.
Now as in the past these mistaken ideas serve to rationalize doubts,
failures to bring about assimilation and, for some, a wish to live in the
past. It is clear that in every generation we must re-educate ourselves
to understand the facts.

There can be no doubt that the components of intelligence, like all
genetically determined traits, are inherited by the individual not from
a group but from his direct ancestors—two parents, four grandparents, eight great-grandparents, and so on. In a very small population that has lived isolated from other groups for many generations,
resemblances are numerous, for the range of traits that are heritable
(genetically based) is relatively limited. Through marriage within the
group over a long period of time everyone comes to share (though in
different ways) much the same ancestry and so also (in a great
variety of combinations) the potentialities of the original ancestral
group. One famous modern example of a population of this kind is
that of the Pitcairn Islanders in Polynesia, all of whom are descendants of two English mutineers from the *Bounty* and eleven Tahitian
women who accompanied them to the island in 1790.

In contrast, in a large population the range of individual differences
is very great, because of the number and diversity of ancestral lines.
Yet even after a long period of isolation, the number of traits peculiar
to that group is likely to be extremely small. What chiefly distinguishes two large, relatively stable populations from each other is not
particular traits, but differences in the statistical distribution of traits
(as, for example, the number of persons who belong to the A, AB or
O blood group), which are present in both of these groups as well as
in many other human populations. It is this intricate statistical patterning as it occurs in different populations to which biologists and
population geneticists are referring in the technical use of the term
"race."

By this scientific criterion Negro Americans are not a race at all.
They form a group not by racial but by social designation: they are

those individuals who have any visible African traits or, lacking these, are known or believed to have some African ancestry. They vary from individuals who may have thirty-one white ancestors and one ancestor who was African in origin, to some who have American Indian as well as African and white ancestors, and to the very few persons who, on the basis of superficial appearance, may be wholly African in descent. By inheritance they are an extraordinarily diversified group; their categorization as members of one group is entirely arbitrary.

This arbitrary social designation in the United States has carried—and in most cases still carries—a terrible burden of discrimination that has the most potent influences on health, length of life, education, economic and social opportunity and freedom of choice. The designation does not change substantially with a black American's economic circumstance or social class. Its deeply punitive effects are part of the experience that shapes the expectations of all black Americans, including what education can offer them.

The fact that, considered as a group, Negro school children, compared with their white (or other) peers, do less well on intelligence tests or tests of achievement is the definitive measure of the complex and multiple pressures to which they are continually subjected as a social group. In special circumstances of trust or hope, the inhibitions depressing their potential may lift somewhat; in circumstances of despair, the inhibitions may weigh more heavily than usual. The fact that, over time, individual Negro children's test scores tend to be consistent does not necessarily mean that we know what their potential is. It means that their feelings of denigration are fixed; all we know is what use they can make of available potential.

The newly burgeoning aspirations of black Americans and the drive for black autonomy can mean that those who have suffered most from the combination of white indifference, lack of knowledge and limited social vision can act, not only out of anger, but also with a new sense of dignity and inner strength. But I believe that the effectiveness of action will depend on our determination to bring our thinking up to date, so that we cannot be misled by the assertions of provincial, naïve or bigoted experts nor even welcome the drive for black autonomy for the wrong reasons.

I would like to think that schools and colleges and universities, where so many contenders in this and other conflicts meet, will be able to carry the major responsibility for creating a community of all Americans. For however inadequate, neglected or downright bad particular schools and school systems may be, our American belief in the value of education carries with it a kind of idealism that finds expression in responsible action and concrete results.

But there is also the danger that an overemphasis on education as the instrument of change may blind us to the necessary involvement of the whole community in bringing about change. Education *alone*, no matter how carefully planned and sustained, cannot change people's destinies. Education can only implement what the members of a society are carrying out in their way of life. It is in our communities that social denigration of black Americans must end; we must broaden our conception of what is involved in community—the community of all Americans.

For it was not the schools, or the schools alone, that made it possible for the children of immigrants in the past to become part of the mainstream of American life; it is not the schools alone that have failed in the task of helping disadvantaged black American children to realize their potential. It is the state of our beliefs, individually and collectively, on which the creation of an open society depends, and this in turn depends, I am convinced, on the matching of belief and reality through scientific knowledge.

Where Is the Wilderness?

❧❧❧❦❧

AUGUST, 1969

Each summer more urban Americans move out of doors. But how long can our outdoor enjoyments last? As millions of us pour across the land, the open places we are looking for may disappear. How shall we solve the dilemma of wanting to use and wanting to keep intact some parts of the natural world?

This year, before Labor Day, when vacation time draws to its close, some 1.5 million people will have converged on Yellowstone National Park. Traveling by plane or crowded bus, packed into cars, pickup trucks and trailers or roaring down the highways on motorcycles, visitors are arriving at the entrances to the park by the thousands and tens of thousands every day.

Hundreds are herded past the principal sights on conducted tours. Tourists on long trips pause here for a day, taking time for a picnic, a hasty glimpse of Old Faithful's skyward gush of water, a boat ride on ice-blue waters or a stagecoach ride, snapshots of the adults gazing up at Mount Washburn or the children feeding the animals—and then they are off again, weaving through the traffic headed for another famous park.

Others, if they are lucky enough to find a place, park their trailers or set up tents for a family vacation. Here fathers can fish, sons go boating, daughters try horseback riding and mothers, between bouts of housekeeping, can sun themselves and compare notes with other homemakers away from home about the problems of mass outdoor living and playing.

A few people—bird watchers, serious amateur botanists and geologists, and searchers after woodland quiet—move off from the crowds into the more remote parts of the park that still (but for how long?) speak of the grand American wilderness.

Yellowstone, the oldest of our great national parks, is only one of the thousands of parks, monuments, reservations, wildernesses and recreation areas where the National Park Service and a dozen other national, state and local services play host to vacationing Americans in search of campgrounds, picnic areas, beaches, lakes, wooded hills and playgrounds for adults and children in the midst of nature. But almost everywhere holiday-makers go, they find traffic jams, noise and litter and organized pleasure—the very things they hoped to escape.

In a recent summer it was estimated that some 532 million day visits and 52 million overnight visits were paid to these public outdoor vacation spots. It is true that the number of persons and the number of "visits" are not the same. Many tourists stopped at half a dozen parks on a cross-country trip; other families drove out to the same lake to swim and sail almost every sunny afternoon during the summer, and each occasion counted as a separate visit.

But it is also true that even these staggering figures from our government-managed parks tell only part of the story. Private and commercial marinas, more of them opening each year on the shores of lakes, the banks of rivers and along the seacoasts, are crowded with the boats on which families are lavishing care. "Second homes" for summer and winter holidays are mushrooming as fast as builders can set them up. Every outdoor sport has its practitioners, experts and novices, who crowd private as well as public recreation areas.

Most of this has happened within the last fifty years, the years since Americans have become city-and-suburb dwellers (rapidly approaching 80 per cent of the population) and the people of small towns and country places have learned to take over the styles of urbanites. In this same period, since 1920, we have grown from a nation of just over 100 million to one of 200 million people, doubling our numbers within years that mature Americans can remember. This is one reason for the immense pressure on every facility, including the out-of-doors, where people feel they should be free to move as they wish and enjoy a vacation from crowded living.

But the end is not in sight. Less than ten years ago, when the Outdoor Recreation Review Commission prepared its monumental report on the use and protection of our environment, studies were made of our outdoor activities. Surprisingly to me, it was found that just driving and walking or easy hiking—activities requiring no special skills—were still by far the most common outdoor pleasures. But it was found also that interest and proficiency in almost any one activity—swimming, boating, fishing, skiing, skating—bred interest in many more. Once someone discovers the delight of mastering one skill, however slightly, he is likely to try out not just one more, but a whole ensemble.

This means that since Americans (except for adolescents and quite elderly adults) usually go on vacations in family groups, particularly on a traveling holiday, the demand for clusters of the most varied recreation facilities—something for every member of a family—is expanding at a tremendous rate. And every few years a new fashion—for example, boats in the 1950's and snowmobiles in the 1960's—widens the range of what people are looking for and feel they have the right to enjoy.

So we must foresee that by the turn of the century, when our children are parents with families, "visits" to recreation areas will number not in the hundreds of millions, as now, but in the billions. The idea staggers the imagination. But unless we can visualize now the land and the resources that will be needed within just thirty years, the millions of Americans whose expectations are rising and the millions more who are still deprived of outdoor holidays will have no wide open places to enjoy themselves, no chance to listen quietly to the play of sounds of a protected wilderness.

A hundred years ago the imagination of only a few men, rare visitors to the boundless, scarcely touched wilderness areas in the West, was enough to shape our first thinking about conservation. Europeans, hemmed in on every side, had long since set aside huge tracts of land, such as the king's forests, and until the late eighteenth century the Alps and other high mountains were a feared and lonely no man's land. But Americans, beginning with the three million spread thinly along the eastern seaboard when we became a nation, were beguiled by their sense of the boundless land stretching out beyond the western horizon, which seemed limitless in its promise of rich resources, and gave little thought to conserving any part of it for the future.

By the 1860's, loggers and cattlemen were taking over western lands, threatening the unique beauty of wild areas like the Yosemite region. And in 1864, Frederick Law Olmstead (who also created New York's Central Park), working with a handful of other far-sighted men, persuaded Congress to pass a bill setting aside Yosemite Valley for the enjoyment of future generations. This represented our first real conservation effort.

Later, in the 1880's and 1890's, such open-handed generosity with national treasures of land no longer was possible. It took the concerted efforts of men like Carl Schurz, Gifford Pinchot and John Muir, highly trained naturalists, who became politicians and lobbyists, to save our dwindling forest reserves. Support came from the outdoor enthusiasts who formed the Sierra Club, the Boone and Crockett Club (founded by Theodore Roosevelt and other game-hunting enthusiasts), and similar organizations that proposed and fought for the next necessary legislation.

Even so, their success would have been doubtful without the forceful rhetoric of an outdoor-loving President. In *The Quiet Crisis* Stewart Udall tells us that Theodore Roosevelt saw himself as the "trustee of the lands owned by the people." His high-handed authority saved millions of acres of public land, from Grand Canyon to great river sites for the development of power, areas that are now our national pride.

In each generation it has taken much more widely distributed and intensive effort to protect and extend the open resources of our country. In the 1930's, when another conservation-minded Roosevelt came into the Presidency, the national disaster of unemployment and a new, horrified awareness of the spreading dustbowl wilderness, where neither human beings nor plants and animals could survive, made a tremendous rescue effort possible in which man and land entered into the same equation. In the Civilian Conservation Corps, Franklin Roosevelt put thousands of unemployed men to constructive work across the country; enormous stretches of the "natural" forests we enjoy today are the product of their labors.

This set a precedent for saving and re-creating resources. But we tend to remember the CCC as a make-work organization, not as the beginning of a new kind of venture in caring for the land that is becoming the most priceless heritage of generations to come.

Now, without delay, we must decide on the kind of outdoor world we want our children's children to inherit. As I see it, this decision will require some understanding by all Americans of what can be gained—or otherwise will be lost forever.

Up to now our true wilderness tracts are safe—larger ones like Jackson Hole and the protected section of Gila National Park and smaller ones that private conservationists are bringing into public care. But the pressure on the park lands open to vacationists is becoming explosive. Americans cannot bear to be fenced in—or fenced out, as happens when they are excluded from the wilder areas of parks and refuges.

And the new roads carrying heavy traffic, the new lodges, trailer parks and camping grounds, the new ski trails, the waters newly opened to motorboats, all threaten the continued existence of living creatures, trees and plants that cannot thrive in the near vicinity of man. The question, "What does a trumpeter swan, a timber wolf, a grizzly bear, need to be happy?" is not really facetious. It is not a matter of putting the needs of wild animals in their habitat before those of civilized men, but of protecting the rights of future generations to experience—as well as to read about in archival records—the wilderness world.

Part of the solution is, I think, for us to acquire and gain protective custody over as much land as we can everywhere within driving distance—two to three hundred miles—of every town and city. Although we cannot count on private ownership alone to guard stretches of unspoiled countryside, mountains, lakes and beaches, we are developing the legal means of protecting both private and long-term public interests.

What we need most is a humanized natural world where people can move safely, can come to know natural phenomena, caves and woods and mountains and prairies; a natural world where we can enjoy the kinds of growing things that prosper, with care, in our daily presence. Where these already exist, we must try to save them. But much of the land we can acquire will have to be re-created, following designs that will both conserve its life and give people the outdoor diversity they seek.

But this will not be enough. So far, most Americans have treated outdoor areas mainly as playgrounds. We shall also need tremendous human resources to keep them safe for our play. Having moved into cities, we shall now have to develop a multitude of professions and careers, other than those concerned with feeding ourselves and other people, centering on the land.

All Americans, not only the ardent hard-working conservationists, will have to participate responsibly in care for the land. I believe the basis for this kind of participation can be laid through the work of a conservation corps of young people in national service. They would be paid for their work, as members of the Peace Corps and Vista are or a new teachers corps would be, and they would be eligible for educational benefits.

Their work would help to re-establish the links between the man-made and the natural world, as the young people themselves would come to understand better the cycles of growth and decay and the deeper attachment of human beings to outdoor life. It would give them time to learn and a chance to choose ways of spending a life at work that is both ancient and, in its base in science, always new.

Play on the land, vacations from city living, will be true recreation for all of us when we can respond with wonder to a world we know, a world that nourishes our imagination as it claims our care.

III

THE
PRIVATE GOOD

The Gift of Autonomy

❧❦❧❦❧

DECEMBER, 1966

Every gift we give carries with it our idea of what a present is. Perhaps it expresses our personality; perhaps, on the contrary, it is what we believe the recipient really wants, a choice based on careful listening for the slightest hint of what he longs for or needs or should have, even though he may not realize it.

Gifts from parents to children always carry the most meaningful messages. The way parents think about presents goes one step beyond the objects themselves—the ties, dolls, sleds, record players, kerchiefs, bicycles and model airplanes that wait by the Christmas tree. The gifts are, in effect, one way of telling boys and girls, "We love you even though you have been a bad boy all month" or, "We love having a daughter" or, "We treat all our children alike" or, "It is all right for girls to have some toys made for boys" or, "This alarm clock will help you get started in the morning all by yourself." Throughout all the centuries since the invention of a Santa Claus figure who represented a special recognition of children's behavior, good and bad, presents have given parents a way of telling children about their love and hopes and expectations for them.

When I was a child, my parents used to give me a pair of books each Christmas. One was "light," easy reading; the other was "heavy," a book I had to think about if I was to enjoy it. This combination carried with it the message that there are different kinds of pleasure to be gained through reading and that I should discover each kind for myself.

If we think about all the presents we have given our children over the years, we will see how they fit into the hopes we have for each child. I do not mean this in the simple sense that we delight in a little girl's femininity, and so give her dolls, or that we implement a boy's masculinity by giving him model planes and boxing gloves. We do, of course, speak to our children in this simplest form of symbolism. And we do, of course, personalize what we say when we give our outdoors son a fishing rod and his experiment-minded brother a microscope.

However, our giving also carries more subtle and complex messages. For example, we can ask ourselves: "What am I saying to my children about growing up to be independent, autonomous people?" An abstract question of this kind can be posed in relation to a whole range of presents for children of both sexes and of different ages. Where the choice to be made is between a simple toy engine that the child himself can wind up and a more complicated one that I shall have to wind up for him, which one do I give him? Choosing a doll for a little girl, do I buy her a perishable costume doll with one beautiful dress, a washable doll with a wardrobe or a doll for which she will make dresses out of the materials I also give her? The costume doll can perhaps be dressed and undressed, but that is all. A bath would be ruinous. A sturdy doll with a ready-made wardrobe places choice in the child's own hands. She herself can dress and undress it, bathe it safely and decide whether her "little girl" will wear pink or blue, plaid or plain. Giving my child materials out of which to fashion doll dresses is a lovely idea, and may perhaps encourage her to learn how to sew. But choice and autonomy both are reduced because now I must help her at every step.

We can ask questions of this kind also about the presents of money that are given our children by grandparents and godparents, aunts and uncles and family friends. What do we tell our children about the bright silver dollar tucked into the toe of a Christmas stocking or the grown-up-looking check that is made out in the child's own name? Is the money meant to be used now for some specific purpose—for the charm bracelet a little girl has admired or the radio a boy wants for his own room? Or is it an inducement, perhaps, to begin saving for the car a teen-ager must wait five years to own? Is the child told, directly or indirectly: "This is your money to do with as you like"? Or is the child asked: "Would you rather spend it or put it in the bank?"

By defining the alternatives so sharply, we are, in effect, robbing the child of choice. In fact, when you tell him that the money is his and then give directions, hint at alternatives or reproach him for spending it in one way instead of another, the gift carries a very definite message: "I don't really trust your choices. I don't really want you to choose." If, on the other hand, the message is simple and direct ("This is your money, yours, to dispose of as you like"), then the child may even solicit your advice. But there is no real turning back once you have said, "This is your money."

Over the years, there are always new ways of reinforcing or detracting from our children's growing sense of independence. For example, if you give a boy a box of stationery imprinted with his name and a supply of postage stamps, you are showing him that you expect him to write, address and mail his own letters. This means, of course, that you may never see the letters he writes, or you may become a consultant on appropriate terms of address or the correct abbreviations of names of states. At this point you can give him an almanac in which he himself can look up the answers to his questions—or you can keep the almanac on your own desk and become the mediator between his questions and the information he needs.

Giving a girl a diary with a key is a way in which a mother can tell her daughter (boys, on the whole, do not keep diaries) that she respects her child's growing sense of identity and independence. Giving a boy a desk is one way of fostering his sense of personal privacy; but if we continually tidy it up or complain about its untidiness, as we see it, the original message miscarries.

In many families the climax, and in some the crisis, of their individual pattern of giving comes as the children approach college, when their parents prepare to give them the most expensive "gift" of all—a college education. Of course, parents are not, as a rule, literally "giving" their children an education. What they are giving them is the opportunity to become educated.

Many parents today meet the responsibility of supporting their children through the college years, wholly or in part, by taking out insurance policies for this special purpose. Usually such policies, whatever their specific form, are payable to the parents. Then the choice of a college and the course of study remains firmly in the parents' hands. Americans believe very strongly that he who pays the piper calls the tune.

This is the *customary* way of doing things. It carries with it the message that our children, although approaching adulthood, are still children in our eyes. But this need not be. The money instead can be set up as a fund available to the boy or girl. Its purpose can be specified: This is not money for just anything. It is money for higher education, intended to give you freedom and choice within this area of your life.

For children who have grown up with an ever-enlarging sense of their own autonomy and independence, intelligent handling of the opportunity for further education will come naturally and easily. They are free, if they like, to postpone going to college for a year. Or they can drop out for a semester or a year without fearing that the tuition money will have vanished when they want to go back. A girl can marry before she goes to college, or while she is still a student, knowing that the choice of when and where she will continue her education remains open to her. Next year or ten years from now the money will be there, waiting, ready for her when she wants and needs it.

Like the small presents of early childhood that carry the message "You need my help," the educational insurance policy in the parents' name places responsibility in the parents' hands. In many cases parents are not even required to spend the money on the education of the child in whose interest the policy was acquired. But when money is placed in the child's own name, a trust for a special purpose, the parents are saying: "This is what I hope to give you—the right of choice. I respect your right to choose. My gift is intended to underwrite your freedom to be a person. Long ago I gave you stamps so you could mail your own letters. I gave you an allowance so you could move more freely in your own world. Now, as then, I want you to be an autonomous, self-starting person, someone who enjoys interdependence with other people because instead of fighting for your independence, you have grown into it."

All our giving carries with it messages about ourselves, our feelings about those to whom we give, how we see them as people and how we phrase the ties of relationship. Christmas giving, in which love and hope and trust play such an intrinsic part, can be an annual way of telling our children that we think of each of them as a person, as we also hope they will come to think of us.

What, in Fact, Is Parenthood?

❦❧❦❧❦

NOVEMBER, 1962

Childlessness is a state which American couples are very reluctant to regard as their fate or as an act of God to be accepted with resignation. We Americans have a strong conviction that just as it is our right to choose our marriage partners, it is also the right of all married couples to have children. It is not surprising, therefore, that childless couples very soon turn their thoughts toward adoption as a way of creating a family.

Since we are so deeply committed to adoption as a way of compensating for childlessness, it may be worth re-examining how we handle adoption and how the relationships of adoptive parents and children affect the relationships of biological parents and children.

Over the years an enormous folklore has grown up about the "unreasonableness" of adoption agencies which demand far more of adoptive parents than anyone would think of demanding of natural parents. Once a couple are legally married, it is their right to have a child without interference. No one gives either husband or wife a physical examination, inquires into their health history or their heredity, counts the books in their home or inspects the kitchen to see if it is neat and clean. No one checks on whether the husband has a steady job, investigates the mortgage on the couple's house, asks whether they have living parents who may become a burden or, on the contrary, can be counted on for help if husband or wife takes sick, finds out whether their religious affiliations are the same or different and what their parents' religious affiliations were, or, finally, investigates their emotional stability.

When a married couple decide to have a baby, no one asks the opinion of the husband's employer or the bank manager or the doctor or the neighbors. It is accepted practice, however, to ask adopting parents for references and to investigate them fully before a baby is placed in their home. Nor, of course, does anyone say to natural parents, "There will be a trial period of six months [or a year]. If everything goes well and you are suited to each other, you can keep the baby." When a baby is born to legally married parents, none of these questions is asked by society—and often they could not be answered.

One reason for the striking contrast in our attitudes toward actual parenthood and adoption is the sheer scarcity of ideally adoptable babies. The kind of baby that the majority of adoptive parents would like to have is even scarcer than are the parents approved of by adoption agencies; for the fact is that many would-be parents, looking for an ideal baby, make far heavier demands on the adopted child than any parents in the world can make on their own children.

The ideally adoptable baby is expected to be tested in every possible way to make certain he is without detectable defects. His parents must be known and he should be certified as coming from fine, healthy stock, preferably enough like that of the adopting parents so that later he will resemble them. He should be intelligent and capable of climbing to any academic heights his adoptive parents may have reached or may aspire to. Furthermore, he must have been born in such circumstances that his two fine, healthy, well-bred parents are perfectly willing to sign away their rights to him forever. (Though the inherent contradiction in this position is a glaring one, it is seldom commented on.) The popular mythology about adoption focuses on the one hand on the unreasonable exactions of the adoption agencies and on the other hand on the terribly bad luck of adoptive parents when, heartbreakingly, the child does not turn out to be the paragon that all the precautions have been designed to produce.

But what, in fact, is parenthood? Do actual parents have any guarantee that the baby born to them will be healthy, free of hereditary handicaps, beautiful and brilliant? Is not the essence of parenthood the willingness to accept and love, cherish and provide for children whatever they are like—intelligent or stupid, handsome or plain, troublesome or amiable, sturdy or sickly, dark-eyed or ash blond, boys or girls?

Every self-conscious and responsible future parent, knowing his or her family history well, realizes that a child *could* turn out to be like Great-aunt Susan, who was silly in the head, *could* have a cleft palate like those two boys of Uncle Willie's. No family is without defective individuals, without unfortunate as well as fortunate traits that may appear in a new generation. Yet all parents take a chance. Only under very special circumstances are they likely to feel that hereditary taints justify their adopting a baby. In such cases, even though a couple are acting responsibly, they are turning from the real to the ideal.

And unfortunately, this concept of the ideal child not only lays an intolerable burden on adopted children, it also decreases our ability to be the kind of courageous and flexible parents on whom society has always depended. Our adoption procedures counterpoint the demand of parents for the perfect child (not the real child) with the demand for the child of the perfect home (not the real home). And the unreal standards with which we have invested adoption can reinforce the difficulties of actual parents and their own children in accepting each other.

At its worst, the demand for the ideal child sanctions the most self-centered kind of parenthood. People who feel they are entitled to perfect children are usually more concerned with their own needs than those of the children. An adopted child in such a case becomes an instrument of its parents' self-centeredness, a way of helping them simulate the kind of family life that they feel is socially necessary and desirable.

In view of all this we may well ask: What right have we to set up standards by which the adoptive parents demand a perfect baby and conversely, to make demands on adoptive parents that we would never make on natural parents?

There *are* people in this country, after all, who approach adoption with a very different attitude, people who admit frankly that adoption is not a good imitation of biological parenthood and that no matter how early you acquire a baby or how lovingly you care for him, this does not alter the fact that it is a relationship with different needs. These are people whose adoption of children is based not on their own needs but on the needs of children—particular children or whole categories of children, including the so-called "unadoptable" children, among whom an untold variety of gifts may be found.

Certainly the attitude of people like this deserves our consideration. It recognizes honestly that adopted children present a special problem and make a different kind of claim on adult care from what natural children do. And at the same time, it throws the doors open for adoptive parents to some of the hazards and joys and uncertainties of the natural parenthood that was denied to them.

The American Takes a Wife

MAY, 1962

Unlike the older societies of Europe, where men have very limited expectations of marriage, the American husband tends to feel that his wife and home should provide him with all the major satisfactions in life. When his marriage fails to do this the American, unlike the European, does not philosophically seek those satisfactions elsewhere —at a café, in his club or with a mistress. He decides instead that he has made a terrible mistake and that the only answer may be to start over again with a new wife and a new home.

Americans today feel that a successful marriage is not only a desirable way of life; it is the *only* way of life in which they can achieve independence, happiness and adulthood. In other societies a boy's recognition as a man may depend on his reaching a certain age, passing an examination, beginning to earn a living, inheriting a farm or even taking an enemy's head. But in the United States it depends on his getting married.

For this a man needs the right kind of girl. Not, be it noted, the right girl, but the right *kind* of girl: a girl who has the same picture of marriage and whose looks, intelligence, education and experience suggest that she will be able to live up to the picture. The man is asking the girl not only to help him make a home and have children; he is asking her also to help him be the kind of person whose parents can't order him around, whom employers will be glad to hire and insurance agents will pursue instead of evading, who can rent an apartment, get a telephone installed, obtain a bank loan, buy furniture on credit—who will, in fact, be treated as a grown-up, responsible member of society.

Young men look at girls as prospective partners from the time they begin to take part in the adolescent rituals of dances and house parties and double dates. And they share with their families the fear of getting entangled with the wrong kind of girl—a girl, in other words, who will not help them find their place in the world. For a man's wife today is expected to have the strength, the organizational ability, the *savoir-faire* to help him professionally as well as personally. Precisely what the expectations are depends on the education and the aspirations of the husband-to-be, but they are always there in the background.

Also in the background is a kind of composite image of how his wife should look and act. This is made up in part of what his friends expect or already have in a wife, in part of images from advertising and the mass media and in part of the things he admired in his own mother.

Ideally, this woman with whom he hopes to share his life, his ambitions and his relaxations should stay at home the way his mother did. He is not so old-fashioned, however, that he will object to her taking a job—until the first baby comes. After that she should devote herself (charmingly and efficiently) to housekeeping and child-rearing. Beyond this she should *look* like the right kind of wife. She need not be beautiful, for beauty may be a little dangerous; she need not have a great deal of sex appeal, for this would make a man continually anxious. Rather, she should take the trouble to dress, wear her make-up, do her hair, walk and talk in the ways prescribed by class and period and locality.

The American man wants a wife who can make as much of herself as the wives of other men with similar incomes and expectations—a wife of whom his friends will be appreciative but not covetous.

The one thing the happily married man in this country wishes to guard against at all costs is temptation for his wife or for himself. Any smallest temptation to respond either sexually or tenderly, by displaying the gentle responsibility a man reserves for his own wife and children, is seen as a danger. There is, to be sure, a certain amount of exploitation in relationships with the women he meets at work, while he is traveling and in other situations from which his wife is absent.

But these relationships are deliberately kept on such a casual level that they seldom threaten his marriage partnership.

Since marriage is our only acceptable way of life, dissolving one partnership means setting up another like it, and this is extremely troublesome, especially if there are children. One must be constantly on guard, therefore, against the danger that some small transitory attraction outside the home, some small disagreement at home, some failure to match an adolescent daydream or to meet the currently reported standard of success in marital relationships, may destroy a marriage and make it necessary to get a divorce and start over again— with another girl of exactly the same kind.

In some great civilizations men have kept their women indoors behind barred windows or hidden beneath black veils. Happily married American men wish that all women were happily married, attractive but unprovocative, and absolutely inaccessible—an attitude that seems to extend even to the women they encounter in subways and buses and trains. Nowhere in the civilized Western world do men show less public consideration for women heavy with pregnancy or with children in their arms. These are other men's children, they seem to be saying, and by rights the other men should be there.

In the home a man wants his wife to keep sex where it belongs. In fact, this is something he wants as soon as the marriage is agreed upon. During the period of their engagement, when the modern girl is often dangerously relaxed, it is the man who stays alert to protect his future marriage from premature paternity. After marriage, however, it is the wife's duty to keep her husband so well satisfied and contented that he will never look at another woman. In addition she must underwrite his successes, deny his failures and keep him working toward the kind of life for which they planned. If a man becomes fatigued and irritable, if he begins to look for someone to tell his troubles to over the third cocktail, it is subtly his wife's fault. He has, he believes, given her a half interest in the company and now it is up to her to do her share to maintain it.

What does the American man expect in a wife? Probably more than has been expected by any other husband in history. If the American wife fulfills his hopes, however, her rewards are supposed to be great.

Her husband will try to come home every evening and never go out on the town with his friends. He will spend his nights in strange cities telephoning to her. He will try never to accept an invitation or take a vacation that doesn't include her. He will carry the biggest life-insurance policy he can afford. He will help every evening and on weekends, even with the newborn baby. He will carry all her heavy packages. He will try to remember to bring her flowers and small presents and never to give her cause for serious jealousy.

He will, in short, be one of the most devoted husbands the world has ever seen—mass-produced by the thousands and safely indistinguishable from every other husband.

Apprenticeship for Marriage

❦❧❦❧❦❧

OCTOBER, 1963

In training people for most professions—doctors, teachers, social workers, nurses—we realize that all those who have to do something must have a chance to learn how it is done—how to treat a patient, teach a child, size up a family situation, give a bedridden patient a bath. Books are not enough; practice also is necessary. So every young person who wants to enter a profession of this kind must spend some time doing field work—whether it is called an internship or practice teaching or has no formal name.

Yet young married couples, young parents, are asked to do something far more complex than is demanded of any young professional. All alone, with no one to guide them, living in their self-contained homes, often in a completely strange suburb near no one they have ever known before, they are asked to care for each other, to budget and plan ahead, to cook and eat nutritional meals, to look after newborn infants, to combine work and study and play in ways that would puzzle any vocational counselor who was asked for advice—mothers before they are women, fathers before they are men.

In our grandmothers' day most girls had some experience of caring for babies, planning meals, buying food, helping with planned housework, helping out in a family struck by illness or accident or death. Boys had a chance to see how and when men intervened in family affairs, how they planned to plant another field of wheat or buy a house or a new team of horses. But today the different ways in which different men and women meet emergencies are seldom visible to the eyes of teen-agers. Each family, living its self-contained life, tries to

solve its problems in its own way, or else the parents look for advice
and help from impersonal agencies outside the home. The teen-agers'
parents, reared in a different age, have weathered many years of marriage and do not present very good models for families in the making.
Today's teen-agers, looking forward to marriage, expect that their
life will be different from that of their parents, whose decisions, con-
ditioned by an economic depression and a world war, often seem so
penny-pinching and inexplicable. Yet most teen-agers in middle-class
families today have very little chance to see how other families live—
least of all young families, where the parents are just a few years older
than themselves.

Unlike the professionals who work with some aspect of human
life—as doctors, social workers or teachers—the young parents-to-be
have had no ward work, no casework, no practice teaching. They are
like surgeons who have never learned to use a scalpel, social workers
who have never listened to a client, teachers who have never faced a
class, chefs who have never cooked a meal, pilots who have never sat
at the controls of a plane. In fact, in these marriages the pilot and
navigator are equally aspirants when the plane taxis down the field.

But, it may be objected, you can't practice marriage. No matter
how much you may practice the skills—cooking or budgeting or
child care or even sex—you can't practice the responsibilities to
which a husband and a wife are jointly committed. In marriage it is
this commitment and these responsibilities that matter. In marriage
two young people are, for better or worse, part of a new social unit
into which children will be born or adopted, for whom they (and no
one else) will have the sole responsibility—for the children's health,
well-being, character, minds and souls and bodies. In marriage these
two young people are suddenly responsible to and for each other.
They (and no one else) are the ones to whom the doctor will turn for
permission to operate, to whom the police will come in case of an
accident or a crime, who must share the questions of the tax collector,
the home-relief investigator, the credit investigator, the insurance
agent. One will sit up and wonder and worry when the other doesn't
come home when expected. How can these things be practiced? Isn't
it the essential, grueling day-in-day-out responsibility for which
young people are not prepared?

True, no boy or girl can practice the final and continuing responsibility of being a husband or wife, of being one of two parents. But neither can the surgeon practice the final responsibility of an actual operation. The difference is that the medical student, the student teacher, the apprentice, can observe others doing the things they themselves will do later. They can observe with instruction. The surgeon-to-be learns anatomy and physiology; he watches operations, first from a distance or on films, then closer, and finally close enough to see the tightened lips, the sudden tension in the skilled surgeon. With his own empathically tautened muscles, he absorbs some of the surgeon's own responsible attention. And when that first time comes for him, he will be prepared.

What we need today is field work in preparation for marriage and parenthood. The skills of managing a home and taking care of children should be learned, like any skill, by practice and observation— not merely out of books. The first temperature one takes should not be that of one's husband or wife. The first baby one holds in one's arms should not be one's own. The first cut finger or scraped knee one bandages should not be that of one's own crying child.

I propose that every school—public or private, in city or suburb or country, in rich neighborhoods and poor ones—teach a course in family life that involves field work and that every student, boy or girl, must pass in order to graduate. Books and films are a necessary part of teaching; learning to know what goes into homemaking is a necessary part of training. Class teaching and discussion are essential. But in addition, we need field work for marriage and parenthood— assignments in which each student would have to spend several periods of twenty-four to forty-eight hours on active duty in the home of a young family with small children and no other help.

Many of the difficulties in carrying out family-life education in schools arise from religious differences about the kind of family life that should be taught. To a large extent these difficulties could be met by allowing young people to do their field work in families with backgrounds like their own—Catholic young people in Catholic homes, Baptist young people in Baptist homes, Orthodox Jewish young people in Orthodox Jewish homes, young people from secular homes in other secular homes. Obviously, even with careful instruction, a few weekends spent in the home of a young family do not provide a complete preparation for marriage any more than short periods of practice teaching are a complete preparation for taking full charge of a class of six-year-olds. But the experience, in both cases, is illuminating and sobering. It would give a great many young people who are ready to leap into marriage—now, immediately, with only a picture-magazine idea of how it works—a chance to reflect, a reason for pausing, some experience on which to base a choice, a firmer grasp of reality in answering the question "Are we really prepared to try it?"

But how could this kind of field work be planned in our hundreds of different kinds of cities, large and small, in our suburbs, new and old? We could not begin with one over-all plan, since the field work would have to be flexible—as different as the different kinds of communities in which it was done. As a first step, plans would have to be made experimentally, in connection with particular schools and related to classes in marriage, home economics and social relations in those schools.

Preparing for this kind of field work would be halfway between preparing a community to take a batch of foreign students to live in individual homes and organizing a community sitter service. Families would have to volunteer, and students would have to be screened and briefed for their experiences. One of the requirements for a family to qualify for this free and eager help might be that they themselves do something that would enrich the experience—make a set of snapshots or write a short report of what went on. And one of the requirements for the students might be that in order to get a good mark, they be invited back for a second weekend. After all, in marriage one is asked to stay—permanently.

The very fact of enlisting in such a plan would bring isolated young families into touch with the wider community, as well as teenagers with those who are just one step ahead of them. All sorts of community groups could take part in working out the plans—church groups, PTA's and women's clubs, and child-study groups, well-baby clinics and prenatal clinics to help in selecting the families. Through field work for parenthood, young people can help younger people forge a new tradition with the support of the community.

Marriage in Two Steps—A Proposal

JULY, 1966

The June bride evokes memory pictures of her mother and her mother's mother as just such a happy girl, caught between tears and laughter. The newest bridegroom, describing his difficulties, awakens memories of other crises, each story a different one, and yet in its happy outcome the same.

For everyone taking part in a wedding each small event, like the solemn ritual of marriage itself, binds the generations in the shared belief that what has been true and lasting in the past is true and lasting today and will remain so safely across time. On such occasions sentiment and loving hope for the young couple—these two who are entering the most important relationship of their adult lives—join in renewing our faith in traditional forms. This, we believe, is how families begin.

But in the cool light of everyday experience a different picture emerges. As a society we have moved—and are still moving—a long way from the kinds of marriage our forefathers knew and believed in. We still define marriage as essentially an adult relationship. But now, in a period in which full participation in adult life is increasingly delayed, the age of first marriage for boys as well as girls has been declining steadily. And although people can look forward to longer years of vigorous maturity, young couples are entering parenthood not later than in the past, but even earlier.

We still believe that marriage entails financial responsibility. Yet we indulge in endless subterfuge to disguise the economic dependency of the majority of very young marriages. Significantly, we have devised systems of loans and insurance to ease our financial burden of seeing children through years of higher education. However, we have not invented any form of insurance to cover the care of children born of student marriages or born to teen-aged parents who are struggling to find themselves. If we encourage these young marriages, as in fact we do, then we must think more clearly about the long-term economic problems for which we, as parents, may have to take some responsibility.

We still believe that marriage is the necessary prelude to responsible parenthood even though, in every social class, pregnancy is to an increasing extent preceding marriage. We still strongly believe that children born of a marriage should be wanted. In the past, this meant accepting the birth of children no matter what the number and circumstances; but today, with existing methods of conception control, every child could be a chosen child.

We still believe that the continuity of the family, based on marriage, is fundamental to our way of life and to the well-being of every individual child. Yet there is clear evidence of the fragility of marriage ties, especially among very young couples who become parents before they know each other as husband and wife.

The disparities are plain to see and the outlook is unpromising. We might expect this to force us to recognize how great are the discrepancies between our expectations, based on tradition, and what is happening to young American families. The truth is, we have not really faced up to the many conflicts between belief and experience, precept and practice, in our current, muddled style of marriage. It is not enough to say, "Yes, marriage patterns are changing." What we have not fully realized is that we do not have to stand by helplessly while change sweeps over us, destroying our hopes for a better life for our children.

Instead, we can look steadily at the changes that have brought us where we are.

We can ask, "How can we invest marriage forms with new meaning?"

We can move toward a reconciliation of belief and practice that is consonant with our understanding of good human relationships.

Of course, there is no simple way of defining the changes that have already taken place, but two things are crucial in the contemporary

situation—our attitude toward sex and our attitude toward commitment. Today, I am convinced, most Americans have come to regard
sex, like eating and sleeping, as a natural activity. We lean toward the
belief that people who are deprived of sex will be tense and crotchety,
and perhaps unreliable in their personal relationships. We have come
to believe also that asking physically mature young people to postpone sex until their middle twenties is neither fair nor feasible. And as
we have learned to deal more evenhandedly with boys and girls most
of us have ceased to believe in any double standard of morality. This
is in keeping with our belief that sex, like marriage and parenthood,
should involve social equals who are close in age. When the age gap
widens—when the man is much older than the woman or the woman
older than the man—we disapprove. And although we may not
express our doubts, we do not have very high expectations for
eventual happiness when two people must bridge wide differences in
upbringing. We believe that young people should learn about sex
together, as equals. But this means that both are likely to be equally
inexperienced. Our emphasis, in the ideal, is on spontaneity. It is this
combination of beliefs, together with our continuing certainty that
sex is safe only in marriage, that has fostered that has, in fact,
forced—our present acceptance of very young marriage.

But in accepting early marriage as the easiest solution to the problem of providing a sex life for everyone, we confront new difficulties.
No matter how many books adolescent boys and girls have read or
how freely they have talked about sex, they actually know very little
about it and are very likely to bungle their first serious sex relations.
Certainly this is not new; an unhappy honeymoon all too often has
been a haunting prelude to marriage. What is new is that the young
husband and wife are as yet inexperienced in living through the initial
difficulties that can enter into any important adult relationship of
choice. They are, for example, inexperienced in making friends and
living through the give-and-take that adult friendships require.
Young men today rarely know how to make friends with girls; and
girls, looking for mates, are unlikely to be much interested in a man as
a friend. Heterosexual friendships therefore are postponed until after
marriage, and then entered into only with other married couples.
Thus friendship, which ideally should precede marriage and help the
young man and woman better understand the adjustments that any

adult relationship requires, now comes too late to help a first marriage.

Inexperience is one hazard. But it becomes especially hazardous because we also believe that no one should be trapped in a final mistake. Individuals as they grow and develop are permitted to change their jobs and occupations, to move from one part of the country to another, to form new associations and develop new interests that bring them into contact with new people. And as part of our expectation that people change as they grow, most of us have come also to accept the idea of divorce. When a marriage does not work out, most of us believe, each partner should have another chance to start over again with a different man or a different woman. We believe in commitment, but we do not believe that commitments are irrevocable.

But divorce also is a hazard. It is true that for two adults without children who now find that they cannot carry out a commitment made at an earlier stage of their lives, divorce can be an end and a beginning; but because of the role children play in the present style of marriage, divorce becomes a widespread hazard. For whereas in the past a man, and especially a woman, might marry in order to have children, now having a child validates marriage. Pregnancy often precedes marriage, and even where it does not, the style is to have a child quickly. It is as if having a child sets the seal of permanence on a marriage that is in truth far from permanent, and that at this stage is still in the making.

The child thus becomes a symbol. This use of a child is out of keeping with our belief that each person should be valued as an individual for his own sake. And when the marriage breaks down, the child is sacrificed to the changed needs of the man and woman, who are acting not as parents but as husband and wife. The child—a person in his own right, growing toward the future—stands as a symbol of an unreal past.

Perhaps we can catch a glimpse of what we might make of marriage and parenthood if we think in terms of a new pattern that would both give young couples a better chance to come to know each other and give children a better chance to grow up in an enduring family. Through what steps might this be accomplished?

It should be said at once that changes as important as those involved in creating a new style of marriage can never be brought about through the actions of a few people, or even all the members of a single group. In a democracy as complex as ours, in which one must always take into account a great diversity of religious, regional, class and national styles, success will depend on contributions made by all kinds of people. Ideas will arise out of discussions in the press, from the pulpits of churches, on television, in the agencies of government, in the theater and in community organizations. Some will come from those whose work brings them face-to-face with the failures of the present system and who are aware of the urgent need for new forms. Some will be shaped by the actual experiments in which lively, imaginative young people are engaging. And still others will arise out of the puzzlement and questions of the people who listen to the suggestions made by all those who are trying to become articulate about the issues. Out of all these discussions, carried on over a period of time, there will, I hope, evolve the kind of consensus that will provide the basis for a new marriage tradition. We are still a long way from the point at which we can consider the new tradition in such pragmatic terms as its formal social framework—in law and religious practice. No one, it should be clear, can write a prescription or make a blueprint for a whole society.

What I am doing here is advancing some ideas of my own as one contribution to an ongoing discussion. First I shall outline the goals that I personally hope we may reach.

I should like to see us put more emphasis upon the importance of human relationships and less upon sex as a physiological need. That is, I would hope that we could encourage a greater willingness to spend time searching for a congenial partner and to enjoy cultivating a deeply personal relationship. Sex then would take its place within a more complex intimacy and would cease to be sought after for itself alone.

I should like also to see children assured of a lifelong relationship to both parents. This, of course, can only be attained when parents themselves have such a relationship. I do not mean that parents must stay married. As long as early marriage remains a practice, it must be assumed that some marriages—perhaps many marriages—will break down in the course of a lifetime of growth, mobility and change. But I should like to see a style of parenthood develop that would survive the breaking of the links of marriage through divorce. This would depend on a mutual recognition that coparenthood is a permanent relationship. Just as brother and sister are irrevocably related because they share the same parents, so also parents are irrevocably related because they share the same child. At present, divorce severs the link between the adult partners and each, in some fashion, attempts—or sometimes gives up the attempt—to keep a separate contact with the children, as if this were now a wholly individual relationship. This need not be.

Granting the freedom of partners to an uncongenial marriage to seek a different, individual commitment within a new marriage, I would hope that we would hold on to the ideal of a lifetime marriage in maturity. No religious group that cherishes marriage as a sacrament should have to give up the image of a marriage that lasts into old age and into the lives of grandchildren and great-grandchildren as one that is blessed by God. No wholly secularized group should have to be deprived of the sense that an enduring, meaningful relationship is made binding by the acceptance, approval and support of the entire society as witnesses.

At the same time, I believe, we must give greater reality to our belief that marriage is a matter of individual choice, a choice made by each young man and woman freely, without coercion by parents or others. The present mode of seeking for sex among a wide range of partners casually, and then, inconsistently, of accepting marriage as a form of "choice" arising from necessity, is a deep denial of individuality and individual love. In courtship, intensity of feeling grows as two people move toward each other. In our present system, however, intensity of feeling is replaced by the tensions arising from a series of unknown factors: Will pregnancy occur? Is this the best bargain on the sex market? Even with sexual freedom, will marriage result? Today true courtship, when it happens, comes about in spite of, not because of, the existing styles of dating and marrying.

These goals—individual choice, a growing desire for a lifelong relationship with a chosen partner and the desire for children with whom and through whom lifelong relationships are maintained— provide a kind of framework for thinking about new forms of marriage. I believe that we need two types of marriage, one of which can (though it need not) develop into the other, each with its own possibilities and special forms of responsibility.

The first type of marriage may be called an *individual marriage*, binding together two individuals only. It has been suggested that it might be called a "student" marriage, as undoubtedly it would occur first and most often among students. But looking ahead, it would be a type of marriage that would also be appropriate for much older men and women; so I shall use the term individual marriage. Such a marriage would be a licensed union in which two individuals would be committed to each other as individuals for as long as they wished to remain together, but not as future parents. As the first step in marriage, it would not include having children.

In contrast, the second type of marriage, which I think of as *parental marriage*, would be explicitly directed toward the founding of a family. It would be not only a second type but also a second step or stage, following always on an individual marriage and with its own license and ceremony and kinds of responsibility. This would be a marriage that looked to a lifetime relationship with links, sometimes, to many people.

In an individual marriage the central obligation of the boy and girl or man and woman to each other would be an ethical, not an economic, one. The husband would not be ultimately responsible for the support of his wife: if the marriage broke up, there would be no alimony or support. The husband would not need to feel demeaned if he was not yet ready, or was not able, to support his wife. By the same token, husband or wife could choose freely to support the other within this partnership.

Individual marriage would give two very young people a chance to know each other with a kind of intimacy that does not usually enter into a brief love affair, and so it would help them to grow into each other's life—and allow them to part without the burden of misunderstood intentions, bitter recriminations and self-destructive guilt. In the past, long periods of engagement, entered into with parental consent, fulfilled at least in part the requirement of growing intimacy and shared experience. But current attitudes toward sex make any retreat to this kind of relationship impossible. In other societies, where parents chose their children's marriage partners, the very fact of meeting as strangers at the beginning of a lifelong relationship gave each a high sense of expectancy within which shared understanding might grow. But this is an impossible option for us because of our emphasis upon personal choice and our unwillingness to insist on maintaining a commitment that has failed.

Individual marriage in some respects resembles "companionate marriage" as it was first discussed in the 1920's and written about by Judge Ben Lindsey on the basis of his long experience in court with troubled young people. This was a time when very few people were ready as yet to look ahead to the consequences of deep changes in our attitude toward sex and personal choice. Today, I believe, we are far better able to place young marriage within the context of a whole lifetime.

Individual marriage, as I see it, would be a serious commitment, entered into in public, validated and protected by law and, for some, by religion, in which each partner would have a deep and continuing concern for the happiness and well-being of the other. For those who found happiness it could open the way to a more complexly designed future.

Every parental marriage, whether children were born into it or adopted, would necessarily have as background a good individual marriage. The fact of a previous marriage, individual or parental, would not alter this. Every parental marriage, at no matter what stage in life, would have to be preceded by an individual marriage. In contrast to individual marriage, parental marriage would be hard to contract. Each partner would know the other well, eliminating the shattering surprise of discovery that either one had suffered years of mental or physical illness, had been convicted of a serious crime, was unable to hold a job, had entered the country illegally, already had children or other dependents, or any one of the thousand shocks that lie in wait for the person who enters into a hasty marriage with someone he or she knows little about. When communities were smaller, most people were protected against such shocks by the publication of the banns. Today other forms of protection are necessary. The assurance thus given to parents that their son or daughter would not become hopelessly trapped into sharing parenthood with an unsuitable mate also would serve as a protection for the children, not yet born.

As a couple prepared to move from an individual to a parental marriage they also would have to demonstrate their economic ability to support a child. Instead of falling back on parents, going deeply into debt or having to ask the aid of welfare agencies, they would be prepared for the coming of a child. Indeed, both might be asked to demonstrate some capacity to undertake the care of the family in the event one or the other became ill. Today a girl's education, which potentially makes her self-sustaining, is perhaps the best dowry a man can give his son-in-law so he will not fall prey to the gnawing anxiety of how his family would survive his death. During an individual marriage, designed to lead to parental marriage, a girl, no less than a boy, might learn a skill that would make her self-supporting in time of need.

Even more basic to the survival of a marriage, however, is the quality of the marriage itself—its serenity, its emotional strength, its mutuality. Over long years we have acquired a fund of experience about good marriages through the inquiries made by adoption agencies before a child is given permanently to adoptive parents. Now, if we wished to do so, we could extrapolate from this experience for the benefit of partners in individual marriages but not yet joined in parenthood and for the benefit of infants hoped for but not yet conceived. And in the course of these explorations before parental marriage the ethical and religious issues that sometimes are glossed over earlier could be discussed and, in a good relationship, resolved. Careful medical examinations would bring to light present or potential troubles and, beyond this, would help the couple to face the issue: What if, in spite of our desire for a family, having a child entails a serious risk to the mother, or perhaps the child? What if, in spite of a good prognosis, we, as a couple, cannot have a child? And then, even assuming that all such questions have been favorably resolved, it must not be forgotten that in all human relationships there are imponderables—and the marriage will be tested by them.

As a parental marriage would take much longer to contract and would be based on a larger set of responsibilities, so also its disruption would be carried out much more slowly. A divorce would be arranged in a way that would protect not only the two adults but also the children for whose sake the marriage was undertaken. The family, as against the marriage, would have to be assured a kind of continuity in which neither parent was turned into an angry ghost and no one could become an emotional blackmailer or be the victim of emotional blackmail.

Perhaps some men and women would choose to remain within individual marriage, with its more limited responsibilities; having found that there was an impediment to parental marriage, they might well be drawn into a deeper individual relationship with each other. And perhaps some who found meaningful companionship through parenthood would look later for more individualized companionship in a different kind of person.

By dignifying individual relationships for young people we would simultaneously invest with new dignity a multitude of deeply meaningful relationships of choice throughout life. First and foremost, we would recognize parenthood as a special form of marriage. But we would also give strong support to marriage as a working relationship of husband and wife as colleagues and as a leisure relationship of a couple who have not yet entered into or who are now moving out of the arduous years of multiple responsibilities. By strengthening parenthood as a lasting relationship we would keep intact the link between grandparents, parents and children. Whether they were living together or were long since divorced, they would remain united in their active concern for their family of descendants. The acceptance of two kinds of marriage would give equal support, however, to the couple who, having forgone a life with children, cherish their individual marriage as the expression of their love and loyalty.

The suggestion for a style of marriage in two steps—individual marriage and marriage for parenthood—has grown out of my belief that clarification is the beginning of constructive change. Just as no one can make a blueprint of the future, so no one can predict the outcome of a new set of practices. We do know something about the unfortunate direction in which contemporary marriage is drifting. But we need not simply continue to drift. With our present knowledge, every child born can be a child wanted and prepared for. And by combining the best of our traditions and our best appraisal of human relations, we may succeed in opening the way for new forms of marriage that will give dignity and grace to all men and women.

Marriage in Two Steps—A Continuing Dialogue

APRIL, 1968

Fundamental changes have taken place, and are continuing to take place, in our ways of rearing our children, our attitudes toward sex, our ideas about the relations between men and women and our acceptance of divorce and remarriage.

All these changes are reflected in contemporary social custom and law; all have had a profound effect on the viability of contemporary marriage. Yet we continue to have but one form of marriage for everyone of every age and circumstance. And the fragility of the marriage bond, especially among the very young, is more clearly demonstrated each year. Statistics show that the divorce rate is three times as high among girls who marry before eighteen as it is among those marrying between the ages of twenty-two and twenty-four; and one recent study of marriage and birth rates in two states found that one bride in six was pregnant.

Believing that open discussion is the beginning of clarity, I presented a tentative but deliberately provocative plan for revising our traditional form of marriage. I proposed that we work toward the development of two forms differing both in the commitments made and the responsibilities accepted.

When my article, "Marriage in Two Steps—A Proposal," appeared in *Redbook*, the editors invited comments from readers and from various professional men and women. These comments, along with discussions with audiences at some of my lectures, have given me

more insight into the ideas of students and other young people whose
views are crucial for the future.

From these expressions of thought and feeling I have learned a
great deal. Publication and discussion of this kind, continuing over a
period of time, provide a new form of research, a way of tapping
opinion that is both more spontaneous and more carefully considered
in its expression than the responses to a public-opinion survey can be.
I know now some of the things that were wrong with the way I
presented my proposal, and I understand better how we can go on to
the next stage of constructive discussion.

It seems to me, however, that it is important to examine the statements of the experts and of the readers who responded. Unfortunately, it is possible to present only a few of these opinions, chosen
because they express individually and vividly the different kinds of
things that many others said and wrote. What is most impressive is
the underlying agreement as to the problems that face us, even where
there is disagreement as to what can and should be done.

The readers who took the time to write letters in response to my
proposal came from every part of the United States and from Canada.
As might be expected, most were married women and the mothers of
children. Only a small proportion was enthusiastically in favor of the
proposal as I presented it.

From Portland, Oregon, a mother of three teen-aged children who
is working with school dropouts, "mostly premaritally pregnant girls
and homemakers under eighteen," wrote:

"There is truly much space yet for genuine pioneering in the field
of human relations. Human dignity shall not be realized until we call
a halt to unwilling parentage of unwanted children. A reverence for
human life is a prerequisite to moral decision making. Somehow I feel
we must make it possible for young people to reach this type of
decision by virtue of their own intelligence without dependence upon
fading absolutes which refuse to be revived."

A college instructor wrote from Muncie, Indiana: "Possibly the
relaxed conditions of 'individualized companionship' not only will
allow sexual exploration and development, but also will stimulate
friendship between the sexes. In fact, if 'individualized companionship' does not serve this dual purpose, it will fail to bring about the

emotional stability necessary for Step Two—'marriage for parent-hood.' "

The majority of writers, men and women, looked at the proposal critically and found it wanting in some respect. Some rejected it outright.

Reflecting the views of a considerable number, one woman wrote: "I still prefer God's one-step plan, which is *only* for mature couples, united for life, who *are* prepared for responsible parenthood."

In a similar vein, a young engaged girl wrote: "Some people fall in and out of love every few months. I know this because my girl friends do, and it makes me sick to hear them and everyone else call it love, because it isn't. If love doesn't last forever, then it isn't love. . . ."

A few writers thought, as did a twenty-seven-year-old bride of two years, who wrote from Toronto, Canada, that "unknowingly, many couples are following Dr. Mead's plan." She added, in part:

"For the first one and a half years of our marriage we concentrated on establishing a home complete with *both* furniture and understand-ing of each other. Marriage combined with my job of teaching young children seemed to make me a whole person. I don't believe you can completely know a person in less than two years, but you can secure a relationship that blooms more each day. We have found that we are now ready to enter into the second step . . . and I am thrilled to say our first baby will be born next winter."

Some women phrased their criticisms in very vivid, concrete im-agery, as when a writer from Westbury, New York, commented: "Sex is not a shoe to be tried on, and if it does not fit, try another." Writing from Highland Park, Michigan, another woman asked: "Wouldn't this be near to legalized prostitution? No, it is surely better to teach the young that sex, like food and sleeping accommoda-tions, is *not* free. They are worked for, paid for, by someone; and sex entails considerably more responsibility. . . ."

Some women also felt that individual marriage would be somehow dehumanizing. More than one phrased the point as a woman did who wrote: "What an opportunity 'individual marriage' would give couples! Do you think the majority would stop with one individual marriage? No! People would live like animals."

There were some women who favored stricter rules for marriage and emphasized the economic responsibilities of marriages involving children, but who also leaned toward the viewpoint of many of the "new" generation regarding earlier sexual experience. One mother, living in a California town, wrote: "It seems it would be better to be engaged and have sexual freedom and become better known to one another than to rush into marriage for sexual freedom and the 'playing house' of individual marriage. . . ."

Finally, there were the wives and mothers who protested that very young marriage could work because they had made it work. It is the experience of courageous young people like these that continues to sustain the belief in traditional marriage. A very young wife, married at fifteen to an eighteen-year-old husband who was in the eleventh grade, wrote of her three years of marriage:

"Everyone predicted the worst for us and no one believed my husband would graduate from high school. It wasn't easy. I thank God my husband is the good, decent, hard-working man he is. He often worked at two jobs while going to school, and in his senior year he had his own dry-cleaning business. I was pregnant in his senior year and could no longer work, but with careful budgeting we managed. We may have been young and poor but our baby was a wanted and a loved child. . . . Our little girl was born in time for her father's graduation. Our son, who arrived just a year later, was wanted just as much. . . . Now we are expecting a third child, and I can say in all truth, it is a wanted child. . . .

"Life was never meant to be easy here on earth and there is no easy way to make a marriage work. But with love and God's grace we *can* make our marriages work. . . ."

Although the experts differed widely in their viewpoints and conclusions, there was consensus on the seriousness of the situation and the need to take action of some kind. No one thought there was an easy solution; many hoped that this proposal would lead to further research and other proposals.

The experts' statements fall into two general groups: those who agreed with some aspect of the proposal; and those who, disagreeing, made suggestions for other courses of action.

Speaking from the standpoint of a psychiatrist specializing in student mental health, Dr. Alan Frank wrote, in part:

"I, for one, have plenty of reason to agree with Dr. Mead as I watch our college students struggling to reconcile reality and what they have been taught is reality. . . .

"We believe in 'progress' but not in change; perhaps someday we shall begin to recognize that change is inevitable and a dimension of time itself. Perhaps [then] we shall begin to accept our responsibility for guiding change into humanly constructive directions. . . . I believe we need more such proposals about all kinds of social forms and patterns and values to help us begin to think about constructive possibilities for increasing genuinely human living."

Judge Anna M. Kross, former Commissioner of Correction in New York City, commented:

"The parental marriage . . . could, if the terms of the contract were binding enough and the prerequisite education for the role were stringently observed, be the way to mental health for coming generations. As she works out the details, which have not assumed definitive form in her article, I would hope that Dr. Mead would lay great stress on specific education for the role of parenthood. In a society that relies almost completely on the biological fact of parenthood to confer the Solomonic wisdom needed to fulfill parental duties, there is no greater reform necessary than a consensus that parenthood is not an inalienable right of the father and mother, but is rather a privilege that should be conferred only on those who have been taught the duties of parenthood and how to fulfill them."

Professor F. Ivan Nye, sociologist and former president of the National Council on Family Relations, pointed out that "early marriage is continuing to increase, especially among men of twenty or younger," and he commented:

"Dr. Mead's objective of 'every baby a wanted baby' will touch a responsive chord in every trained professional in child development and in the study of the family. Her point is timely, too, that not all couples want, need or are competent to be parents. . . .

"We know we can improve medicine, government and technology, but we have recoiled from proposing and considering social inventions which will serve us better—especially those that involve the family. It is time that we pass our social institutions, including the family, under the same serious and intelligent scrutiny which we have long directed toward the physical and biological world."

Among the experts who thought that an individual marriage would not be desirable or feasible, many raised such questions as: How would it be possible to prevent a couple from having children? Who would be the judge of a couple's readiness for parental marriage?

Clark Blackburn, general director of the Family Service Association of America, pointed to these and other difficulties. He commented:

"We need more research, but we feel sure that many of these problems can be attacked directly within our present patterns of marriage and sex mores, and do not have to wait until we have established new forms. In any case, new forms would have to be preceded by changed attitudes and real efforts to reach our high goals. . . . In our discussions, we urgently need to involve young people themselves. . . ."

A contrasting stand was taken by the Reverend William H. Genné, director of the Commission on Marriage and Family of the National Council of the Churches of Christ. In his opinion, the proposal for an individual marriage "begins at the wrong end." He wrote:

"Rather than seek to legalize the immature relationship (which Dr. Mead admits we adults encourage) in the hope that it will grow into a mature one, Dr. Mead would do better to look at the preparation for marriage which we are offering our young people. . . .

"Let us try to be honest with our young people. . . . Let us help them understand and appreciate this gift of their Creator and let us help them mature into manhood and womanhood before offering them a counterfeit marriage."

William Phelps Thompson, stated clerk of the General Assembly of the United Presbyterian Church, thought that restriction of parenthood enforced by statute would be "unthinkable politically—an incursion into the most intimate of personal relations of all citizens." He commented further:

"The Christian Church recognizes that in marriage and parenthood, as indeed in all of life, human performance will always fall short of the Christian ideal. The solution is not to abandon the ideal for something approximating human performance. Rather, with spiritual guidance, church members will strive more nearly to attain the ideal."

Dr. Nathan W. Ackerman, psychiatrist, and director of the Professional Program of the Family Institute, conceded that individual marriage might be feasible economically and socially, merely as a "stopgap" solution to the sexual problems of today's young people, but he condemned it on other grounds:

"Marriage is *yes* or *no*, not maybe. There are three important events in life: birth, marriage and death. Marriage is the symbol of maturity and of a readiness to cope with life. It means commitment, closeness and responsibility. It is sharing a whole way of life; it is mutual aid in the struggle for existence and devotion to children. It is a grown-up business, not kid stuff. The tragedy in early marriage today is precisely that these young people, immature to begin with, stay this way. The decision to marry must be a genuine one, not make-believe. Only after a preliminary period of exploring and experimenting with relationships is a true joining in marriage possible. . . .

"What to do? I just don't know. Of one thing we can be sure: there is no easy way."

Student audiences made me see the same set of problems from still another point of view. Discussing the possibility of an individual marriage, a great many of them asked bluntly: Why get married?

In their eyes, marriage is meaningless without children. The idea of a cherishing relationship between two individuals through marriage does not appeal to them. Arguments about protecting unborn children are not very real to them. Before marriage, uninstitutionalized sex relations—companionship, as they see it—or, for the religious and conservative, decorous waiting, is appropriate.

What they chiefly insisted was this: No new laws, no more laws, no one to tell us when we are mature enough to marry, mature enough to have children.

I cannot reproduce actual student discussions, but a letter written by a young New York woman is representative of the thinking of many articulate students. She said:

"Because our life experiences are different . . . the most complete freedom to choose and change is necessary. Our goals may even be mirages, but we are all entitled to the 'pursuit of happiness.' . . .

"But rather than leave us the hopeful uncertainties of the greater acceptance of greater sexual freedom, Dr. Mead wants to bottle up freedom, to hedge it with ceremony and publicly acknowledged responsibility. The marriage ceremony is precisely what, in my opinion, should be dispensed with—because it announces publicly an intimate relation which should be kept private. . . ."

It now seems clear to me that neither elders nor young people want to make a change to two forms of marriage. They want to reserve the word "marriage" for a commitment that they can feel is permanent and final, no matter how often the actual marriages may fail.

But the need for some kind of answer, some kind of change, is even greater than it was when I wrote the original article. Attitudes toward contraception are changing rapidly as the recognition grows that unbridled increase in population threatens the quality of life everywhere, even in the United States.

Oral contraceptives are now in use all over the country. We face an unprecedented situation in which society and religion no longer can give moral support to a high birth rate, and we have contraceptive methods that are almost completely reliable.

And the young people are clamoring for a new morality, a morality that will put some kind of seal of approval on premarital sex relations. Ten years ago, their parents' fear of pregnancy meant that they had to finance premature marriages, either to prevent the dreaded event or after the conception had occurred. When contraception was still uncertain, premature, parent-supported marriages seemed the only answer. So parents helped rent an apartment, helped buy the car, helped pay the tuition for sons and daughters who married before their education was complete. And many, many of these marriages later ended in divorce, leaving young children with broken homes.

Today this is changing, especially among those young people who go to college. Today instead of implicitly threatening their parents with pregnancy, they are taking the opposite course and demanding the right to a full sex life without pregnancy and without marriage. "Why get married?" they ask. "Why can't we simply live together until we are ready to get married? Contraception is reliable. No unborn baby is being wronged; no girl's honor will be ruined; no young man, his education unfinished, will be trapped into marriage." This is what they are asking; and how are their parents, their teachers, the Church, their employers, going to answer this request for new standards?

For it is important to realize that this is a request for new *standards*.

There are, and there always have been, young people who want no standards of any kind, who have never learned to value or see the need for any kind of code. These are not the young people who present the acute moral problem today. It is the earnest and responsible young people who are requesting sex freedom with a single, chosen lover who present the dilemma. As the president of one of our best coeducational colleges phrased it to me: "It's the good girls who want us to approve their receiving boys in their rooms. The bad girls have found the answer long ago, in the parking lot at the other end of town."

It's the good girls—and the boys they love—who are asking parents and heads of dormitories and schools to give tacit approval to the new state of affairs. These are not the ones who are interested in sex as a form of rebellion against authority or revenge against unloving parents. They want parental approval; they want to feel that what they are doing, or would like to do, is right. They have absorbed the changed attitude toward sex itself that has been growing in the United States. They have been told, and they believe, that full sex relations are important for full and healthy relationships. They have now seen that marriage too early is not a good thing.

They don't want to compromise their future, especially the future of the boys, by a grueling domesticity too soon. They know how many years must be given to education today, and they have taken to heart all that they have heard about the importance of degrees for careers. They are increasingly willing to wait for marriage, but they no longer understand why they must wait for sex.

So parents and advisers, teachers and clergy, are in a quandary. Many of them no longer believe that sex is intrinsically wrong, something to be barely tolerated within the confines of a marriage devoted to propagating the race. The pregnancies they feared, the possible pregnancies with which they threatened the young and with which the young in turn threatened them, can now be prevented. So they say one thing out loud, one thing from the rostrum and the pulpit; and privately they sympathize, condone and connive to give particular young people the happiness they are demanding. The churches that failed to exact any penalties in the way of a simpler wedding ceremony from the pregnant bride are finding it increasingly difficult to justify—in private—a condemnation of premarital sex that doesn't lead to pregnancy. Young people, looking at the way their older brothers and sisters were treated—hurried into marriage, blackmailed and bribed by the society around them—ask, understandably: What arguments do you have left?

Yet there are fears even in the hearts of those who feel that in today's world we must put off marriage much longer than we used to and who feel that it is reasonable for young people to demand a right to live together honestly and openly and not be forced to lie, to cover up, to live a hole-in-corner existence. These fears are real because living together outside the law *is* against the law, and will subject their children to possible blackmail, public exposure, public penalties and later dangers.

Evidence of a sex relationship can be used to expel a boy or girl from college. And the very thing that the young people want, a chance to live together, to eat meals they have prepared together, under the same roof, means—even if the parents do concur and the dormitory authorities close their eyes—that the young people are open to censure, punishment, disgrace and damaged careers. The heads of dormitories may close their eyes—and lose their jobs. The parents may permit sexual freedom between their underage daughter and her perfectly suitable and trusted lover—and themselves be censured and ostracized by neighbors who use the old standards instead of the new.

In any case, asking compliant and sympathetic elders not only to close their eyes but also to aid and abet their children to live in a way that many people still consider sinful—and that the laws of the land treat as criminal—puts them in a position that is unbearable, both for them and for their children. The children are asking for moral support of new standards. The most they can get is collusion in the kind of behavior that is still branded as immoral and illegal.

This is the dilemma. A loosened moral code in which people close their eyes, look the other way and subject themselves and their children to social condemnation is not the answer to the question the most thoughtful of the young people are asking.

They are not asking for the right to be delinquent; they are asking that the stigma of delinquency be removed altogether. They have read the books that tell them sex is good and necessary for a well-balanced life. They have listened to the lectures on the importance of being sure you are marrying the right person, someone you can live with all the rest of your life. They have been taught and they still believe that marriage should be for life.

Any solution at present is unsatisfactory. In states in which divorce is easy and cheap and does not demand an abhorrent resort to lying or defaming of character a couple can, of course, "just get married," with the tacit agreement on all sides that if it doesn't work, they can "just get a divorce." The more devoutly their parents believe that marriage is a sacrament and remarriage after divorce a sin, the more the parents may counsel a civil marriage—not so serious, socially more easily dissolved—in case it "doesn't work out." And many young people are taking this course—which is again a compromise and a concealment of their real intentions. They are accepting such a marriage as a real marriage, with the hidden proviso—in their own, their parents' and their friends' minds—that "if it doesn't work, we can always get a divorce."

Yet I do not see how the senior world of parents, teachers, preachers and counselors can give any other advice until the laws are changed. However much we respect the integrity of what the young people are asking for, there is no way we can give it to them, inside the law. We have seen the effects on the moral fiber of the country and the lawbreaking that came with the lack of belief in the Prohibition law, which was felt to be unfair and was therefore evaded. Lawbreaking by the lawless is a matter for better education and better police, but lawbreaking by resentful, normally law-abiding members of society can in the end bring the whole social order down.

I believe we have to say at present: If you want the experience of full-time companionship with someone you love—and this is what you should want, for it is the most satisfactory and fully responsible relationship—you had better get legally married, use contraceptives responsibly and risk divorce later. You are risking even more if you don't.

On Educating Women

✂︎❦❦✂︎

JANUARY, 1962

"Women don't really need a college education. It's a waste of time and money!" A hundred years of women's education have not changed this thought, even though today it is often expressed less bluntly. It is a thought that occurs to fathers whose business is not going too well and who have sons as well as daughters to educate. It occurs to practical school advisers who suggest that boys who are good at mathematics learn mathematics and that girls who are good at mathematics learn typing. It occurs to legislators as they think about the state funds that will be needed to meet the growing demand for a college education for everyone. It occurs to young men who are hurrying toward marriage and fatherhood long before they are mature or even economically self-sufficient. It peeps out of the pages written by presidents of women's colleges about educating women as women—that is, in the "lesser arts."

What these detractors of higher education for women mean is not that *women* do not need a college education but that *mothers* do not need a college education. Almost everyone will agree that a woman who does not marry and have children can use a college education. There is no place for her at home, and some sort of higher education is necessary even for modest schoolteaching or a good department-store job.

Since single blessedness is abhorred in all known forms in the United States, however, a girl's need for a college education is, in fact, a kind of disaster insurance. If she should not marry, or if her husband should be disabled or die young or want to marry somebody else, she can, if she has an education, "take care of herself." A grim phrase that echoes disaster—after the flood or the fire, after the plane goes down. . . .

Barring such disaster, a college education obviously is not necessary. In fact, the kind of job that a young college-educated wife is likely to take today—to help her husband through college, law school, medical school or motor mechanics school, or to help make the down payment on the house—is a short-term affair often requiring the least alert part of her mind. After spending the first few months or years of marriage sorting, filing, typing or operating a business machine, she is only too ready to stay at home, to have some time to herself and start a family.

Once the babies start coming, it is brilliantly clear to everyone that whatever college education the girl had was "wasted." Her work begins at dawn and she falls into bed at night so tired that no bedside reading is necessary. She spends the day washing, ironing, cleaning, cooking, shopping in supermarkets, driving the car, following her active, well-fed children, who never learn to be quiet, from room to room. It is not literature and philosophy that she needs to know now, but how to shop wisely, how to plan for her children's physical and mental health, how to comfort and support her husband. Her life gives her no time to use a college education, no time to read, to write, to reflect. Or so it is said by those who claim that women don't really need a college education.

It sounds simple enough. If it is the chief aim of a woman's life to find an appropriate husband and then to keep his devotion, why should she spend four long years discovering subjects she will probably never think about again?

Implicit in these biased arguments are several very odd assumptions about college, and about marriage as well. One is that a college education is only a preparation for a "career." Another is that marriage is *not* a career. Another is that "doing something" with an education means turning it, conspicuously, to some advantage in the world. And still another is that wives and mothers, busy caring for their families, have little to offer the world—that motherhood somehow relieves them of the responsibility as well as the desire to be enlightened citizens and thinking people in their own right. Granted that women's manual labor is needed to keep homes going and their affection and support are needed to keep husbands and children going, working and growing—what does all this have to do with a college education?

Fortunately, answers to questions like this are sometimes given unwittingly by the very people who ask them. Even the most hardened detractors of education for women, for example, agree about the need for educating men. And yet where does a man's education really begin—his love of learning, his respect for knowledge, his ultimate concern with serious rather than trivial matters? Isn't it likely that an educated woman will guide a child toward these interests more readily than a woman in whom such interests may never even have been awakened?

Clearly the best way to start boys toward education is to provide them with educated mothers who can open their eyes and ears to the world around them. And the easiest—though not the only—way for us to have educated mothers is for girls to go to college.

"Mothers should take care of their children and not leave them with nurses" is another conviction that is almost axiomatic with the opponents of higher education for women. If you ask *why* this is true, invariably you will be told (among other things) that it is because the nurse may be too "ignorant" or too "uneducated" to give a child the kind of care a mother can give him. Despite their theories about college and women, these people, too, apparently value an educated mother far more than an uneducated one.

For a mother, after all, not only feeds and loves her children; she talks to them and thinks with them. Consciously or unconsciously, ignorantly or wisely, she shapes their values and guides their opinions in directions that are very often never reversed.

And even when her education seems to be dormant, it is never completely so. During the early years, when the babies are little, there will be a kind of "rainbow nuisance" of memories in the back of her head—an unanswered question, a half-forgotten poem, a lecture that now makes explicable the fight for desegregation, for better hospitals, for the repeal of capital punishment, for help to refugees.

In giving a woman a chance to become a more complete human being, a college education also gives her a chance to become a more complete mother. It gives her a backlog of thought to carry her through the nursery years; it helps her nourish her children's minds as well as their bodies. It keeps her from being fenced in by endless, routine tasks. And when her family is grown and there is time, the college education with which she began her adult life makes it possible for her to continue that life with dignity and self-respect.

The Working Wife—Two Full-Time Jobs

NOVEMBER, 1963

In 1961, President Kennedy appointed a Commission on the Status of Women, and in 1963, that commission reported to him and to the people of the United States. This was a momentous event—the first full-dress report of its kind. Mrs. Eleanor Roosevelt actively participated in the early stages of the commission's work, providing a link to work on the same problems on a world-wide scale in which she participated in the United Nations.

In the present climate of world opinion, when the attention of governments is directed toward improving the position of those who are held back from fullest development through race or nationality or geography, the report treats women too as a disadvantaged segment of society; it regards the problem of their status as one aspect of the larger problem of all second-class groups, and makes clear that their advancement depends on over-all advancements—economic, educational and legislative—within our society.

Working women in the United States would be better off—much better off—if the practical recommendations of the commission were carried out and we had better working conditions for women, better minimum wage laws, better provisions for maternity leave and loss of income because of changes of residence, better education, better educational counseling, more opportunities for continuing education at all ages, better community services, fairer allowances for widows and divorcees. In the face of the facts, it takes no imagination at all to realize how important it is for the government and the country as a whole to see to it that this very significant portion of our population is treated fairly. In discussing women's economic and professional disadvantages, the commission has avoided feminist diatribes and special pleading and has covered its ground equitably and well. Just because it has done so, it raises the question of the real position of women in a very acute form.

For in reading the report it becomes evident that the commission deals with women simply as a group of people—not unlike men except that they happen to bear children, are expected to run a household, live longer than men and may have more leisure time in late middle age. The report views women as economic individuals—as partners, as property owners, as recipients of state and federal benefits and primarily as workers.

Unquestionably, the consideration of the woman as a worker is basic to any discussion of the status of women today. The figures in the report show that one out of every three workers today is a woman, that more than eight out of ten women work at some time during their lives and that, increasingly, married women are taking jobs. In 1940, married women made up one-third of the female labor force; in 1950, one-half; in 1962, three-fifths. Today one-third of the married women in the white population are working at outside jobs; in the nonwhite population, one out of two.

The tendency of more and more women to take jobs is obviously a significant trend, and it has many serious implications—particularly for the working wife and mother. Yet some of these implications become apparent only as one considers certain information contained in the report—and certain considerations that have been omitted from the report.

Putting together the information on the underprivileged, who must work to live at all, and the information on the privileged, it is apparent that for a great many married women the reasons for taking jobs are largely economic ones. The United States is developing an economy that is geared increasingly to two jobs for each family. As women are forced into income-earning jobs they leave the care of their children and their homes to sitters, unemployable grandparents or institutions. Increasingly the home is understaffed and precariously balanced as women try to do two jobs or as a man and a woman each do a job and a half, and that not very well.

The report also indicates, however, that while economic pressures are pushing women out of the home, the women who can make a choice—the well-to-do and the well educated—are choosing *for* the home. Often, although they *could* prepare themselves for rewarding and useful careers, they leave college and, as young women and later as mature women, work far below their potentialities. In most cases, highly educated and well-to-do women choose to subordinate their jobs to marriage. They may work from time to time, but they shy away from full commitment. In general they choose to spend most of their lives at home, with their families.

Yet, throughout the report it is assumed that women want to work and that they should be encouraged to do so, both as a personal right and because the economy needs them. None of the specific recommendations of the report are directed to the emotional conflicts and problems created for a married woman and her family if the woman takes a job. Nothing is said about women who would rather center their lives in the home. There is no real discussion of the values involved in a choice between working outside the home for money and inside the home for love. There is no emphasis on the mother's role as an educator of her children (except a lip-service speech about passing on tradition), and the concept of a woman as a *wife* to her husband is missing entirely from the report. In fact, it is assumed that once the children are grown, women can stay away from home for months at a time, if a career should require it, and no one will suffer.

The report also omits one of the most significant facts about women in the United States today—that working women, working at lower-level jobs than men, give over a tremendous amount of their time to repetitive drudgery related to things rather than to people. No cognizance is taken of the sacrifice most women make every time the needs of the individual—their traditional concern—have to be subordinated to a time clock, an assembly line or a deadline.

There is no real recognition of the principal historical difference between women's and men's roles—no recognition of the fact that while men generally have devoted themselves to organizing and exploiting the outside world of nature and society, women have devoted most of their time and attention to the care and well-being of individuals, primarily to their families.

Through the ages, human beings have remained human because there were women whose duty it was to provide continuity in their lives—to be there when they went to sleep and when they woke up, to ease pain, to sympathize with failure and rejoice at success, to listen to tales of broken hearts, to soothe and support and sustain and stimulate husbands and sons as they faced the vicissitudes of a hard outside world. Throughout history, children have needed mothers, men have needed wives. The young, the sick, the old, the unhappy and the triumphantly victorious have needed special individuals to share with them and care for them.

If the full recommendations of the commission's report were carried out, we would have more women working at capacity, better working conditions for women, fewer completely neglected homes and fewer neglected older women; but we would not have gone one step further in reconciling the conflict between a woman's working away from her home and her providing the thread of continuity on which her husband's and her children's lives are strung. For the essential question remains unanswered. Who in the population will be free to care—with continuity—for human beings?

The hard facts are that if individuals are to be treated as individuals, someone must be free—at home—to care for them. Some working wives are fortunate in having relatives who will care for their homes and their children; some are fortunate enough to find warm and competent paid substitutes; but they are in the minority. Domestic work in this country has never been honored as a profession. And though the problem of increasing the dignity and the benefits for domestic servants is discussed in the report, it is not discussed in relation to the need for help if women are both to marry and to work outside the home.

Yet every mother of young children who goes out of the home to work leaves a gap, and the tasks she leaves undone must be done by another woman or man—or must be dispersed among a number of people or agencies. Every woman who devotes part of her time to a job has less time to be a wife—to listen to, to play or travel with, to "understand," her husband. And in the future there will be greater—not less—need for the individual care traditionally provided by women. There will be more vulnerable children, more gifted children, more handicapped children, more men under pressures of their own, who will need their wives' sympathetic attention. There will be more of the very old, who need the same kind of tender care little children do.

By concentrating primarily on women as workers and neglecting to deal with the whole of a woman's life, except in economic or social terms, and by assuming that more and more women will and should work (even in an automated world in which fewer and fewer people will work), the report has obscured issues central to its subject. In fact, the report cannot be considered a complete report on the status of women. It is, instead, a report on the opportunities, possibilities and handicaps affecting women working outside the home, and an exploration of how to make it possible for more women to work, more of the time, under better conditions, closer to their skills and potentialities. With little recognition of the pressures that lead increasing numbers of women to work outside the home, this report simply reinforces those pressures. The implications, the problems, the dangers, in this trend—these are questions to which the commission does not adequately address itself. We shall need to devote a great deal of further attention and study and imaginative thinking to the question of whether we should build a society that encourages, and even forces, wives and mothers to leave their homes, and to the ways in which we can fill the gap resulting from their absence.

When Women Help Each Other

❧❦❧❦❧

APRIL, 1964

Women often ask me how, in practice, I have reconciled the demands of a full professional life and the need of a young child for continuity of care. My daughter now has a home and a professional life of her own. But an account of how I worked out my life when my daughter was a child may be of some value to other women.

I believe that when a woman goes out for a day or even an hour, leaving young children at home, another woman must take over or the children will suffer. But I also believe that women as well as men who have the aptitudes or the training for tasks that society needs to have done or who are specially gifted, as poets, for example, or musicians, should have an opportunity to exercise their skills and gifts. They should not be forced to sacrifice all their talents as individuals to rearing children.

In the recent past women who wished to work hard at some special task usually found it necessary to remain single and celibate; in some periods of history the same requirement was made of men. If we do not now make such a requirement, we should make it possible for both men and women to engage in their chosen professions and also to have their children well cared for.

I was lucky because I myself did not have to design a life style that combined work and homemaking. My grandmother and my mother had both been professional women, and I grew up believing that it was natural for women to use their brains *and* to have children. Furthermore, my mother, who was deeply interested in dignifying domestic work, invented a plan of employing women who had young children of their own to support. In this way a woman who needed a job could free the mother of another household and at the same time keep her child near her. So I grew up in a household that never contained fewer than three women and often other children besides my brother and sisters.

Even before I had a child of my own I was dependent on the willingness of other women to help me in my household and to do the hundred small jobs that only a woman can do, such as finding dress materials that would not fade, pins that would not rust, or toys for South Sea children—things I needed for my field trips. And at work I was dependent on the generosity of the women with whom I worked, who by taking details from me left me free to think and write. From my first book on, my godmother copy-edited my manuscripts and my mother made the indexes.

When my child was a baby I reorganized my work, by doing extra teaching, so that I had to give only half-time to my regular job. A highly trained nurse-housekeeper with a fourteen-year-old daughter in high school came to live with us, reconstituting the kind of household my mother had believed in. Then, when my daughter was about two and a half, war work began to keep me away from home for longer periods of time and more drastic planning was needed.

We arranged to move in with friends, and for the next several years we lived in a great composite household. The host family had six children, and the domestic staff consisted of two women, one of whom had her baby with her while her husband was away at war. This complex arrangement freed the husbands from worry, left the younger mother free to care for the small children, provided a backlog of baby sitters, and also left me free for the travel and writing my war work required. Later, after the war, I was especially indebted to a friend who took her daughter and mine home from school to play at her house in the afternoons.

The gist of the matter is that it is unrealistic to expect that professional men or professional women can do their exacting work and at the same time carry out the daily small unremembered acts of kindness and love of which homemaking consists.

But neither can we expect that the kind of care which a small child needs can be paid for with money alone. The main reason that mothers take better care of their children than most other people can—even if they are poor cooks, poor housekeepers and have little patience or skill with small children—is that they love them. And only if a professional woman—or any woman who must spend many hours away from her home—can establish relationships of shared responsibility and mutual respect with other women can she hope to create the kind of life in which neither her home and children nor her work will suffer.

"But doesn't a child need continuity of care?" many women ask. Yes, but a child need not be cared for by only one person. Two or more persons together can provide a continuous thread on which its hours are strung. Children in the modern world need to learn to trust and understand a variety of people and a variety of life styles. The narrow nuclear family, with only two adults of opposite sex as models and resources, is too fragile a protection against a changing world. We cannot start too early helping our children to feel at home with many different people—people who differ in physique and ways of doing things, some who are fussy and others who are casual, some who are temperamental and others who are even-tempered and serene. Except for the hypersensitive infant who must be shielded from overstimulation, most children who are loved and cared for by several older children, adolescents and adults will be better prepared for the unforeseen vicissitudes of the modern world.

"Doesn't a young child need its mother's attention and care in order to develop intellectually as well as physically?" Yes, but the working mother who has adequate help can give her child her un-divided attention—and often for a longer time than the busy and preoccupied mother who must carry all the burdens of housekeeping. This depends, of course, on having the kind of help that makes it possible for her to sit down, when she comes home in the evening, and talk with or read to her children. When the day's work ends in a desperate scramble to get dinner, iron clothes, sew on buttons and clean house, then the whole family—children, husband and the wife herself—suffers. Yet this is the impossible situation we are imposing on women who work either from choice or necessity.

"Aren't there always emergencies, even if children go to school, when a mother is needed at home? What if there is an accident?" True, there must be someone to telephone to, someone to take over, if a child gets sick or is hurt in school. But one mother on a block, on any particular day, who really is at home is a more reliable safeguard than ten mothers who are nominally at home but in fact are shopping, or taking another child to the dentist, or attending a PTA committee meeting. During World War II, in some states the PTA's set up an institution called "block mothers"—mothers who took turns in being on call. One of the fictions of our present style of homemaking is that because a woman does not have a job she will be at home; another is that because she is at home she will be developing her child's mind.

What it comes to in the end is the need for co-operation among women—women of the same and of different ages, women who are needed out in the world and others who enjoy devoting all their intelligence and love to the minutiae of everyday life, women with young children and those whose children are grown, women who have never had children, and women who, husbandless, must care for their young children by themselves. To be meaningful and effective, alliances among women must be personal and warm; there must be a willingness to put up with another woman's different way of stacking leftovers in the icebox, or braiding a child's hair, or shopping for "specials."

In the final analysis, what the individual woman can do depends not on involving her overworked husband in more and more domestic tasks but on the methods of co-operation and help that groups of women can work out among themselves. Instead, today, single women who work are coming to resent married women who work, whose activities are always subject to interruption by calls from poorly staffed homes, and women who stay at home are coming to complain about having to put up with the children of neighbors who work away from home. Out of a generation of narrowness and lack of co-operation among women, we are developing a state of active unco-operativeness. Yet, actually, only a few women really want to combine the double task of work and homemaking and many women have less homemaking than they desire.

We need, now, to develop a new style of real co-operation. But the plans a woman makes to co-operate with other women depend, of course, on where and how she is living. A woman who is on the point of moving can consider the possibility of living close to relatives or good friends who can complement the needs in her life and whom she can help in some other way in return. Or, by combining their resources, a group of women may be able to guarantee a neighbor who needs money a steady income based on occasional or regular care of all their children. Or, in a neighborhood of young mothers, a woman whose children are grown and who may be on the point of moving away because she feels she has nothing to do, may be persuaded to stay. A neighbor who enjoys the task may be encouraged to care for the child of a working mother, in her own home, every day and for the children of other mothers some days. A housebound mother might be persuaded to run an informal answering service to deal with telephone calls from school, from husbands, from the garage, from children; in return, others could do her shopping for her. This would eliminate the endless waiting for telephone calls, and a group of mothers would know that there was someone who could deal with an emergency. For women who work, most forms of co-operation will involve some payment of money, but money alone is never enough. Many things that need to be done cannot be done for money, but they can be done for mutual help, respect and love.

Double-Talk about Divorce

MAY, 1968

Young couples—despite their search for a "new morality" and new ways of life—still hold firmly to an old ideal: that marriage is a lifelong commitment, binding husband and wife to each other and to the children born to them. This conviction, this faith, they imply, is the only basis on which marriage should begin.

But for most Americans, particularly the younger generations, divorce is a familiar fact of life. How, then, do we reconcile our feelings about marriage with our feelings about divorce? How soundly and realistically do we handle marriages that fail?

To me the answer seems clear: not very well. Our attitudes toward divorce are confused, contradictory and often harmful. They urgently need clarification.

We Americans believe that people have the right to correct mistakes, to do what they can and must in order to make better lives for themselves and those for whom they are responsible. We approve of cosmetic surgery for young girls who want their noses altered. We approve when a man leaves a job for a better one, when a family moves to a better home or a better community. Our standards are high; our expectations of happiness are great; and in general, when we find ourselves dissatisfied with our lives we are optimistic enough to want to remedy errors of the past.

This view carries over to marriage. In this country we make great demands on marriage, expecting it to supply each couple with sexual fulfillment, congeniality, companionship and the sharing of virtually every aspect of life. Obviously the greater the expectations, the greater the possibilities of disappointment and failure. Husbands and wives keep asking themselves whether they are really in love, whether they are as happy as they have a right to expect.

Where there is no prospect of divorce, married couples have to make the best of a bad bargain. But if divorce is permitted, it will be seen as offering the chance that another marriage will be a better marriage, a *true* marriage. And we who believe that marriage should be for love, not for convenience, feel that when two people find they have made a mistake, they have the right to get a divorce and seek more compatible mates.

But what if there are children? We don't face the fact that every time we emphasize the importance of a happy, secure home for children, we are emphasizing implicitly the rightfulness of ending marriages when homes become unhappy and insecure. We want to avoid the destructive effects of a bad marriage on children. Thus devoted fathers and devoted mothers come to realize that keeping the family together at all costs may exact too high a price from each other and from their children. Divorce for them is not only an honest, heartbroken recognition of failure; it is also a moral imperative based on the belief that it is wrong to bring up children in an unhappy home.

So we Americans seem characteristically pragmatic in agreeing that if a marriage proves a mistake, it should be ended by divorce. But then we reverse ourselves and stigmatize those who get divorced. Instead of treating divorce as the recognition of a failed marriage which it is wise to leave, we see it as a sin or a disgrace. On a sociological level we place divorce in practically the same category as crime. In measuring the breakdown of society it is customary for researchers to group together statistics on crime, juvenile delinquency, alcoholism, drug addiction, mental illness—and divorce.

To some degree, of course, divorce statistics do serve as a measure of social problems. The divorce rate for adolescents and very young adults indicates our failure to cope with too-early marriages, while the divorce rate for young couples with a single child indicates our failure to cope with too-early parenthood (and may well reflect marriages of pregnant brides). On the whole, however, I think it is a misrepresentation to use divorce statistics, as we do crime statistics, to measure social disorder.

One reason we lump together crime, illness and divorce is that we cannot free ourselves from our Puritan heritage. Not too long ago divorce was still considered sinful and wicked. The divorced woman would not be asked to dinner; the divorced man was considered a dangerous kind of man to have in the community and might well be forced to resign his job and move elsewhere. Divorce, like drinking and playing cards, was a sin—and still is, in the minds of many.

If we are to handle divorce more intelligently, we have to learn to overcome these emotional prejudices of the past. We should realize that when every marriage is expected to be an ideal one, failures are inevitable. We should realize that in a society where people from diverse backgrounds move so often and so far, where they change their social position and social preferences, where they marry without parental consent (or else force that consent by premature pregnancy) and where long-life expectancies mean that couples will be together for a great many years, divorce must be accepted as a regrettable but necessary resolution for unhappy marriages.

This means we can no longer sit as judge and jury, condemning the immorality of divorce. After all, we have learned not to stigmatize illegitimate children for the acts of irresponsible parents, and we understand that in our complex modern world men who are unemployed or women who are on relief cannot be held individually responsible for their plight. Now we must learn to accept the fact that, given our social system and our cherished ideals of marriage, some marriages are bound to fail, and that these failures require compassion, not the passing of judgment.

We should discard the notion that in a divorce one partner is in the right and the other in the wrong. Friends and relatives could then stop choosing sides and allying themselves with the husband or wife—for when they do, they divide the family still more. These struggles put a further strain on those whose lives are already deeply disrupted.

Only when we revise our confused, contradictory and outmoded notions of divorce can we begin to work toward some new customs that will make life easier for those who at the time of a divorce most need emotional support and encouragement—the children.

In this regard, some primitive societies provide greater security for the children than we do. Among the Manus, for example, marriages can be dissolved but family relationships endure forever. A divorced mother and father may live in two different villages with their own clans. Their children, however, who will live with either their mother's or father's clan, will be accepted and "belong" in both villages and both clans. Aunts and uncles and cousins, on both sides, will remain committed aunts and uncles and cousins.

In the village whose ways I have been studying since 1928, I've watched children shift their clan as they choose. They may take their mother's new husband's name, for example, and ten years later decide to join their father's clan, changing their name and being happily reassimilated. It is even possible for them to change once again and return to their mother's clan. The important point is that all the alternative family relationships are safeguarded.

Should we do less? We must find ways of keeping open all possibilities for vital personal ties for the children of broken homes. To achieve this, we have to change our whole approach to divorce.

The first fundamental change requires a revision of the law similar to that which has been authoritatively advocated in England in a joint report (1967) of the Law Commissioners and the Church of England. By recommending divorce "upon proof that the marriage has irretrievably broken down," the idea that a divorce necessarily represents the violation of a marriage compact (which means that there must be an innocent and a guilty party) is changed to the contrasting view that it simply formalizes the fact that the marriage compact no longer applies. (This requires neither blame nor recrimination.)

Such an approach would permit couples to achieve a civilized divorce, and while it cannot relieve their anguish, it would remove the bitter legal dueling that is now virtually unavoidable. In addition, it could lay the groundwork for a less antagonistic post-divorce relationship between the parents, so that they would be able to give a greater sense of security to the children.

By accepting divorce as the termination of a marriage and not its violation, we as a society can develop other, more constructive ways to handle the situation. One highly desirable procedure, it seems to me, lies in the establishment of pre-divorce counseling to prepare parents and children for the pain and anxieties they must anticipate. I began advocating such counseling twenty years ago; I can only hope it will not take another twenty years before we accept this.

There is another step we can take that could prove beneficial beyond all proportion to the simplicity of the step itself. I believe we should establish some forthright way of announcing a divorce. A brief, highly formal announcement could be used, varied to accommodate individual tastes. This would place divorce in the category of those private events that must be publicly noted as a matter of record—birth, marriage, retirement, death—and it would spare the former husbands and wives the pain and awkwardness of repeatedly explaining their breakup to shocked friends who have not yet learned the news.

But more important still, for the children's sake we must keep all the family bonds intact after the marital bond itself has been severed. This cannot occur if before (or during or immediately after) the divorce, relatives join in the bitter and futile battle of assessing blame. It is particularly harmful when grandparents take sides. They represent a special kind of emotional security for young children, and if either set of grandparents attacks the mother or the father, the children suffer.

Awareness of the importance of grandparents in a child's life does in fact lead many mothers to do all they can, after a divorce, to cement relations with their former parents-in-law. I think this is one of the bravest things that young mothers are doing today—even if this means postponing remarriage for a while. For although such relationships can be made to work immediately after the divorce, they are likely to break down if the mother remarries and her children call her new husband "Daddy."

This highlights a generally overlooked but acutely important problem. We do not have terms for newcomers to families where divorce and then remarriage have occurred—and words are very important for young children. If a child calls the new husband "Father," he repudiates his real father; if he doesn't, what can he call his mother's husband? Or his father's new wife? We need terms for *my father's wife* (who is not my mother), *my mother's husband* (who is not my father), *my child's father* (to whom I am no longer married), *my grandchild* (from a family divided by divorce).

Terms like "stepmother" and "stepfather" are inappropriate because the new husband or wife does not, as in the case where death has occurred, step into the missing parent's place. Furthermore, the term "stepmother" remains emotionally loaded for any child who has ever read a fairy tale, and it is unfair to apply such a negative word to the kind young second wife who is struggling hard to care for her husband's children or to make them welcome when they visit her home.

The lack of kinship terms is more than just a vocabulary defect. It reflects our inability to think clearly and calmly on the whole subject of divorce, and it complicates life for all those whose lives are touched by divorce. Without terms to identify former wives and present wives, former husbands and present husbands, we tend to deny previous relationships, if only by not talking about them because of the awkwardness of language.

We can no longer afford to indulge in the notion that the perpetuation of any relationship between formerly married couples, except a hostile and distant one, is in some vague way immoral. We need ways in which divorced parents can meet without embarrassment at important moments in their children's lives. If we are to encourage young people to work toward the real, lifelong, highly committed marriage that is our ideal, even though their own parents have been divorced, we must not make them cast their mother or father in the role of the wrongdoer just because archaic laws have phrased it that way. These young people need to grow up within a new kind of extended family—new and old relationships stemming not only from second marriages, but perhaps third marriages as well.

Whether we like it or not, we are almost certainly going to have divorce occurring as frequently in the future as it does today. Our choices, therefore, are clear. We will either continue to handle divorce as badly as we do now, scarring those who married in good faith but failed to succeed and wounding the children of those marriages, or we will move forward to a realistic acceptance of society's obligation to help all those who are caught in a difficult period of reorganizing their lives.

Limiting Large Families in America, I

AUGUST, 1963

Mankind today faces a new prospect—the prospect of too many people. With our present ability to care for every child that is born and to protect the health of adults, more and more children live to adulthood and more adults live to old age. Yet our hope for a warless world, a world of people who are well fed and clothed and educated, has raised a new fear. Will the peace and plenty we foresee vanish in a new kind of havoc? Will there be too many hungry mouths for the earth to support?

Looking ahead only a few years, we can see that the prospect for the world's children—including our own—depends on what we do *now*.

In poorer countries overpopulation is already striking, and the rate of increase has become a terrifying threat. But it is temptingly easy to believe that Americans face a very different future. Our country still has some wild and empty parts. Our vast productive machine is not working at full capacity, and our fields produce more grain than we eat. Surely countries with little industry, poor soil, a crowded landscape and only a rudimentary educational system to build on are the ones to worry. Shouldn't we, who are so fortunately placed, devote ourselves to having more, not fewer, children?

It is hard to realize that something has deeply changed since the time when it was the duty—the religious duty, the patriotic duty, the personal duty—of everyone who could to rear a large family. In most of the world and for most of human history, the fear lest there be too few children in one's own family, one's own tribe, one's own country, one's own religion, was very real. The desire, the hope, the need, to have children is a theme that runs through the myths and tales and histories of the world's peoples. "Lest the people perish"—words like these express the age-old need to keep up the strength of one's own group. Looking to the past, we can be proud that we have fulfilled the American dream of populating and building up an almost empty continent. Now, in the midst of success, why should the size of our families concern us?

The reasons are simple. All over the world people think of Americans as living a good life. They may disdain our "materialism"—as they see it. They may carp at the inequalities among us. They may shudder at the pace of American living. But everywhere they long for the well-being that makes it possible for Americans to rear children in the way three-fifths of the nation actually does and the rest of the nation could. Depicted in a million advertisements, ours is the good life.

Like it or not, the place we have created for ourselves in the world and the role we play for other peoples entail responsibilities. In the way that we live our lives, others will aspire to live theirs. If fortunate Americans regard it as the most desirable aim in life to bring up large families, other peoples of the earth will count themselves unfortunate if they cannot do likewise. The large families of the past, when many children were born but few survived, will gradually shade into the large families of the American present. If we are unwilling to change our own present ideal of parenthood, can we expect others to work out and accept a different solution?

True, thinking about parenthood and families in terms of the future is a task Americans share with other industrialized countries—England and France and Germany, Scandinavia and Switzerland, Japan and Russia. But our share of the responsibility is perhaps the greatest because we ourselves have glamorized our way of life in the eyes of the world.

And even those who would be willing to shirk or suppress this responsibility cannot escape the fact that in the end, the world's fate will be ours. Or that even though the direst consequences of over-population are still in the future for Americans, there will be severe consequences for us nonetheless. For if our population growth goes unchecked, there will be, in the foreseeable future, a serious lowering of our standards of a good life. Our cities will sprawl in unending stretches along each coast and reach far inland. Parks and playgrounds will be so crowded that the outdoors in any form will be denied to millions of children. Schools will become increasingly inadequate as the ratio of teachers to pupils rises. Everywhere, every facility and every space will be strained and crowded beyond endurance. Failure to act now will jeopardize all the values for our children that we have worked so hard to create and defend and perpetuate.

As parents, cherishing and enjoying our children, we can see the need for a new ethic of parenthood. We can no longer say that everyone should have a child, that families should have as many children as they can afford, that all couples have a right to have as many children as they wish, that parenthood excels all other virtues and is to be commended above all other ways of life. We cannot now, as a people, continue to extol a way of life which—however much we enjoy it in the present—will all too soon destroy what we have worked so long to achieve and will ultimately turn the earth from a habitable place into a grim, overcrowded prison where individuals will survive only by stepping over the bodies of those struck down by hunger and despair.

In the past, little could be done to avert disaster. The new element in our present situation is the possibility of choice. What does this mean for the individual? Who is to start the change? The answer is that everyone has to take part in the change—for everyone has some stake in the future.

The first step in the change that must come is to start to think. Instead of wholehearted approval and excitement about every young marriage and every baby—a pause. If everyone has this many children, and they all live, what will life be like in another generation—within two generations?

In order to check our population growth it will be necessary to take big steps, especially to organize massive research to find methods of controlling fertility that will fit our different religious beliefs and that are safe and economically possible for everyone. But in a democratic country, demands for action at the top are meaningless without public opinion to support the actions that might be taken.

First must come the recognition that every choice, every individual decision about whether or not to have a baby, matters.

What this recognition means is that we must turn the generosity and concern for children that have led us into prolific and energetic parenthood into a new concern for the fate of individual children. In the kind of world in prospect, we shall have to develop a climate of opinion in which the emphasis will not be on the quantity of children, but on the quality of childhood. In a world in which the number of children must be limited, many adults—aunts, uncles, friends, neighbors—may be involved in caring for each child that is born and in giving it a full chance to become a human being. This is how we can best implement our belief that each individual is important and that the world is a better place when all individuals accept the responsibility of valuing and being valued by others.

Above all, we must recognize that the time to limit the size of our families is *now*, that the living must take precedence over the unborn *now*, if future generations are to be born into a livable world.

Limiting Large Families in America, II

✣✣✣✣

JANUARY, 1964

One way of recognizing a living issue is by the controversy it arouses. Unquestionably, the problem of large families is an issue of this kind, for any discussion of it today evokes immediate and vigorous response.

Clearly, a new kind of understanding about the future should not affect our feelings concerning the families we already have. As one father of ten children said to me recently, "They are all here, and there isn't one I would do without." I was talking about the future—about American attitudes toward large families in the future, and what these attitudes can and will mean to the world.

Nothing I—or anyone—can say will have much meaning to those who are concerned only with their own private right to do exactly as they feel they should, without taking thought for their neighbors, for the rest of society and the rest of the world, or for the children of tomorrow. I was not dealing with anyone's individual life except as he or she cares to live it so that it is relevant to the needs of others, now and in the future.

Those who responded to my actual comments raised a number of questions, but almost all of them, I feel, spoke in the light of our existing emphasis on large families and our present feeling that having children is the single most important thing a woman—or a man—can do. I would ask those who are old enough to do so to go back in memory to the years of World War II and the Depression. How would they have phrased their questions then? For many people in those years felt that it was against the will of God for them to marry and have children they could not adequately care for. In an article written in 1944 I myself asked what our society needed to do so that all groups in it could have children and provide for them. Demographers of that day, however, still tended to think that in a world of plenty, people would *automatically* limit the size of their families so that each child could have a better share of a better life. Our experience then was an insufficient guide to what prosperity—or even the hope of prosperity—might mean in a changing world. Today we must ask—and answer—current questions in the light of our changed and still-changing world.

To take the questions raised in order: By a "livable world" I mean a world in which children are safe and well, loved and cared for, in which city children have space to play and all children, even in the most remote places, have access to good education and medical care. Many families today are spending an indefensible amount of money on meaningless luxury—smothering their children with toys, loading down their adolescents with clothes and gadgets and cars. This is not what I had in mind. Those who associate the good life only with poverty, chastity and obedience are, for the most part, living without families, serving God within religious orders apart from the world. But the real needs of most people for human growth and the development of a full personality have their material aspects—and these have a place in a livable world.

Those who ask why we should not put our trust in science to provide food or to provide colonies in outer space miss the point that it is the scientists themselves who have alerted us to the present crisis. Science in its application must be concerned not only with the development of new resources, such as new foods, but also with making a sober appraisal of what is happening and what is possible. And it is scientists, using their best knowledge, who are warning us of the dangers of a runaway population and of the importance of getting our world population into balance. It is scientists who foresee the stresses that may result, even with the best use of our resources. We run no risk of running out of people for space colonization in the future; we do run the risk of suffocating the next three or four generations.

It was argued by some that it is contrary to nature to consider how many children we can rear in the next generation—and the next and the next—and still have a good life for each child. What is involved here is the question of what we mean by "nature." One view is embodied in the religious conception of natural law—man's understanding of nature as the will of God. Those who accept this view do not argue against celibacy, or late marriage, or continued marital relations in the case of those who know they are unable to conceive or bear children. And I know of no religious group that, in the name of natural law, advocates marriage for all adults under all circumstances or the bearing of an indefinite number of children. What is important, from this religious viewpoint, is a willingness on the part of those who are married to accept the children sent by God. For religious men and women who take this view of nature and who also take seriously their responsibilities to the future of the world, measures to protect that future will take the form of fewer marriages, or later marriages, or marriages with periods of continence.

There is also the viewpoint that regards nature simply as the order of the universe in which we live, about which we are continually learning new things. Among those who hold this view, including those who believe it is part of a religious life to live in accordance with nature, there is a recognition that as our knowledge of nature changes and grows, so does our ability to include nature in our chosen actions—and that this is also natural. There was a time when human beings had to accept as natural the death of infants whose mothers had no milk to feed them and those who were stricken by diseases for which no remedy was known. Today our scientific knowledge—our greater knowledge of nature—has made it possible for babies to live on carefully devised formulas, and scientific medicine protects their health; yet few argue that such advances are wrong or that they contradict the will of God.

In every form of human behavior as civilization has advanced, the means that men use to follow their understanding of the will of God have changed. At some periods in the past, this meant a great number of celibates, some of whom devoted their lives to the protection of learning; at other periods, large families were needed. What we are now considering is the particular need of a particular period when, because of the sudden increase in our ability to save infant lives, we must include nature in our plans and actions in a new way. Living in accordance with nature is not a matter of prescription but of the spirit in which men carry out what they believe to be God's will.

Then there are those who think that we could solve the problem of overpopulation if we could solve the problem of illegitimacy. It is true that the social situations that lead to a high rate of illegitimacy in some groups in our population also lay a heavy burden on all the children who are so born—and on the whole society. But altering these situations alone would not resolve the problems of overpopulation; it would merely mean that we would have more legitimate children born, with the same chances in life as other children like themselves. Without a change in style, we would still have large families.

Others have raised the question whether it would not be the best educated and the most responsible sections of the population—the people who are best able to bring up children—who would be most likely to limit the size of their families. The answer to this question is not far to seek. It is the educated and the responsible who *set* the style in size of family and methods used in child-rearing.

As long as very early marriage for everyone and large families for everyone are the ideal, this style will be followed not only by the educated and the responsible but also by those with less education and fewer resources. And so will a different style of marriage and family life.

Moreover, there need be no danger that we shall lack educated children. If we can establish a new style of family living, which emphasizes fewer children and more time for adults to care for each child, more children in every group will be given more care and a better chance at education. We are steadily opening education to more people. If that education includes a greater emphasis on responsible and thoughtful parenthood, we shall have a larger proportion of well-loved and well-reared children a generation from now.

Discipline—To What End?

AUGUST, 1967

In the matter of childhood discipline there is no absolute standard. The question is one of appropriateness to a style of living. What is the intended outcome? Are the methods of discipline effective in preparing the child to live in the adult world into which he is growing? The means of discipline that are very effective in rearing children to become headhunters and cannibals would be most ineffective in preparing them to become peaceful shepherds.

The Mundugumor, a New Guinea people, trained their children to be tough and self-reliant. Among these headhunters, when one village was preparing to attack another and wanted to guard itself against attack by a third village, the first village sent its children to the third to be held as hostages. The children knew that they faced death if their own people broke this temporary truce. Mundugumor methods of child-rearing were harsh but efficient. An infant sleeping in a basket hung on the wall was not taken out and held when it wakened and cried. Instead, someone scratched on the outside of the basket, making a screeching sound like the squeak of chalk on a blackboard. And a child that cried with fright was not given the mother's breast. It was simply lifted and held off the ground. Mundugumor children learned to live in a tough world, unfearful of hostility. When they lived among strangers as hostages, they watched and listened, gathering the information they would need someday for a successful raid on this village.

The Arapesh, another New Guinea people, had a very different view of life and human personality. They expected their children to grow up in a fairly peaceful world, and their methods of caring for children reflected their belief that both men and women were gentle and nurturing in their intimate personal relations. Parents responded to an infant's least cry, held him and comforted him. And far from using punishment as a discipline, adults sometimes stood helplessly by while a child pitched precious firewood over a cliff.

Even very inconsistent discipline may fit a child to live in an inconsistent world. A Balinese mother would play on her child's fright by shouting warnings against nonexistent dangers: "Look out! Fire! . . . Snake! . . . Tiger!" The Balinese system required people to avoid strange places without inquiring why. And the Balinese child learned simply to be afraid of strangeness. He never learned that there are no bears under the stairs, as American children do. We want our children to test reality. We teach our children to believe in Santa Claus and later, without bitter disappointment, to give up that belief. We want them to be open to change, and as they grow older, to put childhood fears and rewards aside and be ready for new kinds of reality.

There are also forms of discipline that may be self-defeating. Training for bravery, for example, may be so rigorous that some children give up in despair. Some Plains Indians put boys through such severe and frightening experiences in preparing them for their young manhood as warriors that some boys gave up entirely and dressed instead as women.

In a society in which many people are socially mobile and may live as adults in a social or cultural environment very different from the one in which they grew up, old forms of discipline may be wholly unsuited to new situations. A father whose family lived according to a rigid, severe set of standards, and who was beaten in his boyhood for lying or stealing, may still think of beatings as an appropriate method of disciplining his son. Though he now lives as a middle-class professional man in a suburb, he may punish his son roughly for not doing well in school. It is not the harshness as such that then may discourage the boy even more, but his bewilderment. Living in a milieu in which parents and teachers reward children by praise and presents for doing well in school—a milieu in which beating is not connected with competence in schoolwork—the boy may not be able to make much sense of the treatment he receives.

There is still another consideration in this question about discipline. Through studies of children as they grow up in different cultures we are coming to understand more about the supportive and the maiming effects of various forms of discipline. Extreme harshness or insensitivity to the child may prepare him to survive in a harsh environment. But it also may cripple the child's ability to meet changing situations. And today we cannot know the kind of world the children we are rearing will live in as adults. For us, therefore, the most important question to ask about any method of discipline is: How will it affect the child's capacity to face change? Will it give the child the kind of strength necessary to live under new and unpredictable conditions?

An unyielding conscience may be a good guide to successful living in a narrow and predictable environment. But it may become a heavy burden and a cruel scourge in a world in which strength depends on flexibility. Similarly, the kind of discipline that makes a child tractable, easy to bring up and easy to teach in a highly structured milieu, may fail to give the child the independence, courage and curiosity he will need to meet the challenges in a continually changing situation. At the same time, the absence of forms of discipline that give a child a sense of living in an ordered world in which it is rewarding to learn the rules, whatever they may be, also may be maiming. A belief in one's own accuracy and a dependable sense of how to find the patterning in one's environment are necessary parts of mature adaptation to new styles of living.

There is, in fact, no single answer to the problem of childhood discipline. But there is always the central question: For what future?

A Summer in the Woodlands, a Summer by the Sea

❧❧❦❧❧

FEBRUARY, 1968

I have been looking through a crop of booklets about summer camps.

Camping for children of every age is an American invention, and each spring thousands of perplexed parents leaf through pamphlets, just as I have been doing, reading descriptions of camps in the mountains, camps by the seaside and on the shores of lakes, ranch camps and farm camps, camps that specialize in riding or sailing, music or science, tennis or mountain climbing, camps for the all-around boy, camps where the shy child will blossom or the plump adolescent girl become slim, camps that will engage the fitful energy of the teen-ager or open a new play world to the active and curious six-year-old. Camps are considered part of a child's growing up, and there seems to be a kind of camp to match almost every daydream of summertime.

The words and pictures conjure up an entrancing holiday setting full of promise for children: swimming in sparkling lake water, sailing in a cool and sheltered bay, riding gentle horses along shady woodland trails, games on sunny playing fields, tennis and archery, dancing and crafts, cookouts on a blueberry mountain, singing by a campfire under the stars.

There are implicit promises to parents too. Their children will be safe and well, eating good food, sleeping restfully in comfortable housing, protected in their adventures by the friendly vigilance of an experienced staff. They will be helped to enjoy the benefits of group living and to find congenial companionship. The way will be made easy for all of them, but especially for the smallest campers—the juniors, the little people, the boys and girls living away from home for the first time.

Two weeks, a month, two months away from home, in camp, a setting designed for children's enjoyment. It isn't a very long time, and parents can come for a visit. Yet, looking ahead to summer, parents hesitate and wonder. Is our youngster ready for camp? Can we bear missing him for so long? What is there that is special about camps?

Camps are, in fact, the American answer to helping a child learn how to live away from home at night, for many nights, just as schools are our answer to teaching children how to be contented, happy and busy away from home in the daytime. Discovering themselves, away from home and their own family, is something children in every society must learn. But each society has its own way of framing the situations within which children take their first steps into a larger world, learn to meet the strange with equanimity and come to know themselves—their likes and dislikes, their strengths and weaknesses, their thoughts and opinions and their own ways of seeing things.

The American custom of sending children away to camp during the vacation months is in complete contrast to the traditional British style of handling these early experiences away from home. For in England, parents who can afford to do so send their children to boarding school for what they regard as the cold and miserable, hard-working, character-forming part of the year, and they bring the children back to spend carefree holidays at home. English parents have often wondered aloud to me about our American way of keeping children home during the winter months, when they are preoccupied with studying and the rest of the family is also busy, and of sending them away during the pleasant summer holidays.

But the difference is entirely in keeping with two very different conceptions of "home." In England home is where you want to be. Informality and familiarity are centered on home. Coming home is coming to the heart of things. For us, home is essentially the place from which you start out. Home is a beginning. It is a place to eat and sleep and study and rest—and get ready. For children it is a kind of launching pad into the future.

We take for granted that children will go to school, day by day and year by year. Neither parents nor children think of it as a matter of choice. But going to a summer camp is optional. And children's camps are expensive, even a Scout camp where a whole troop may have worked hard to earn the money for the stay. For most families the decision to spend money for camp for one child (even more so for several children of different ages and with different interests) is a serious one. Is it really worthwhile? Wouldn't it be better to plan a vacation for the whole family? Wouldn't the family enjoy a camping vacation?

Every summer a larger number of Americans decide in favor of family vacations. Without spending a very large sum of money it is possible to buy a handsome tent, hire a trailer and go off together to a family camp or one of our great national parks. And there, in the outdoors, everyone can enjoy many of the pleasures so vividly described in the booklets on children's camps: swimming and boating, fishing and walks on wilderness trails, cookouts and views of distant mountains at dawn. And later the family will have a shared set of memories of the fun, the mishaps, the intended and the unintended adventures.

What is more, a three-week vacation for the whole family is likely to cost little more than the camp fees for one child for a summer. In a children's camp, parents are paying for supervision and for expert and friendly attention to each child's needs. Counselors not only are teaching children how to swim or ride or make pottery; they also are watchful for a runny nose or an infected ear, for hurt feelings or timidness in a strange situation or sulks over a slight or a failure. These all are things that parents do anyhow, and they do not get charged to the vacation trip.

And then, reasonably, parents feel that childhood is all too short. Why shouldn't families enjoy their summers together?

Increasingly today, the decision to send a child to camp is losing the old appeal of introducing the child to the wilderness—a very gentle wilderness—and of helping a girl or a boy learn how to stand physical effort and physical fatigue. Instead, the question centers on whether a child is ready for new experiences among strangers, age mates and older people or whether family camping will yield greater rewards.

Of course, modern children learn a great deal about going away from home, far more than children did in the past. Moving around begins when the small baby sleeps in the car while his mother picks up the older children at school. The baby rides not only in his familiar carriage, but also in the supermarket cart while his mother shops up and down the long aisles. He sleeps not only in his own bed, but also on someone else's sofa while the parents play bridge. In fact, American children in general have a great deal of very varied experience in being away from home *with* their families. For many children, home is wherever the family may be for the time being. Many children have slept in a dozen different houses and in innumerable motels long before they are old enough to stay overnight with a friend.

Fifty years ago adventure for most children was a visit to the mountains or the seashore and a trip that involved long preparation and hours of travel by train or on a boat. Or it could be a visit to a grandfather's farm or the home of a city-dwelling uncle. The fascination of such a trip lay in the strangeness of the landscape scene from the train window and the strangeness of the new place—the *clip-clop* of the milkman's horse on a cobbled street, the crowing of the rooster before dawn, the treasures found in dusty brown trunks in the attic and the taste of new foods: baked clams or beans cooked without bacon or gingerbread made with cinnamon.

Nowadays children are surfeited with strange places, unfamiliar foods, lonely ribbon highways, scenery scarcely glimpsed. But at the same time the group of people whom they know well is circumscribed, and the more they move from one place to another, the smaller the circle. The world of people may be limited to their own family, a few neighbors and relatives, the children in the same grade at school. Really getting to know any people outside this confined circle is often more of a new experience than a transcontinental trip.

It is in this sense that summer camp may be of more benefit to a child than a camping trip with his family. It is a chance for him to live with and learn to know people he is meeting for the first time. A generation ago children went to camp so they could live out of doors, learn new skills, stay in a place new to them. Today these activities have become the setting within which children can widen their human experience.

And having the children at camp gives parents the same respite that it has given them in the past—an opportunity to vacation by themselves, to travel or to live quietly at home. Often a father has only two or three weeks' vacation a year. But the children have a whole summer, two months or more, away from school. Spending at least part of the summer at camp may be a choice welcome to both youngsters and their parents.

The wide diversity of camps means that children can choose the kind of setting that meets their interests and parents can make choices in terms of their children's particular needs. For camps no longer follow a single pattern. In one a child can enjoy the freedom of voluntary choices, as opposed to the rigors of winter schooling. In another a well-structured program of group living can help a child to bridge a period of disorganization.

And camping can help a child make a new start. This is an explanation parents give privately, though it is one the camp brochures do not emphasize. Making a new place for himself, finding new interests, can be especially important for the shy, unsocial child or the child who is overshadowed by a brother or sister; it can help to break the deadlock between an adolescent girl and her mother or between the unathletic little boy and a father who cannot bear his lack of athletic skill. Camp can be a place where the child can find, by leaving home, something that home cannot give him at a particular time.

Yet all this essentially becomes part of the setting, the human setting within which children can gain a wider experience of their own age mates or of children of diversified ages as well as of adults who enjoy children.

Leaving home, sleeping among those who are initially strangers, learning to share exacting physical conditions, learning to put up with stress and accident, all these are prefigurative experiences for going away to college, going abroad, joining the Peace Corps or even going to the moon. Finding among strangers friends who share one's own interests, coming to know oneself within a group whose judgments are diverse, learning to protect the privacy of the friends with whom one shares all the experiences of a day, all these are prefigurative experiences of living comfortably in a very complex adult world.

Camp is not the only way we can provide these weaning experiences for our children. But the realization of what this kind of step away from home can mean for modern children is itself a step parents can take in their thinking about the nature of their children's relationship to a wider world.

Education for Diversity

❧❦❧

MAY, 1967

How can parents give their children a solid education today and at the same time prepare them for life in a racially diverse world?

Traveling around the country, I meet a great number of parents who are deeply troubled about what action to take to achieve both these ends. Should they try to stick it out in a changing neighborhood? Should they struggle with all the difficulties of a newly integrated school? Should they move to a different kind of community for the sake of the children's education? Should they decide in favor of private schools?

Urgency is part of the problem, because the time for children's education is always *now*.

Parents want schooling for their children that will give them access to the knowledge and the skills that will open the doors of the world to them in later years. But farsighted parents also realize that their children must acquire a readiness to move into a highly diversified world in which they will live and work with men and women of markedly different backgrounds. No one can predict where these children, just taking their first tentative steps away from home, will be working twenty years from now, on what continent or at what tasks. And it is this double demand on education that poses the parents' dilemma.

In the past, schools did prepare American children to move freely in what was then a more circumscribed world. Two factors seem to have been important in achieving this. Most American families lived in small communities, where rich and poor jostled elbows and the children of new immigrants learning to speak the language and eat the food of the new country mingled with those who had come before them. And most children attended public schools, where our fundamental belief in the value of free public education gave meaning to their meeting and learning together. However much they differed in their background and in the prospects for their future, their common experience in school taught them the easy give-and-take, the friendliness and trust that made them into people who were at home anywhere in the country.

There were, of course, regions of the country where this was not so. Schools in the southeast were segregated, and in our largest cities immigrants of one nationality often were crowded together in one grim reception slum. But for most Americans in small towns and in the mixed neighborhoods of larger cities, the public school was a good preparation for the kind of diversity they were likely to meet in later life. Children learned what we then understood to be democracy —how to get along comfortably with people of many different backgrounds.

But young children today will move into a world that is global in its dimensions. They will face a far more complex diversity. As adults they may have to learn to speak any one of forty or fifty languages, and they may find themselves working as supervisors or subordinates, colleagues or neighbors, with individuals of any of the world's races. Instead of learning what they must so that they can get along as well in Chicago as they can in Boston, whether with second-generation Italians, Germans, Irish or their parents' own ethnic group, today's children must learn how to live and work with people anywhere in the world.

And they are ill prepared to do so, for our schools long ago ceased to be small replicas of a larger world. Great numbers of Americans now live in neighborhoods and communities where their principal associations are with families very similar to their own, of the same class, color and religion, having the same kind of education and interests, and even, within a narrow range, the same kinds of occupations. Where those belonging to ethnically disadvantaged groups have become isolated, we speak of their crowded slum neighborhoods as ghettos, borrowing the term used to describe the old segregated Jewish settlements in Europe. Where the community is made up of more-privileged people, we call it a suburb or a "nice residential section." One result for the ghetto children has been an ever-increasing inequality of opportunity for good schooling. But from the point of view of human experience, segregation is equally damaging for the privileged, who are cut off from experiencing others—and themselves —as full human beings.

What we are facing now is the hard struggle to reverse this process. In most of what we are undertaking in rezoning neighborhoods, changing real-estate regulations, trying to integrate housing and schools, attempting to open up employment and to give everyone access to recreational facilities, the emphasis is on the rights and needs of those who have suffered from poverty and prejudice. However tardily, we have come to realize that it is devastatingly destructive for children to grow up trapped in ghettos. But we are much less clear that it is deeply damaging for children to grow up isolated in suburbs and in "select" sections of a city.

Instead, where privileged children are concerned our attention is focused on the more limited problem of how they will get a sound basic education. And in the midst of the uneasy process of transition and the pressures that are brought to bear on everyone, there is a real danger that the diversity we once valued for all children will come to be defined as a privilege for the deprived and as a penalty for the previously privileged.

Talking all these problems over with parents today, I have been struck both by the similarity and the contrast between their situation now and mine twenty years ago, when my own daughter was ready for school. I knew what I wanted for her. I wanted a school where she could learn all that we depend on schools to teach. But I also wanted her to grow up able to move freely, responsibly and with sophistication anywhere in the world. I wanted her to feel at home and welcome anywhere in the New World, where all the great races of man have mingled, and in the Old World, where so many groups have lived apart from one another. I wanted her to understand that skin color and eye color and hair form are signs of special ability and disability only where, temporarily, people have treated them as such.

Particularly I wanted her to overcome the peculiar American belief that African heritage, in whatever proportion, is determining as no other heritage, European or Asian, is. I wanted her to know members of other groups so that she would not classify individuals by such categories as skin color, language or religion, but would be able to respond to each of them as a person whom she liked or found uncongenial for individual reasons. I wanted her to experience living with others as full human beings.

But we lived in New York City, and there seemed to be no way of providing good schooling based on diversity within the then-deteriorating school system. I was faced, as parents now are faced, with the fact that children are young only once. If they are to have the right kind of education, they must have it now, not in some far future when we have reorganized the school system. And so, very reluctantly (for I grew up believing firmly in public schools), I joined with a group of parents in starting a new school where a few children, at least, could have the things we wanted for all children: a good formal education, a rich artistic experience and the daily give-and-take of growing up with children and with adults—teachers, trustees, maintenance staff—of diverse ethnic, religious and cultural backgrounds.

My conscience troubled me. A good school should be rooted in the community, and our children came from distant parts of the city. The long bus trips were hard on the children, and keeping the school going was hard on the parents. Most of them were young and had little money. They were scarcely able to afford tuition for their own children, much less contribute to the many scholarships that were needed.

The school often faced disaster. We paid the staff less than they could have earned in a different kind of school, and sometimes we couldn't pay them on time. The Negro families faced the greatest difficulties. Their children had the longest bus rides and the Negro parents made the greatest sacrifices in sharing the costs. No one now can count the hours everyone gave to make that school a living thing. Our children had a good education, but at great cost.

Today we have the legal framework for creating such diversity in all our public schools. But we are still a long way from having created the social climate in which each child can have both a good formal education and a happy experience of human diversity. Our attempts nationally to bring together children who differ from one another in color, religion, language and in ethnic, economic and social back-ground are still clumsy and crude. Breaking old neighborhood patterns, bringing together children and teachers and parents who are strangers to one another, using old schools and new schools, finding methods of teaching the deprived and the privileged simultaneously—all this is hard on everyone, the children most of all.

Can we make it work? Can we give our children, all our children, the kind of education they will need? Some parents I know have given up and are sending their children to private schools; others are founding new private schools. Even the parents who care the most are discouraged. We are finding that what we want is expensive in time and money, and especially in effort. We are discovering that it is not enough to try to work toward our older, already existing standards. If a fully integrated school is to benefit all its students, it must have better teachers and better facilities than any ordinary school. And everyone will have to work much harder—the teachers, the school boards, the parents, the children themselves and the whole community. It will not be easy.

But I think we can succeed—on one condition: that is, that we continue to value diversity. Today this is not simply an ideal. It is the reality of our children's world.

How Our Children Face the Future

❧❦❧❦❧

MARCH, 1962

Long ago, in a different world, when children asked questions about war and the implements of war they got fairly reassuring answers. The coat of mail hanging in the great hall, they were told, was what Father wore so that he wouldn't be killed when he went off to fight the enemy. Later, as soldiers marched in a patriotic parade and children asked, "What are soldiers for?" they were told, "To fight for us if an enemy attacks us. To protect our country and our homes." The armor, the soldiers, the great fighting ships of the line, the massed planes of World War II, all became parts of the world that could be trusted to give protection. This was especially true for American children living in a country on whose soil no war had been fought for almost a hundred years, where no living person could teach a child out of his own experience here that soldiers are also invaders, that ships sailing into our quiet harbors and planes circling in the sky may carry menace.

But now there is the atom bomb. From the day of Hiroshima on, children have heard about the bomb, dreamed about the bomb, made pictures of the bomb.

Until adults explained the bomb to them, however, there was no way for children to know whether it was a good thing or a bad thing. For children have to *learn* what is frightening. We all are born with the ability to be frightened—to jump at a loud sound, to respond spasmodically to the loss of support, to spit out something with a strange taste—but it is other people who teach us about the many things in our world that can be frightening. Is the whir of the vacuum cleaner as soothing as a lullaby because it means that Mother is nearby, or is it a monstrous roar from which Father flees? Is Father's motorboat as safe as a cradle, or is it something that always makes Mother sick when she goes out in it? Are people with different-colored skin friendly and reliable, or are they somehow strange and menacing?

Children learn their fears from words, from the tone in people's voices, from the look on their faces.

And ever since 1945 children have been asking and learning about the bomb. In different homes, in different schools, at different times they have been given very different answers. "It's a terribly powerful bomb that kills a lot of people." . . . "What for?" . . . "To stop the war, so no more people will be killed"—this in 1945. "To keep anybody from attacking our country"—this in 1946 and 1947.

In 1948 when the Soviet Union exploded its first bomb, it was described in a Russian poem, written in the form of a lullaby, as a power strong enough to move mountains. Russian children also were taught that the bomb made them safer.

A few years later, during the Korean War, American children who wanted to know why they were having air-raid drills at school were told, "Because something might go wrong. Someone might make a mistake. A bomb might be dropped by accident. A war might start by accident."

In 1961 there was only one answer parents could give to the question of what would happen to the people where the bomb fell. That answer was: "The people would be dead." So children today know not only that atom bombs are tremendously powerful, they know also that these bombs may go off, that there is no protection if they do go off, that the knowledge of how to make them is here to stay.

Are modern children, then, destined to be constantly afraid? Or, to rephrase the question, is danger always frightening? The answer is, not necessarily.

Danger can be exhilarating, as on a ski jump. It can be challenging, as in a parachute jump. It can be disciplining, as in learning to drive a fast modern car with responsibility and precision.

The way children learn to respond to danger depends on how they encounter it and, most of all, on how adults and older children interpret it to them. A factual account of what to do if the house should catch fire suggests that here is a danger that can be met by some kind of action. But if the very idea of fire evokes only a shudder of horror, blanches a face with fear, this too will be communicated.

One thing that can help people face and meet danger today is our greater understanding of fear itself, of bravery and cowardice and of what makes a man act like a man. While we have been inventing bigger and bigger bombs we have also been learning by systematic observation what are the most effectual and ineffectual ways of meeting fear. We have learned that it is not necessary to be "fearless" in order to be brave. Bravery consists in recognizing danger clearly enough to prepare for it and to try to protect the things one is living for. We have learned that the greatest psychological hazard is to have to remain passive and helpless in the face of danger.

The parents who can look their children in the eye today and admit that they are afraid of what a modern war would do have taken the first step in teaching their children courage—the courage to admit to an informed, real fear. The next step, of course, is how one handles such a fear. Human beings who can think of nothing better to do than to build individual shelters to crawl into in case of an attack are a hazard to everyone around them. But those who are involving themselves in preventive tasks, however large or small, are teaching their children an invaluable lesson—that the new dangers can be faced and met by new kinds of action.

Today's children are the first generation to grow up in a world that has the power to destroy itself. But if they must face the horrifying implications of scientific war, they also have the new protection that comes from the sciences of human behavior. They do not have to pretend that they are not afraid of modern warfare. Nor do they have to feel that it is unmanly to work for peace. Their heroes need not be daredevils, but men who can soberly assess just how dangerous the new projects are that mankind must undertake—projects that admittedly may not work out, that are subject to disastrous accidents. The children whose birthright is this new age will be saved from psychological disaster if they see around them men and women who estimate danger carefully and accurately, who work soberly to prevent war and who invent safer ways of keeping the peace.

IV

DIALOGUES

On Telling Children about War and Peace

❦❧❦❧❦❧

In the spring of 1965 in New York City, eight women sat down with us to talk earnestly and thoughtfully about their fears for the world and their hopes for world peace. They were young mothers who had been invited by *Redbook* to take part in the discussion. Two were old enough to have been teen-agers in the era before the atom bomb; one was only twenty-one. One was Japanese. One was a lawyer, another a bachelor of divinity; four had not finished college. Among them, they had seventeen children ranging in age from twenty years to ten months, and one young mother was pregnant.

Our conversation was tape-recorded; part of it, a very lively exchange, is set down here.

DR. MEAD: The year 1965 is the twentieth anniversary of Hiroshima and the twentieth anniversary of the signing of the United Nations Charter, and it is International Co-operation Year. So it's a good moment in history to look both backward and forward in time. How far have we come since World War II and how close are we to peace? Let's see, does anyone here besides me have a child who was born before August, 1945—before Hiroshima?

EDITH HUNTER: My daughter was twenty this April 18.

DR. MEAD: Then her lifetime almost coincides with the period that the world has lived with the bomb. My daughter was born in 1939, the year the war began in Europe. So apparently all our children have grown up never knowing a world without war or without the bomb. I think if we talk about what we tell our children about the state of the world, what we tell them about the bomb and what we tell them about the United Nations—what it is and what it is attempting to do—these will be the most important things. It might be a good beginning if we start with what you tell your children about Hiroshima. How about you, Mrs. Crueger?

NANCY CRUEGER (*smiling*): The subject hasn't come up yet. My oldest is just six, still in kindergarten. We have television, however, which is a very broad source of information for children, and we *have* had quite a bit of discussion about the relationship of the United States and Germany. He is interested to know that Hitler was a bad man, that Germany was our enemy during the last war and yet at the moment is one of our staunchest friends. Why? We say simply because human beings change. You know?

VANCE FEINBERG: Our three daughters are ten, fourteen and sixteen. We try not to put any pressure on them to think the same as we do, but we are very outspoken, my husband and I. We don't muzzle what we think in order to preserve their sensibilities. We've told them that we feel Hiroshima was wrong. Maybe it was tactically necessary. Maybe if we knew more about it and had been sitting in the White House, we would have dropped the bomb. But we tell them we feel it was wrong. And it seems to me that the consciousness Americans have had ever since Hiroshima that maybe America *can* sometimes be wrong is one of the things that has given politics a new look.

VICTORIA SHARVEY: Well, I'm a Quaker. My child is only two, but when he was three months old he was taken on a Hiroshima Day peace walk. I intend to keep on doing this sort of thing because this is what I believe in. The only thing I can do is go on a Hiroshima peace walk. I have to protest this barbarism somehow, and my child will go along with me because I feel he should be a part of it. When he gets older he can make his own decisions. But meanwhile I will tell him over and over again that the ends do not justify the means. I will say, "It doesn't matter if you're promoting democracy. You don't kill people."

DR. MEAD: Mrs. Hunter, what would you say about this?

MRS. HUNTER: I have a longer history than some of you. We're a pacifist family too, but I have very ambivalent feelings about World War II. Our eleven-year-old William is very interested in politics. He and his father and I have been watching a series of television shows on the life of F.D.R. on Friday nights. To me it's been very interesting, reliving the dilemma of the terribly hard decisions Roosevelt made and being awfully glad that he did something about Hitler. I agree with you in theory one hundred per cent, that the means seem perfectly terrible. And yet I have to be honest with myself and say I was darn glad that F.D.R. got us involved in stopping Hitler from killing the Jews. I expressed this feeling to my children.

MRS. CRUEGER: As far as Hiroshima goes, wouldn't it have been possible for President Truman to announce to the Japanese that we had X number of powerful bombs and that they were invited to watch the display?

DR. MEAD: But we have to remember that no one could be certain the bomb would go off, and we had only two. They really *did* believe dropping the bomb would save millions of lives—not only American lives but also Japanese lives. One estimate at the time was that it would take about three million American lives and three million Japanese lives to fight the war to a finish. The contrary position was, of course, that the Japanese were beginning to make moves toward peace that were not picked up. But the notion—and it *is* a dramatic notion and it would have been a good notion—of dropping the bomb on an empty mountainside with people watching from box seats, this you would dare to do only if you were sure the bomb would go off.

Mrs. Matsumoto, you are the only Japanese here. I'm not going to ask you to represent your entire country, but can you tell us something of how the Japanese feel about Hiroshima today?

NOBUKO MATSUMOTO: I am not going to say this only because you are Americans, but if we did—if we, the Japanese, had had a bomb, we think we would have bombed the Americans.

MRS. SHARVEY (*sharply*): And would that have made it right?

MRS. MATSUMOTO: No, that's why I think I'm going to tell my children that the bombing itself was very wrong. But you had to do something to end the war, and it could have been either the Americans or the Japanese. It just happened to be the Americans because they had the bomb.

RUTH LEVITAN: Were you there? Were you in Japan?

MRS. MATSUMOTO: No, I was in China at the time.

MRS. LEVITAN: I was opposed to the bomb as soon as it was dropped and I've been opposed to it ever since. But I do think we have to remember the climate in which it was dropped. There was a lot of killing going on. There was the fire-bombing of Germany. England had been bombed. People were almost saturated by numbers at that point. There were these figures coming back from Russia of armies upon armies being destroyed. Hiroshima wasn't as far out of context then as it would be today, and we have to remember this in evaluating the decision. Even though I think it was a completely wrong decision.

MRS. SHARVEY: Well, but we still talk of dropping bombs. We're mad at China. We might bomb China.

DR. MEAD: But we *haven't* yet. We're in a different world now. We have to face the knowledge of the bomb. The Soviet Union has it, France has it and China has it. What do you tell your children about this? What do you tell them, not only about the Hiroshima bomb but the bomb today?

MRS. FEINBERG: We point out to our daughters that the world has always lived with danger. We've tried to point out that none of the people of the world want to use the bomb, that the people of Russia want peace, that the people of Vietnam want peace, that the people in America want peace, and that if the people, preferably through the United Nations, can make themselves felt strongly enough, the leaders will not use the bomb.

MRS. CRUEGER: But people feel so helpless! It seems to me this is why they're so afraid of the bomb. What can they do about it?

MRS. FEINBERG: We try to teach our daughters that they can march, that they can vote as soon as they are old enough—and they can think.

DR. MEAD: And what about the United Nations? You said people could make their feelings felt through the United Nations. Do you give your children a sense that the United Nations is working?

MRS. FEINBERG: I tell them that I think it has faults, but it's the one hope of the world so far.

MRS. LEVITAN: I agree that not only do you have to give children attitudes about right and wrong, about Hiroshima in the past, but also you have to give them a feeling that there is something they can do about the future. I am a person in a democracy. This is not an authoritarian regime. I can make my feelings heard. I can write to my President. I can picket. I can distribute leaflets. And this is something that you can't start too young. My twelve-year-old's been on marches with me, and the eight-year-old too, as a matter of fact. My twelve-year-old distributed leaflets as long ago as 1962, when the Women Strike for Peace was trying to get people to sign a petition against high-altitude testing and the President to sign the ban on testing. I talked to her at the time—she was then, I guess, in the fifth grade—and said, "You know, Debbie, the opinions we have in this house are not the opinions that everybody has. They're not always popular opinions. They're things that Mommy and Daddy and a lot of our close friends think. But not necessarily everyone else agrees with them." My fifth-grader looked at me in disgust and said, "Oh, Mommy, I *know* that already." So they start very early with a knowledge of what they believe and what they can do to promote what they believe, and this gives them a strength which you can't take away. I think it's crucial.

MRS. CRUEGER: And they learn whether holding minority opinions is a shameful thing or a source of pride and strength.

MRS. FEINBERG: Or whether to be embarrassed about it.

MRS. CRUEGER: That's right. Whether to cower before the fact that theirs is the only family to feel that way.

MRS. LEVITAN: We're not an "only family." I might think twice about that. We're very lucky, perhaps, in the friends we have. It's hard to be the only one. I was the only one when I was a girl, and it was hard. I'm lucky in my neighbors and perhaps in the times that I live in. When I went to college in the forties, boy! Nobody was on a picket line. But it's different now. So it's easier.

MRS. SHARVEY: I went on my first Hiroshima Day walk when I was eight years old, with my parents. I remember it. It was in New York City and it impressed me terribly. I saw pictures of what had been done in Hiroshima. Ten thousand degrees! I was eight. This wasn't far out somewhere. This was real to me.

MRS. FEINBERG: It was something physical that you were doing. It wasn't talk.

DR. MEAD: I'd like to go back to Mrs. Levitan's remarks a moment ago about the number of dead in World War II. We who are old enough remember the bombing of Hamburg, the bombing of

Tokyo, the bombing of Britain, the massacres of the Russian armies by the Germans, and the thousands and thousands and thousands of dead. But today what do you think our children feel? Have our children learned to value life more than people did in the middle of World War II?

MRS. FEINBERG: I don't quite get your question.

DR. MEAD: Well, when children today read that, say, there are eighteen American casualties in an encounter in Vietnam . . .

MRS. FEINBERG: Even one man in Selma . . .

DR. MEAD: Well, the question is whether one man in Selma hasn't helped make them more conscious of the individuals involved in death. Has this helped advance the cause of peace?

LINDA FELNER: I think it has. Selma more so than Vietnam. Vietnam is too far away.

MRS. CRUEGER: But what is peace? Do we have it now? Is peace merely the absence of war, which I guess would be the classical definition? We've more or less had an absence of world war, but we've had a couple of limited wars. In the limited wars the big powers and the balance of pressures, perhaps, are able to keep them limited. There was Cyprus. That could have flared up terribly except for the outside pressure. We have a great deal of external pressure, I think, in Vietnam. This is perhaps what's keeping it at a less than global level. Are we about to get into a global war?

MRS. FEINBERG: One of the arguments I use to help my children when they begin to worry a bit about the atomic bomb is to point out that at all these different times the world was on the brink and it would have been so easy for someone to have pushed the button—yet no one did. Perhaps this goes back to Mrs. Levitan's recalling the context of World War II. In peacetime, even in a time of limited wars, it is much harder to make a decision to drop a nuclear bomb than it is in the middle of a world war.

MARLEIGH SIEBECKER: I agree, there has been a very obvious restraint. In a way—maybe I'm just fooling myself—I feel the world is a little bit more—well, let's say *I'm* more at peace now. I think the fear that was instilled in people for a while is lessening now. I think the world is a little bit safer now than it's ever been, simply because of the bomb. Maybe because death has become more meaningful again.

MRS. FELNER: Is this true of the Chinese? I don't think we

know enough—I mean *I* don't know enough—about the Chinese culture and the Chinese mind to know whether or not they're afraid to
use the bomb.

DR. MEAD: What do you think would make the Chinese as
unwilling to use the bomb as the Russians and the Americans?

MRS. FELNER: I don't know that they *are* unwilling.

DR. MEAD: No, but I say, what do you think would make
them so?

MRS. FELNER: The Chinese have so little to lose.

DR. MEAD: That seems to me a point. When did the Russians
start being reasonably conservative about the bomb? When they had
cities they didn't want destroyed. You go to Moscow today and see
the building that has been done. They don't want this destroyed
again. Now, what could happen in China that would make them——

MRS. SIEBECKER: If they become a little more prosperous.

MRS. FELNER: The Chinese have very little to lose. We have a
lot to lose. The Russians have a lot to lose and most of the Western
world does.

RHODA METRAUX: We *think* the Chinese feel they have very
little to lose.

DR. MEAD: I'd like to hear Dr. Metraux go on with that.

DR. METRAUX: The Chinese sense of rebuilding their civilization is a very precious thing. They may not be well off materially,
but from their own point of view they have a two-thousand-year
tradition to lose.

DR. MEAD (*after a thoughtful pause*): We've been talking
about what has happened and what is happening in the world, and
your own feelings about it. We seem to have reached an agreement
that at this moment, at least, the world is a little less tense, that it is
exercising restraint. Now let's talk about how you regard the future.
This will affect your children, you know. Some of them are babies in
arms, and they get what you feel through your arms. Some are two-
year-olds who hear the tension in your voice after you've listened to a
newscast. Some are six or older, old enough to understand what you
say. It's going to make a difference to them whether you feel anxious
or not, whether you are hopeful or pessimistic.

MRS. FEINBERG: You know, that makes me think of something
curious. About two and a half years ago I was doing some interview-

ing. It was during the Cuba crisis, in 1962. Everybody was talking about the world's being wiped out, about the possibility of there being only a handful of persons left, about mass death. Today these possibilities seem more theoretical. I wonder whether this reflects the passage of two or three years—the fact that you can't stay terrified forever; you adapt to it—or whether it reflects a very real hope for the future.

MRS. FELNER: I'm hopeful that my child will grow up, you know, in the kind of world I live in and the kind of America I live in. That's why, I think, I have deep feelings about wars in general. I want my child to grow up, but more than that—and maybe this sounds like a militant thing to say—I want him to grow up in a nice world. I want him to grow up in a world of opportunity.

DR. MEAD: Would you be willing to risk destroying all children to preserve a world of opportunity?

MRS. FELNER: No, I wouldn't be willing to risk destroying all children. That's why I think the bomb on Hiroshima—I don't think I could ever sanction that bomb. I feel very strongly against that, but I do think we should fight for what we believe in, if necessary. I would never go on a peace march. I'm probably different from everybody else here on that score. I would not go on a peace march against nuclear weapons. I could never consider myself a pacifist in any sense.

MRS. SHARVEY: You say you want your kids to grow up in a nice world, but are you willing to sacrifice your advantages for your principles?

DR. MEAD: The major question is: Is there going to be any world at all? A discussion of giving up advantages is rather minor compared with the question "Are we going to refrain from destroying the world?"

MRS. FEINBERG: We haven't been talking as though that were the issue today. We talk as though we fully believed the world would go on like this forever.

DR. MEAD: Yet what about people who say they'd rather be dead than Red? Who see a choice between a nuclear war, which would destroy all of us, and world-wide communism?

MRS. SHARVEY: But do we have to be either/or?

MRS. FELNER: You don't really have to be.

MRS. SIEBECKER: Nothing is black or white. But don't you think there's less of that lately?

DR. MEAD: Exactly! We're discovering there's no need to make such a choice. And this has a great bearing on the future—which is our subject of discussion. Since he has had the knowledge of how to make the bomb man is becoming responsible in a way that he's never been before. That responsibility may transform our capacity to provide some kind of world order. Mrs. Felner, what do you think we can do to help create this world order?

MRS. FELNER: Well, I believe our first responsibility in the new world order should be to admit Red China to the UN. I don't know how we can possibly talk about understanding other people and negotiating with them when at the same time we're saying, "No, we can't admit them to the UN. They're bad."

DR. MEAD: Are you that sure they want to be admitted?

MRS. FELNER: There's a chance they might want to send observers, anyway.

MRS. CRUEGER: I think the basic step toward world understanding—the two basic steps—are education and technology. Education is perhaps the more essential, and then raising the standard of living so people don't have to go hungry every day. If you're hungry every day, you can't think about world peace.

MRS. SHARVEY: That's not true.

MRS. CRUEGER: You don't think so?

MRS. SHARVEY: I *know* so, because when I was in Europe I went hungry every day but I still thought about world peace.

DR. MEAD: Elective hunger is a rather different thing from compulsory hunger.

MRS. SHARVEY: That's quite true.

MRS. FELNER: We still have the enemy syndrome, though, you know. Can education change that? What do you tell your children about the Chinese? Do you say they're nice people and we should live with these people because their ideas are just as good as ours?

MRS. FEINBERG (*to Mrs. Sharvey*): What do you tell your child?

MRS. SHARVEY: I tell him there are better ways of doing things than what we're doing now. I don't say, "I'm on this peace walk and that means I think the Chinese are good."

MRS. CRUEGER: No, you say the Chinese may have bad ideas but even so you want to have peace, and there are better ways of achieving it.

MRS. FEINBERG: You can break down the enemy syndrome on a level that a little child can understand. This summer a very, very good friend of my oldest daughter's, a Japanese exchange student, came to the house. He showed us pictures and all that, and after a little time of being uneasy about it, he and my husband were talking about the fact that my husband had fought the Japanese during the war. I think it was a wonderful example for the children to see. Here was a boy who, if he had been old enough, might have confronted my husband in Iwo Jima. They would have been shooting at each other. But actually they had so much more in common than they had differences.

MRS. FELNER: The trouble is, our educational system does not teach that sort of real understanding of other peoples. People are pointed out as enemies. If people are enemies, how can there be peace?

DR. MEAD: If you want a change in education, you will have to change the adults, because you have to have teachers.

MRS. HUNTER: I can put this in the very practical terms of William. Here he is, eleven, and the other night, listening to this F.D.R. program, he heard a very pro-Chinese remark about our old allies. He laughed and said, "Now they're the *bad* guys." To me, this is the kind of thinking that makes our adult culture seem so stupid.

DR. MEAD: To me, the child saying, "Now they're the bad guys" is an example of the children who've grown up in this world understanding things that we don't. If they understand that first one group are the bad guys, and then another—because you're able to organize national feeling this way—they will be able to think more clearly as adults than people who grew up believing absolutely somebody was a bad guy.

MRS. FEINBERG: And this is one of the ways in which we can change the world. We can change it by making our children, as nearly as we can *make* children anything, the kind of people who'll make it better.

MRS. HUNTER: Let's say we think the Chinese may really go

ahead and drop the bomb on somebody. Is this an adequate reason for us to go ahead and have a nuclear war against China?

DR. MEAD: There is no *conceivable* reason for nuclear war! A nuclear war means risking the end of everyone. It's madness to say one is willing to die for freedom when there's not going to be anybody alive to be free. The real issue is the kind of world we're going to produce as people come to recognize what nuclear warfare means, and learn to live with this knowledge.

MRS. SIEBECKER: There have always been wars before for the simple reason that somebody thought they would win, and that's not true any more.

DR. MEAD: You see, it's not man's basic nature but the nature of war that is relevant here.

MRS. LEVITAN: Dr. Mead, is it true that it is man's basic nature to make war?

DR. MEAD: No. War is simply a social invention. But once it was invented, one group could use it to overcome or defend itself against another organized group. Right through history, war has paid. And as there was always the possibility of being a victor, it was very difficult to eliminate war. All the great religions have declared themselves for the brotherhood of man. But this is the first time in the history of warfare that there can be no victory. This is new. War, as such, has nothing to do with man's "basic" nature. That is, we have no reason to believe that early man had war. There are small groups of primitive peoples who do not have war. But there are also Pygmies who put an army of fifteen men in the field and have all of war's paraphernalia, including the idea of a peace treaty. War is a social invention, and one that was very useful. It was a way of building great kingdoms, and with these went great resources of food and technology that led to advancement. Furthermore, in the past there were different centers of power around which many people congregated. But now the whole world is one picture, and everybody has an interest in keeping the world steady. This is a totally new situation. We have not changed as human beings, but we have created a new situation.

MRS. LEVITAN: Is it fair to say, then, that now that war is no longer an effective technique, man will no longer use it?

DR. MEAD: Well, you have to add that nations also lost wars.

There is no proof that man will act on the fact that nation after nation has been destroyed by war. You have to realize that we've no reason, no scientific reason, for saying that man will save himself through the "instinct for self-preservation," as some people put it. We *could* destroy ourselves and destroy the world. There is no reason to believe this mightn't happen if we don't pay attention.

MRS. FEINBERG: Dr. Mead, don't you think the civil rights struggle could be important, aside from the intrinsic rightness of it, as the first time that the world has been shown a workable alternative to war? This is the first time, isn't it, that anybody has——

MRS. CRUEGER: I've heard Mahatma Gandhi called the prophet of the atomic age because he showed what great political change can be brought about by nonviolence. Dr. King is perhaps the strongest advocate of it in this country. It's a *fantastic* concept, you know. Since World War II most of the British colonies have achieved independence by negotiation, not wars of liberation. The American Revolution was the greatest war of liberation from the British. After we won that, they figured, "We'll have to do it by talking instead of by losing soldiers." But these are great ideas, you know, with great hope for the future. There are people all around the world committed to trying to find nonviolent ways that we can live with this awful bomb.

DR. MEAD: Nonviolence is a magnificent alternative to war if you're faced with an Anglo-Saxon conscience. Gandhi used it on the English. We have no reason to believe it would have worked with the Japanese. Nonviolence is a technique embedded within the Anglo-Saxon Christian Protestant tradition.

MRS. FEINBERG: It didn't work against Hitler when the Jews——

MRS. CRUEGER: That's why I think peace can be attained not by ideological discussion but only by practical applications—like technology.

MRS. HUNTER: What's practical for us isn't necessarily practical for everybody.

MRS. CRUEGER: Practical for everybody is having enough clothes to keep you warm and enough food to eat, a house and the chance to bring up your children in a relatively decent atmosphere.

MRS. SHARVEY: You also have to eliminate hate in the world, because hate is what makes war.

DR. MEAD: *Does* hate make war? I mean, do the Russian people right now hate America? Do we in America hate the Russians? I've never seen a people more committed against war than the contemporary Russian people. You never speak to anyone in Russia who doesn't describe someone being killed in front of his eyes. They lost twenty million dead in World War II, and they're extremely against war. But they are taught that *we* are starting wars, and that it is their duty to defend peace by fighting us. Everybody in the world at present, as far as is known, is one hundred per cent for peace. Yet we still feel threatened by war.

MRS. LEVITAN: It seems to me there are two different levels on which you are for peace. One of them is the vague ideal—"I'm for peace and against the bomb," and I think all of us feel this way. The other is, "What can I personally do about peace in a concrete way?" I've been involved with peace groups long enough to notice that this second level is reached when people begin to feel personally threatened. Our generation has felt personally threatened at certain times. They felt personally threatened before the test ban was signed. That was when women were willing to demonstrate, write petitions, write letters, and so forth. Another time was the Cuba crisis, and today it's Vietnam. More and more people are willing to take action at such times. This is why you're beginning to see a lot of students picketing the White House. This is why you're beginning to see women writing letters to the President and to their representatives and so on. But it's still only intermittent action. Between times we don't feel threatened.

DR. MEAD: The issue that I think Mrs. Levitan is raising is the difference between individuals who are fighting for themselves or their children and wake up only when they feel they themselves or their children are threatened and the people who take a responsibility for the world's children, not only their own. There's been a contrast between young mothers who got out the baby carriages whenever they felt their children were threatened and retired when they didn't and the sort of generosity and bravery that's gone, say, into the civil rights movement in the last year or so. The students who came from all over the country to Selma were not personally threatened, yet they made themselves responsible. I think this is a serious thing. Mrs.

Levitan, are you saying that it's a better basis for peace when one is frightened for one's own and oneself?

MRS. LEVITAN: No. I'm arguing that the hardest way to work for peace is continuously—constantly trying to influence not only your own children but your government, and even strangers. How do you get a whole nation to do this? I would like to ask Mrs. Matsumoto if a deep national experience helps. After all, something very bad happened to the Japanese. There was actually a bomb dropped on that country. I would be curious to know whether she thought this had modified the Japanese feeling about wanting peace.

DR. MEAD: Mrs. Matsumoto, did Hiroshima make a difference in the entire Japanese people's attitude toward war itself, war as an instrument of national policy? Because at the time of World War II, Japan was a very nationalistic country that believed war was a legitimate instrument of national policy. How do you think the Japanese people feel today?

MRS. MATSUMOTO: I think after the war we realized—before the war and during the war we always thought we could win, but after the war we realized that war is not——

MRS. SHARVEY: It's not the answer?

MRS. MATSUMOTO: That's right.

DR. MEAD: When Japanese students demonstrate outside the United States Embassy, are they demonstrating against the United States or against war?

MRS. MATSUMOTO: Oh, against war! Against the war in Vietnam.

DR. MEAD: Is this kind of public activity constructive or destructive? When they demonstrate against the US, what's the next step? Is the next step more anti-American feeling, which leads in a spiral to war, or is it a more active role in peacemaking?

MRS. MATSUMOTO: Peacemaking!

DR. MEAD: And what do you think is the major thing Japan can contribute to keeping a stable world in which we won't have nuclear war?

MRS. MATSUMOTO: The Japanese government sent a group to investigate what was happening in Vietnam. And we were trying to— As a third nation we can watch and wait.

MRS. FEINBERG: Don't you think that Japan acts a little bit as the world's conscience? Don't you think the thing we did in Hiroshima and the things we did to Japanese-American citizens in California during World War II may just possibly make us uneasy enough to keep us from making similar decisions that glibly again?

MRS. MATSUMOTO: Yes.

DR. MEAD: I think it's very important to realize that the American *people* did *not* bomb Japan. They were never given the chance to vote, and they knew nothing about it. This was a decision made by a very small number of men with great responsibility. Only if one feels that one would vote today for nuclear war does one need to feel collective guilt for Hiroshima.

MRS. LEVITAN: But it *is* up to each of us to think through just what we think this country's policy should be today. We really *are* at a crossroads today, we *are* in a position to decide, and I think each of us owes it to herself and her children to do what she can to see that the policy she thinks is right is enforced by our government. The great thing we can do in a democracy is to let the government know how we feel, and I think that every mother in this country has a responsibility to do so. We should let the President know what we think he should be doing—whether he should be pressing for negotiations, whether he should be bombing, whom we should negotiate with and how. These are important issues that should be decided at every breakfast table. It's our responsibility as citizens to let the government know what we want. It's our government.

MRS. FEINBERG: And the local things we do are part of this too. Urban renewal, voting for the school-bond issues—all these things are part of it, because we're creating an impact on the government. This is the best chance we have to make sure we have a government interested in keeping the peace.

COMMENT: The conversation above is marked by the concern, the sense of responsibility and the feeling of moderate hope that together are shaping the prevalent mood of the country. Knowing they must answer their children's questions, these mothers have faced the problems of war and peace straightforwardly and with full consciousness of the difficulties lying ahead.

Though their viewpoints differ, their hopes for an ordered world are based neither on a simple, old-fashioned pacifism nor on the belief that we have only to ban the bomb to save the world. Several of them worked strenuously for the test ban, but they know that this was only a first step. Looking back twenty years to Hiroshima, they condemn the act and yet, placing the event within the context of the death and destruction of World War II, look with sympathy on the decision-makers. None of them shirks the complications inherent in her own viewpoint.

All of them speak with a sense of personal involvement. And on one point all are in full agreement. They are opposed to nuclear warfare. And so in their different ways they are facing up to the problem of how to work—or even fight—for what they believe in and value and at the same time how to repudiate unequivocally the use of nuclear weapons. Instead of falling prey to indiscriminate fear of a show of force or of decisive action, each of these women is struggling to achieve discriminating attitudes toward the exigencies of the contemporary world. This, I think, is one of the key points in this conversation. After twenty years in which the great powers have vacillated, now urging action and now drawing back from the brink of possible disaster, this issue of trying to find other alternatives is just beginning to emerge clearly. How are we to work out a way of reconciling men's willingness to die for what they believe in and the fact that in a nuclear holocaust, dying would be quite useless because no one would be left to enjoy freedom, peace or independence?

The growing awareness of mainland China has had the effect of making the USSR, so recently a country no one could trust, seem relatively familiar and understandable. The present greater hope that we can get along with the Russians is based on the notion that the Russians are somehow more like us, in contrast to the Chinese, who (like the Japanese in World War II) seem strange and "inscrutable." Yet there is no real feeling that the Chinese are unknowable. Instead, there is a feeling that we should know more, that our schools should teach more, that mainland China should be brought into the United Nations and so into face-to-face contact with people from other countries. There are echoes of the older feeling of helplessness in the face of events, but it is being replaced by a new assurance that individual action matters and that each person has the responsibility, as Mrs. Levitan says, to "let the President know what we think he should be doing."

These young women are clearly aware that the era of passivity has ended. They are living in an active world where children should be told what the issues are and should take part, together with their parents, in working for change—marching when their parents march —and yet not expecting all others to share their views. As parents they do not avoid the difficulties, but include their children in the struggle to recognize that one's ideas about "the good guys and the bad guys" may change—that the enemy of yesterday may be the ally of today. They are clear too about the interconnectedness of the various kinds of activity in which they are taking part and about the symbolic value of demonstrations in which a group of people, each of whom is individually unable to attain a goal, band together to walk or sit or stand in a common act of commitment to a purpose.

Speaking as the mothers of children, these women made me aware that their concern is primarily with individuals, beginning with their sons and daughters, whom they hope will be clearheaded citizens of a world that is worth saving and that can be saved if every individual faces his responsibilities. Again and again they emphasize the choice that lies before every woman—whether to make a major contribution by rearing the best possible new generation or by taking part in action now. But they do not treat these as exclusive alternatives. They see their role as parents as one aspect of responsible action. And the child who responds to her mother's explanation by exclaiming, "Oh, Mommy, I *know* that already!" is carrying that responsibility forward. Her awareness is seen as resulting from her parents' willing-ness to think, examine, ponder and plan, day after day, at the dinner table.

No one spoke of Telstar or Early Bird. But the tone of assurance about what individuals can do reflects a new awareness of the power of individuals, widely scattered, to bring about change. As print once made it possible for one well-conceived pamphlet to rouse a whole country, so now this new means of world-wide communication opens the way to new forms of participation and action.

And as the determination to conquer the problems of nuclear war gives us a hope for peace—peace that will, for the first time in history, affect the whole world—so the feeling of the worth of the individual is being restored by the moving reality of the death of a few people, each of whom becomes identified and known as a person in the struggle for civil rights. The willingness to assume responsibility at every level of action has given back to us our sense of the uniqueness of the individual that was lost a generation ago in the numb horror of the unnumbered dead in World War II that culminated in Hiroshima. And our newly awakening sense of the world as a single community, irrevocably joined through what is seen and heard, in which all must take responsibility for some aspect of living, gives a new kind of support to our renewed belief in the irreplaceable value of individual action, our growing belief that each person's voice does count.

On Loving Marriages

AT THE INVITATION of Sey Chassler, *Redbook*'s editor, nine young women came to New York from different parts of the country—New England, Upstate New York, the Midwest, the Deep South and Texas—to talk with us about being wives and mothers in contemporary society. Over the past eight years each of these young mothers had been a contributor to the series, "A Young Mother's Story," and now they were meeting around a table to share with us and one another some of their problems, experiences and thoughts about their children, their marriages and their hopes for the future.

This is a record of part of our conversation on that sunny afternoon in the fall of 1968.

FEBRUARY, 1969

A comment made frequently about our contemporary style of living is that American women have no lives of their own while their children are young. The implication is that somehow, during the years in which they are caught up in the endless round of child care and domestic chores, young mothers cease to be individuals with interests, expectations, hopes and minds of their own.

Certainly making a home for her husband and two or three or four young children is a seven-day-a-week, difficult and engrossing task for the most energetic, well-organized and optimistic young woman. About this there can be no question. But how do women themselves see these years of their lives—as mothers? As wives? As individuals with many years ahead of them when their children are growing toward independence? Do they temporarily lose their sense of themselves as people? Are they cut off from life outside their homes? Is it a period without time perspective?

The answers began to come spontaneously from the young mothers in the first moments of our sitting around the table together in *Redbook*'s conference room. As I listened to these nine young women, each one so different from the others, they gave an immediate impression of great eagerness and pleasure in talking to one another and to us, of enjoyment in putting into words the things they had been mulling over while they were carrying out the myriad duties of looking after their children and keeping their homes running—deciding what had to be done and how, and what could be skipped, making a few moments for themselves or a little time for their husbands. Each was deeply caught up in the life of her family. All of them took the vocation of raising a family seriously. But none of them had settled for motherhood as a lifelong role. Each in her way was planning ahead, even beginning to include activities related to the future. These modern young women, I thought, were partners with their husbands in loving marriages.

We were speaking about the long-term relationship of parents and children, and I asked: How would you like your children to see you? As mother? As a person?

GRACE CHARBONNET: I think the ideal situation is if you can live long enough to see your children as individuals, as people, and they can see you as a person instead of just a mother.

DR. MEAD: Do you think you can't see them as individuals until they can see you?

MRS. CHARBONNET: No. I think they're always individuals.

SEY CHASSLER: How do you think of yourselves? As individuals? As mothers?

HARRIETTE ROBINET: How can you dissociate the two?

NORMA DUERST: I don't think you can be one or the other. I think first of all you must be the mother. Later I think the two merge to be one.

MR. CHASSLER: Looking back, how did you see your own mothers? Have your feelings changed over the years?

MRS. CHARBONNET: I lost my mother when I was fourteen. And of course the older I get, the more I miss her. When I was fourteen, her death was less of a blow, really, than it is now. As I get older I see there are so many things that I could have talked about with her.

MARGERY FACKLAM: But you want to talk to her as your mother.

MRS. CHARBONNET: I want to talk to her as a person.

MRS. FACKLAM: You're saying that as you get older you simply appreciate what your parents are.

SEVERAL VOICES: Right, right.

DORTHY MCNALLY: You build up different relationships with your parents as you get older. I've worked with my mother as teacher with teacher. Then she is Mrs. Wickliffe the teacher and I am Mrs. McNally the teacher. I don't even think of her as Mother. But when I go to her home, she's my mother and then I respect her in that role.

SUSAN LLOYD: I don't think I knew who my mother was until I had children of my own, and then I realized how she had cared for me.

MRS. CHARBONNET: And that was the time I really wanted her the most.

MRS. ROBINET: This is what I appreciate. I know that there is one person in the world who really cares about me, my mother. And any little detail or trifle, I can call her on the phone and tell her about it and she's interested, she's fascinated.

MRS. FACKLAM: So she's still your mother. Even though you respect her as a person, as we say.

DR. MEAD: But how much do you think what happens later is dependent on your seeing your children as persons too—on seeing your six-month-old baby as a person. Does that increase the possibilities of his seeing you as a person?

MRS. CHARBONNET: I think so. This is what I told Margery earlier. It depends on the mother's approach. It can be done, but I think it depends—if you look at him as an individual, then he will see you, too, as an individual and as a person.

MRS. MCNALLY: At six months old, though?

MRS. CHARBONNET: Of course. At two weeks.

DR. MEAD: How many of you feel that, if necessary—with

illness or divorce or death—you could possibly find anybody to take care of your children the way you want them taken care of?

MRS. FACKLAM: I don't. Absolutely not.

MRS. ROBINET: I've lived my whole life so that I could tell my children some of the things I've learned. You've got to pass on some things.

MRS. FACKLAM: The person you hire won't love the children.

ANNE TAYLOR: But look at all the other people in the world who grow up without concerned mothers.

BERNICE BLASI: Right. Who says you're the greatest? Who's to say they'd be at a disadvantage? Maybe the children would be better off!

MR. CHASSLER: Harriette, do you have a definition of the things you want to pass on?

MRS. ROBINET: I think each generation should be far better than the last. I don't want my kids to start off lacking many of the things that held me back. It's not education or money or anything like that. I want them to respect their school and have no prejudices—I want them not to have the hangups that so many people have. I've got to give my children this.

MR. CHASSLER: Why can't someone else give it to them?

MRS. ROBINET: They might. There are other young couples I know who feel the same way about their kids. My kids could be raised by them and I'd feel fairly free.

DR. MEAD: Yes, but they're your friends.

MRS. ROBINET: They think the way I do. It's nobody I could hire.

MRS. BLASI: But other people could care about them.

MRS. FACKLAM: Not in the same way. I love my nieces and nephews, and I care about what happens to them. But a good life for them is the responsibility of my brother and his wife.

MRS. MCNALLY: If it was necessary, though, you'd accept it easily.

MRS. FACKLAM: Yes. If something happened to my brother and his wife and I took his children, then we would raise them as our own. But that wouldn't be hiring me to do it. You cannot hire someone who is going to care the way you care.

MRS. BLASI: No, I'm not saying that money necessarily buys it.

But if someone hands you a human being to mold, you're going to do the best you can.

For half the afternoon we talked animatedly about mothers and children and a very little about the fathers who today are helping to care for children. But what about marriage during these years of concentration on babies and little children? Of course, American women usually talk about their husbands only to women they have known for a long time, for they are wary of delivering the happiness that is never quite won, never quite certain, into any but the most trusted hands. Still, I wondered how clearly these young mothers were thinking about the future of their marriages and whether this was something they would discuss with one another.

DR. MEAD: What kind of wives do you want to be after you've stopped being mainly mothers?

MRS. ROBINET: Most of the gals in our community are more interested in being good mothers than in being good wives. I think it's a very terrible thing. Their marriages are going to pot while they're spending all their energy and time concentrating on the kids' ups and downs. . . . But the husbands have a lot of ups and downs too.

MRS. TAYLOR: We haven't even discussed husbands here today, not at all. We've talked only about our children. It seems to me we're all making the same mistake. Because our husbands are there too. They were there before the kids, and——

MRS. ROBINET: They're there after the kids.

MRS. DUERST: But we have to face it—a baby, I mean, you've got to take care of it immediately——

MRS. TAYLOR: Don't you love your husband more than your kids?

MR. CHASSLER: Or to ask it another way, isn't it necessary to show some kind of evidence of your love every day in order for your marriage to be a happy one?

MRS. DUERST: There are all kinds of love.

MRS. TAYLOR: Yes, but you've got to work both of them in. Put the children first, that leaves the husband out.

MRS. DUERST: But if a baby is crying and wet and your husband wants a cup of coffee——

MRS. TAYLOR: I think you should get the coffee.

MRS. DUERST: I think I'd pick the baby up first, or say, "Hon, would you pour your coffee? I'll be with you in a minute." When they're little, that is—I don't mean as they're growing older—I think you have to take care of the immediate needs.

MRS. ROBINET: Nobody thinks that perhaps the husband could change the baby while you pour the coffee? (*laughter*)

MRS. TAYLOR: I think we take our husbands for granted, and we shouldn't.

MRS. DUERST: I don't think so. I think a concept of love, before you're married, is a kind of awe. He'd never see me with my hair in rollers. But now I think when you love your husband the most is when you look your worst—when you're sitting in a hospital room crying with a sick child. I think times like that . . . It's different—it certainly isn't a romantic type of love, but . . .

MR. CHASSLER: Well, as a man I can tell you that a husband who is realistic doesn't expect romantic love to be the force that makes his marriage happy. He knows that he can neither supply nor expect continuous romance. But a happy marriage is made of *all* the things we are talking about here. A happy marriage, one that has a full share of love, is a kind of interweaving of yourself, your husband, your children and the constant changes that all of you in a family undergo. It's the interweaving that counts. But let's get back to Harriette. How do you think wives are neglecting their husbands?

MRS. ROBINET: I think they're absorbing themselves in their kids, and as little rifts come up between a husband and a wife they grow further apart.

MRS. FACKLAM: I agree with Anne to the extent that while we're talking about how marvelous it is that we're all going to change and be such terrific people as our kids get older, we're neglecting the fact that our husbands are doing this all the time. They're changing as much as we are, if not more.

MRS. ROBINET: I think that maybe we're trying to keep up with their changes.

MRS. FACKLAM: And what makes the whole thing a going concern is the fact that your husband is moving and changing and learning—and this is what gives you the impetus to do likewise.

DR. MEAD: And when the children are grown up enough so

that you can devote energy to whatever job you hope to do, do you think you'll be a different person? Then whom will your husband be married to? A different person or the same one?

MRS. CHARBONNET: The same person. The same person, but on a different level.

MRS. BLASI: Yes, you change even from the day you met. You're always changing.

Unexpectedly, the quality of the companionship between young husbands and wives, parents of growing children, emerged when we began to speak about the need to have some time alone. True, mothers wanted time to be quiet, to think, to read. But what they valued were the hours alone with their husbands—time to talk, time to do things together, time to work out their differences, to disagree and make up. And as they talked I could see how they were changing together, from the years when their babies could be put to bed to the years when they did most things "alone" with the children and, later, the years when a new companionship of just husband and wife was beginning to re-emerge. Listening to these mothers, most of them still with very young children and one with a college-age son, I realized that today parenthood is only one stage of a woman's and a man's life.

MR. CHASSLER: All of you have agreed that one thing you want, now, is time to be alone. Well, I ask, what would you like to do when you're alone?

MRS. CHARBONNET: Just to be quiet. It takes you an hour to realize that someone is not going to charge in and say, "Mummy, may I have this?"

DOROTHY MCDONALD: Think. Just think. Just sit there. Be quiet.

MRS. MCNALLY: I think we solve problems, too. You know, we are learning to raise children as we go along, and every day a new problem comes up, and you don't decide the solution to that problem when people are around. You need time to be alone to decide what's the best way.

MR. CHASSLER: Is this only a moment of quiet or is it a time to be alone?

MRS. DUERST: Alone, yes. At least an hour. The children are excused and they can either play or read. And we always have our coffee alone. It isn't very long, but that's what time there is. No interruptions, and we just visit.

DR. MEAD: You know, Norma, you're doing something that's very interesting. Your definition of "alone" is when you and your husband are there without the children. Does "time alone" mean time with your husbands or just by yourselves?

SEVERAL VOICES: With your husband.

MRS. TAYLOR: By myself.

MRS. CHARBONNET: Sometimes with my husband and sometimes by myself.

DR. MEAD: Well, do you call it alone when you are with your husband?

MRS. CHARBONNET: Sometimes. My husband works mostly at night—he's a newspaperman—and when he comes in around five o'clock on Saturday morning, we go sit out in the yard, and it's heaven because there are no neighbors, and we'll sit there for about two hours and then he'll go to bed. To me this is just . . . I live for it every week.

MRS. MCNALLY: My husband's on the road almost all week, and he usually comes home about seven o'clock Thursday night. I generally have the children fed by then, and they go away to other children's homes until we've had a couple of hours just to talk the week over. And even scream at each other once in a while.

MR. CHASSLER: So time with your husband is another way of being alone. What kinds of things do you enjoy doing together?

MRS. MCDONALD: Go out to dinner, if there's an invitation to dinner, or to a restaurant by ourselves. We seldom go to the movies together. It's so expensive. The one who really wants to see the movie, goes.

MRS. CHARBONNET: It's different with us because we had eleven years when we could pick up and do anything we wanted, and we feel that this is a whole new life. So really, we don't do anything unless it's with the children. But if I hadn't had those years, I'd be climbing the walls.

MRS. LLOYD: We waited four years to have children, on purpose. In those four years our recreations were camping or traveling.

What we like to do best is talk together—but in the last year I've noticed that we've both been so busy, because my husband has taken on some extra community responsibility, that we haven't had time to talk and we haven't had time to argue. So when we get together alone, we've saved up all our arguments that we have to get through. And it's ended up often being a rip-roaring argument, which we both secretly enjoy, I suppose, and we make up and resolve the problem that's been eating at us.

MRS. BLASI: Lately we don't go out much at all because of the kids and the problem of finding a baby sitter. Mostly we sit and listen to hi-fi, which we've just become deeply involved with. And now my husband informs me that I have to become more civic-minded—which I'm not. I've been a *Frau* up until now; I've accepted my role. And now suddenly I'm supposed to become involved with people, through him, by him, for him. [*Laughter*]

MRS. DUERST: Our vacation is spent camping or hiking with the children, because usually we can only afford one vacation a year. But we do golf together. My husband's teaching me how to play golf. And we play bridge with other couples. There are many social things—actually we could go out a lot more if we wanted to.

MRS. ROBINET: Our kids are quite young—five, three and one—so we don't go out a great deal, but we have after-dinner groups, people who are invited over after nine, after the kids are in bed, and we go to their homes quite often. But I think the most exciting thing is when we get all the kids in bed by eight thirty at night, we both come downstairs and we feel like we've been released from everything; we're excited, we have a Coke or a cup of coffee and then we want to talk. Because there's something he's read in a journal or something I've read. And sometimes it's two or three nights before we get a chance to get together to talk. So getting together in the evening after the kids are in bed is a big thing. And we feel guilty because sometimes we have ice cream. . . . We've sneaked away from them, and here we are. [*Laughter*.] It's like we're dating again—like young kids.

MRS. TAYLOR: The biggest thing we do is eating out, and we see a lot of movies. Those two things together. Then we do things separately. We're strong on this; he has his activities and I have mine. He's a bow-hunter, he hunts and fishes a lot, he has his friends at the office. He does all those things without me, and I don't want to join him. I read a lot and I have a very few friends who are a lot like me, and I spend a lot of time with them.

DR. MEAD: Talking?

MRS. TAYLOR: Yes, talking. You wouldn't believe all the talking we do.

MRS. FACKLAM: We bicycle a lot, and we walk and we talk an awful lot. Sometimes we get in the car in the evening and take a ride just so we can talk to each other. We go out to dinner once in a great while; mainly we don't because it's expensive and we're starting this college thing. With our oldest boy at college and my husband studying and going back myself . . . We're lucky, though, because now we have baby sitters at home, which is awfully nice. If the oldest is gone on a date, the second one is there, and we have no problem. We're beginning to feel this freedom a little bit more, and we're beginning to enjoy each other more than we ever have. I think there were years when we wondered if we'd ever make it, because we were both so busy. My husband has been going to school and he has two jobs, and it's been kind of wild. But now life is beginning to look as if it's going to be kind of nice.

MRS. CHARBONNET: I think after forty you level off, and it really gets heavenly.

We had talked about the irreplaceability of parents in children's early years. But I wondered what these mothers hoped to give their children through their care. In traditional societies, children learned what their parents before them learned. But what about today? Are children learning from their own parents ideas and ways of feeling that will form them not only as individuals but also as a generation? And American women often are accused of being overambitious for their children and intent on their being successful, socially and intellectually. What are the values, I wondered, that these mothers wanted their children to take as their own?

MR. CHASSLER: What do you really want to give your children of your own guidelines and your own beliefs?

MRS. MCDONALD: I want to give mine peace of mind, so that they'll be free when they grow up.

MRS. CHARBONNET: Think. Just think for themselves. That's all I want. To make their decisions, right or wrong, but make their decisions—think.

MRS. TAYLOR: And I'm trying to teach mine to read and to love books, to love to read. You have to give them books.

MRS. LLOYD: I think you bring up something that really puzzles me and troubles me in lots of ways, that children now have so many choices. You want to teach them to be courageous and not to have fear of things that are perhaps imagined.

MRS. FACKLAM: I think what you can give them, and I agree with you, Dorothy, is peace of mind. But you can't teach peace of mind. You have to give them—I don't know what. It's kind of intangible. There's got to be a feeling for other people. Care. Care about themselves and the world.

MRS. DUERST: And I think you have to sow this within your own home. You have to sow the seeds of love and brotherhood. Because children are perceptive. If you're dishonest with them, they sense it.

MRS. FACKLAM: It's true. We say one thing in church and go out and do another. My only rebuttal is, "But you keep trying." Certainly we are all failures on that score. Nobody is perfect. But you try.

MRS. CHARBONNET: I think it's great, for instance, that my child will question a truth, a religious truth, when I didn't. I didn't have the guts to. You just accepted it and you didn't think. So I think it's marvelous, but I think we have to help them. We have to have an answer for them.

MRS. LLOYD: How can you have answers? That's what I'm worried about.

MRS. BLASI: Tell him how you interpret it. And if you're wrong, then it's up to him to interpret it differently.

MRS. LLOYD: Could it be that there aren't any answers and that what we have to do is somehow help children to live with *that* fact?

MR. CHASSLER: But what do you want to teach your children about the meaning of love, faith, loyalty, work, hope? What do *you* believe?

MRS. ROBINET: I think the most exciting thing about the era we're living in is that some people—call it a civil rights revolution, a social revolution, teachers striking—what's happening is the *human relations revolution*. People as individuals are looking at other people as individuals and saying, "You have worth. You are somebody." We want the policeman to respect each individual, we want the minister to be respected not because he wears a clerical collar but because he is a tremendous person and not a hypocrite. We want to be a person, not a hypocritical mother who says, "I am your mother, respect me," but, "I am the type of person I want you to respect." It's the worth of each individual that matters, whether he's black or white, whether he's Jewish or Catholic or Protestant, a suburbanite or the kid in the slum standing on the corner who has no background but is still a totally worthwhile person who is to be respected and helped. In my mind the human relations revolution is the most exciting idea of our time—and this is what I want to pass on to my children.

MRS. DUERST: Do you sometimes wonder if what you give your children at home—love, security, faith, faith in human nature—is going to be strong enough to counteract so much of what they see: the violence and the new permissiveness? I'm thinking as they get older now and leave. At college age, is what we give them going to be enough?

MRS. FACKLAM: You can only hope.

MRS. CHARBONNET: We can give them security but also I think we have to give them battles. You have to test them. You can't make it all smooth.

MRS. BLASI: You could be a buffer zone; they get enough conflict outside.

MRS. DUERST: Do you think it will be harder for our children than it was for us?

MRS. FACKLAM: We think about what we see ahead for our children, and see what there is to be afraid of in the world, because we've been through it. Maybe we haven't been through as much—the world has been changing a great deal. But our children look forward eagerly. They don't see these fears, and it's just as well they don't. They're ready for the fight and they're looking forward eagerly. Their only battle dress is really what you've given them, simply in the way you live.

MRS. LLOYD: I think one of the exciting things you talked about, Harriette, is the whole idea that people deserve respect. . . .

This has become a much more sophisticated concept in recent years. When I was a child you respected everybody, and it was a great generalization. This was the land of the free. All men are created equal. But now the Black Power movement means, among other things, that we recognize that there are differences and don't shy away from them and fear them. We have to learn to appreciate them and make them enrich our lives. I think that's an exciting idea to me because I was brought up with a much more generalized feeling about human worth. It didn't check with the facts the way the one we're struggling toward now does.

MRS. DUERST: I think we accepted what our parents said. I did, anyway. But now I think we have to give our children some answers, on sex, for instance—why we believe fidelity is better than unfaithfulness and why premarital sex would be injurious. Whether they go along with us or not. We can't just say, "You can't do that. It's wrong." But possibly we listened more just to authority and paid more attention to the taboos than they do.

MRS. LLOYD: These taboos that you're talking about, Norma— I feel that sex in a sense was *such* a touchy subject when I was growing up that I don't feel capable of judging in lots of ways what young people are doing now. I have my standards. There are certain overriding values such as respect for people. And love and the family—to me these are very important. And whatever can keep a family together is good. And if premarital sex helps that, then maybe it's good. And if it hinders it, maybe it's wrong. But on the whole I just think that we are too much the prisoner of the taboos that existed when we were growing up to make the kind of judgments that our children maybe need.

MRS. DUERST: It will be interesting to see whether our children are happier people because of the permissiveness or whether they will be less happy. And I don't think we will know this for years to come.

When the matter of joining organizations and clubs first came up, everyone reacted negatively. These women, I said to myself, definitely are not joiners. The very word seemed to make them shudder.

But when at last I asked, "Don't you think you will have to change the world a bit for your children?" two things became clear. Their picture of organizations and clubs was one of bridge and spaghetti suppers and meaningless meetings, and they were far too busy and too thoughtful to be interested. At the same time their standards of what they wanted for their children were so high that planning for their children meant organizing for other peoples' children too. Cub scouts, PTA, volunteer library work, teaching Sunday school ("Not just Jonah in the whale, but understanding your fellow man"), civil rights activities—all these were part of life.

A number of them had mothers or fathers who were teachers and several were planning to teach. Making a wider life for children in general was part of their picture of the job they were doing at the present time. More thoughtful than women without their hopes of a later career, more introspective than many less articulate women, they still reflected the very high demands that American women make on themselves while they are busy being mothers and maturing with their children.

During the years in which their attention was focused on their children and hours alone with their husbands were few and precious, they were also maturing as individuals and discovering themselves as responsible members of their communities. They were learning to distinguish among the demands made on them for their time and energy and for conformity to community standards of wifehood and motherhood. And they were finding out how to make choices—how to say yes or no—in terms of their own maturing abilities, their own and their husbands' interests and their view of the world they wanted for their children.

For young mothers like these, learning to choose what one can and cannot do is part of becoming a whole person and of knowing who one is in relationship to others. One of them put it this way: "The sign of maturity is when you can decide: I don't care what they think; I'm *not* going to join. At first you think, Oh, well, I'd better do this. But when you can say, 'No, this is not my cup of tea,' then you feel you have matured—you feel, I'm me now."

V

CATEGORIES
OF BELIEF

New Superstitions for Old

✄✄✄✄✄

JANUARY, 1966

Once in a while there is a day when everything seems to run smoothly and even the riskiest venture comes out exactly right. You exclaim, "This is my lucky day!" Then as an afterthought you say, "Knock on wood!" Of course, you do not really believe that knocking on wood will ward off danger. Still, boasting about your own good luck gives you a slightly uneasy feeling—and you carry out the little protective ritual. If someone challenged you at that moment, you would probably say, "Oh, that's nothing. Just an old superstition."

But when you come to think about it, what is a superstition?

In the contemporary world most people treat old folk beliefs as superstitions—the belief, for instance, that there are lucky and unlucky days or numbers, that future events can be read from omens, that there are protective charms or that what happens can be influenced by casting spells. We have excluded magic from our current world view, for we know that natural events have natural causes.

In a religious context, where truths cannot be demonstrated, we accept them as a matter of faith. Superstitions, however, belong to the category of beliefs, practices and ways of thinking that have been discarded because they are inconsistent with scientific knowledge. It is easy to say that other people are superstitious because they believe what we regard to be untrue. "Superstition" used in that sense is a derogatory term for the beliefs of other people that we do not share. But there is more to it than that. For superstitions lead a kind of half life in a twilight world where, sometimes, we partly suspend our disbelief and act as if magic worked.

Actually, almost every day, even in the most sophisticated home, something is likely to happen that evokes the memory of some old folk belief. The salt spills. A knife falls to the floor. Your nose tickles. Then perhaps, with a slightly embarrassed smile, the person who spilled the salt tosses a pinch over his left shoulder. Or someone recites the old rhyme, "Knife falls, gentleman calls." Or as you rub your nose you think, That means a letter. I wonder who's writing? No one takes these small responses very seriously or gives them more than a passing thought. Sometimes people will preface one of these ritual acts—walking around instead of under a ladder or hastily closing an umbrella that has been opened inside a house—with such a remark as "I remember my great-aunt used to . . ." or "Germans used to say you ought not . . ." And then, having placed the belief at some distance away in time or space, they carry out the ritual.

Everyone also remembers a few of the observances of childhood—wishing on the first star; looking at the new moon over the right shoulder; avoiding the cracks in the sidewalk on the way to school while chanting, "Step on a crack, break your mother's back"; wishing on white horses, on loads of hay, on covered bridges, on red cars; saying quickly, "Bread-and-butter" when a post or a tree separated you from the friend you were walking with. The adult may not actually recite the formula "Star light, star bright . . ." and may not quite turn to look at the new moon, but his mood is tempered by a little of the old thrill that came when the observance was still freighted with magic.

Superstition can also be used with another meaning. When I discuss the religious beliefs of other peoples, especially primitive peoples, I am often asked, "Do they really have a religion, or is it all just superstition?" The point of contrast here is not between a scientific and a magical view of the world but between the clear, theologically defensible religious beliefs of members of civilized societies and what we regard as the false and childish views of the heathen who "bow down to wood and stone." Within the civilized religions, however, where membership includes believers who are educated and urbane and others who are ignorant and simple, one always finds traditions and practices that the more sophisticated will dismiss offhand as "just superstition" but that guide the steps of those who live by older ways. Mostly these are very ancient beliefs, some handed on from one religion to another and carried from country to country around the world.

Very commonly, people associate superstition with the past, with very old ways of thinking that have been supplanted by modern knowledge. But new superstitions are continually coming into being and flourishing in our society. Listening to mothers in the park in the 1930's, one heard them say, "Now, don't you run out into the sun, or Polio will get you." In the 1940's elderly people explained to one another in tones of resignation, "It was the Virus that got him down." And every year the cosmetics industry offers us new magic—cures for baldness, lotions that will give every woman radiant skin, hair coloring that will restore to the middle-aged the charm and romance of youth—results that are promised if we will just follow the simple directions. Families and individuals also have their cherished, private superstitions. You must leave by the back door when you are going on a journey, or you must wear a green dress when you are taking an examination. It is a kind of joke, of course, but it makes you feel safe.

These old half-beliefs and new half-beliefs reflect the keenness of our wish to have something come true or to prevent something bad from happening. We do not always recognize new superstitions for what they are, and we still follow the old ones because someone's faith long ago matches our contemporary hopes and fears. In the past people "knew" that a black cat crossing one's path was a bad omen, and they turned back home. Today we are fearful of taking a journey and would give anything to turn back—and then we notice a black cat running across the road in front of us.

Child psychologists recognize the value of the toy a child holds in his hand at bedtime. It is different from his thumb, with which he can close himself in from the rest of the world, and it is different from the real world, to which he is learning to relate himself. Psychologists call these toys—these furry animals and old, cozy baby blankets—"transitional objects"; that is, objects that help the child move back and forth between the exactions of everyday life and the world of wish and dream.

Superstitions have some of the qualities of these transitional objects. They help people pass between the areas of life where what happens has to be accepted without proof and the areas where sequences of events are explicable in terms of cause and effect, based on knowledge. Bacteria and viruses that cause sickness have been identified; the cause of symptoms can be diagnosed and a rational course of treatment prescribed. Magical charms no longer are needed to treat the sick; modern medicine has brought the whole sequence of events into the secular world. But people often act as if this change had not taken place. Laymen still treat germs as if they were invisible, malign spirits, and physicians sometimes prescribe antibiotics as if they were magic substances.

Over time, more and more of life has become subject to the controls of knowledge. However, this is never a one-way process. Scientific investigation is continually increasing our knowledge. But if we are to make good use of this knowledge, we must not only rid our minds of old, superseded beliefs and fragments of magical practice, but also recognize new superstitions for what they are. Both are generated by our wishes, our fears and our feeling of helplessness in difficult situations.

Civilized peoples are not alone in having grasped the idea of superstitions—beliefs and practices that are superseded but that still may evoke compliance. The idea is one that is familiar to every people, however primitive, that I have ever known. Every society has a core of transcendent beliefs—beliefs about the nature of the universe, the world and man—that no one doubts or questions. Every society also has a fund of knowledge related to practical life—about the succession of day and night and of the seasons; about correct ways of planting seeds so that they will germinate and grow; about the processes involved in making dyes or the steps necessary to remove the deadly poison from manioc roots so they become edible. Island peoples know how the winds shift and they know the star toward which they must point the prow of the canoe exactly so that as the sun rises they will see the first fringing palms on the shore toward which they are sailing.

This knowledge, based on repeated observations of reliable sequences, leads to ideas and hypotheses of the kind that underlie scientific thinking. And gradually as scientific knowledge, once developed without conscious plan, has become a great self-corrective system and the foundation for rational planning and action, old magical beliefs and observances have had to be discarded.

But it takes time for new ways of thinking to take hold, and often the transition is only partial. Older, more direct beliefs live on in the hearts and minds of elderly people. And they are learned by children who, generation after generation, start out life as hopefully and fearfully as their forebears did. Taking their first steps away from home, children use the old rituals and invent new ones to protect themselves against the strangeness of the world into which they are venturing.

So whatever has been rejected as no longer true, as limited, provincial and idolatrous, still leads a half life. People may say, "It's just a superstition," but they continue to invoke the ritual's protection or potency. In this transitional, twilight state such beliefs come to resemble dreaming. In the dream world a thing can be either good or bad; a cause can be an effect and an effect can be a cause. Do warts come from touching toads, or does touching a toad cure the wart? Is sneezing a good omen or a bad omen? You can have it either way—or both ways at once. In the same sense, the half-acceptance and half-denial accorded superstitions give us the best of both worlds.

Superstitions are sometimes smiled at and sometimes frowned upon as observances characteristic of the old-fashioned, the unenlightened, children, peasants, servants, immigrants, foreigners or backwoods people. Nevertheless, they give all of us ways of moving back and forth among the different worlds in which we live—the sacred, the secular and the scientific. They allow us to keep a private world also, where, smiling a little, we can banish danger with a gesture and summon luck with a rhyme, make the sun shine in spite of storm clouds, force the stranger to do our bidding, keep an enemy at bay and straighten the paths of those we love.

The Nudist Idea

❧❦❧

JULY, 1968

Some of the pleasanter parts of the country shelter resorts that are carefully screened from public view and firmly barricaded against invasion by unfriendly or merely curious sight-seers and strangers. Externally there is little to distinguish these resorts from others to which Americans flock for weekend and holiday outings. Why, then, the barriers? Essentially they are a safeguard both for those inside and those who stay outside.

For in these enclosed resorts members of nudist clubs gather, mostly in family groups, to swim and sunbathe, play volleyball, stroll, picnic or just relax in the warm sunshine and tan their bodies from head to toe. They are the outdoor settings in which enthusiasts carry out their conviction that wearing clothes is a hindrance to the health and well-being of men and women and children, their belief that social nudism is truly the way to a new morality and a new democracy in human relations.

In fact, nudists don't object to functional articles of clothing. Sun-bathers wear hats to shield their heads from glaring light and sandals to protect their feet. Other modifications of nudity are permitted, and still others are insisted upon. Newcomers are allowed a period of grace, for instance, before they take the final plunge. Untrained toddlers must wear diapers. Teen-agers, who are welcome only in the company of their parents, may wear clothes if they want to. But the belief that social nudity is natural, good and wholesome sets the style of people's appearance and governs their rules of behavior at each of the resorts.

There are a thousand or more nudist parks across the country. Although each seems to have its own identity and local atmosphere, the parks do have certain things in common. One is the big swimming pool, with a wide sunbathing area around it where people gather to chat in relaxed comfort. Another is a volleyball court—perhaps several courts—for this is the one game most sunbathers seem to enjoy. There is also their protected seclusion. Nudists, as individuals and as organized groups, have had to fight innumerable legal battles for the right to live according to their ideal, but they are still a group set apart.

In other respects there are variations among parks. Some resemble more-familiar kinds of resorts for the well-to-do, with spacious grounds and facilities for many kinds of outdoor recreation. Members may have cottages or cabins. There may be a central lodge with a dining room, a recreation hall, and a great fireplace for chilly hours. At the other extreme are parks that are laid out as campgrounds, with trailer and tent sites and a simple snack canteen. Some parks operate only during the warm summer-holiday season. Others, in milder climates, may be open the year round, and some invite attendance by vacationing nudist club members who live far away. But by and large each resort draws for its membership on an area within which people can travel comfortably for a weekend or for a day's outing.

Clubs also share in their basic rules of membership and behavior. Only adults can join and membership is generally in family units: husbands and wives and their children. The number of "singles" accepted is relatively small. First names only are used in introductions; generally, only as much is known about a person's background and occupation as the individual chooses to confide. This is in keeping with the belief that by divesting themselves of artificial distinctions along with their clothes, people can meet on more natural and equal terms. But partial anonymity also serves as one more protective device for those who feel that they may be ridiculed or even persecuted for their beliefs at any time by a prejudiced outside world. Similarly there is a taboo on religious and political discussions, as inherently divisive and emotion-ridden topics. Much more fundamental is the taboo on touching and body contact. At dances everyone puts on clothes.

The plunge into nudism by novices is reported to be a pretty violent one. But once newcomers catch their breath, they find themselves taking part in a life of domestic bliss where husbands and wives walk about naked and as unconscious of each other as in the days before the serpent entered the Garden. This at least is the hope, and, in some nudist camps, the rule.

Two things seem to make this possible. One is the sense of congenial companionship among the sunbathing families who meet at nudist resorts. The other is the members' firm adherence to accepted practice. Although there have been modifications over time, arising from more general changes in American tastes, nudist groups retain the austere rules and moral attitudes that characterized the movement when it was imported into this country.

Social nudism had its beginnings in Germany around the turn of the century, and the idea spread as a kind of secular cult in the years immediately following World War I. Initially it had strong overtones of righteous rebellion against a society that was conceived of as hypocritical, corrupt and coercive. The nudist idea was combined with a belief in the healthful value of body-building exercises; converts not only swam and sunbathed but also took part in energetic calisthenics. Similarly they denounced the use of stimulants and intoxicants, and many became vegetarians. For social nudists, however, the central aim was—and still is—a new morality based on a shame-free acceptance of the whole human body.

As the movement has grown and spread in the United States over the last forty years most of the faddist characteristics, including the emphasis on exercise, have been lost. There is smoking in many parks, and in some the rules have been modified to permit a modest bar on the premises. At the same time, however, true believers still tend to see themselves as pioneers in a potentially—and sometimes even actively—hostile world.

Yet in the same period we have lived through an almost worldwide revolution in standards of publicly acceptable dress and behavior. There is almost no limit to what can be shown on the stage or screen. And few voices are raised in condemnation as people of all ages, dressed in costumes that combine the barest concession to decency with an almost total surrender to seduction, lie entwined on beaches or romp in the water, touching and tumbling, teasing and courting each other.

Why, then, do nudist resorts continue to multiply and nudist clubs to increase their membership? And why, on the other hand, do out-siders continue to regard social nudism with suspicion and antipathy?

In thinking about this I turn back to New Guinea, where I once lived with a people who wore hardly any clothes, just a G string for the men and a little apronlike grass skirt for the women. Nearby there were a people who went stark naked except for beautiful ornaments of fur and bird-of-paradise feathers that they wore on their heads. Very frequently I saw the stark-naked men striding, heads high and unashamed, through the village of their slightly clothed neighbors. But I also saw the air of disdain with which my own villagers looked on those who had not yet imported the right to dress, and I heard them snicker with squeamish superiority. Lightly clad as they were, they felt shame in the presence of nakedness.

Elsewhere in New Guinea I have lived among a people, wearing as few clothes, who were so puritanical that no woman would com-pletely remove her grass skirt in the presence of another woman even during childbirth. And when a widow ceremonially walked naked into the sea, accompanied by a row of clothed women, all men had to remain inside the houses behind barred doors. Among these prudish and puritanical people, men told salacious stories of hiding, in order to watch, by the paths along which naked women from inland villages walked.

Certainly one function of dress is to create a state of indiscriminate sexual awareness that is unrelated to the individual as such, so that the very idea of taking off whatever is normally worn in public makes a woman—any woman—desirable in fantasy, if not in reality. Such fantasies in turn foster shame and fears of exposure. No doubt the more that women are covered up, the greater are real ignorance and also the artificial excitement and anxieties that fantasies of exposure generate.

Early nudists rebelled against the excesses of Victorian prudery and the burdensome taboos that stifled the human spirit the way distort-ing layers of clothes stifled the human body. Other rebels advocated other kinds of freedom—free verse and free love and a freer enjoy-ment of the good things in life. But the nudists, in breaking down one major taboo, had to give up much else. The price they had to pay for the right to strip off the concealing envelope of clothing was the maintenance of a rigid puritanism in other respects, including the taboo on body contact.

Today we have substituted for Victorian obsessive prudery an equally obsessive and doubtfully healthier exhibitionism. Those things that once were hidden are not merely revealed but publicly flaunted. This reversal—and an emphasis on transparency—goes far beyond dress. Picture windows reveal the life going on inside the home, and vast expanses of glass expose to the outer world men at work in banks and other businesses. Plastic chairs not only contain but also display the persons sitting in them. The "glass lady" exhibited in museums reveals the inner organs of the body, and sound-taped operations give us a surgeon's view of the body's interior. In clothing styles we accentuate all that remains unrevealed. The young wife buys a mother-to-be dress to advertise her otherwise as-yet-unobservable pregnancy when her grandmother or even her mother wore a maternity dress in some hope of concealing her state.

Early social nudists were extreme and cultist precursors of the present situation. But perhaps nudism is coming to have a new contemporary significance in a world that has moved from concealment to transparency and accentuated revelation. What nudists have tried and are still trying to do is break the links between dress and fantasy and shame, by turning what has been shameful and therefore a subject of fantasy into acceptable everyday experience.

It may be that we *are* moving in this direction. But most people have very little opportunity for experimentation. In vast urban areas there is no escape from possibly censorious neighbors. People may hear about the "free" European beaches where bathers of both sexes sunbathe and swim together matter-of-factly and without the slightest embarrassment. And faintly Freudian echoes of the ill effects on children of never seeing human bodies of both sexes and all ages filter through to parents in books and articles. But most adults are still too shy to attempt radical innovations on their own initiative.

Nudist parks, registered, legal and sheltered, give them a chance to make the trial. Here they can depend on the experience of older practitioners and gain assurance through the system of protective rules. Though most new arrivals seem to have last-minute doubts, when they do take their clothes off they make two comforting discoveries. The first is that nothing at all happens; their anxieties were quite needless. The second is that their new companions are families very much like their own.

Although it has been said by some psychiatrists that social nudists do not differ much from their contemporaries in their fantasy life, nudists themselves feel that they have been freed from disturbing fantasies. They feel more relaxed. Of course, even the most convinced advocates can practice what they so firmly believe only on a part-time basis. The rest of the time they live within the larger community, and some of their own rules reflect beliefs they share with the rest of the community. What they have demonstrated is that within limited settings, such as swimming and sunbathing, people can learn to accept their own bodies and the bodies of others of both sexes and all ages without embarrassment.

In the long run it may be that the acceptance of a limited range of social situations in which children can run free and adults can enjoy unexciting relaxation without wearing clothes will be the end result both of the nudist movement and the plastic transparency of everyday life. Mixed swimming under controlled conditions probably is not far away. And swimming and sunbathing are the two activities in which total nudity really makes sense in a temperate climate. Some clothing is necessary most of the time, simply for reasons of sanitation and safety. But not in the water. Beaches and lake shores could be the safe and sensible setting within which everyone could learn relaxed acceptance of the human body as it really is.

This could mean a reduction in puritanism and prudery that would ultimately lead to a decrease in neuroses and certain kinds of crime—but it will not come about overnight. The legacy of prudery is a long one, and fantasies that are fostered in early childhood are hard to outgrow or overcome. The sense of freedom gained in the puritanical setting of nudist resorts is one step away from prudery, but it is also a retreat from the freedom to express affection in public.

Wearing clothes has been one of the conditions necessary for unembarrassed and easy physical contact between human beings in public situations. What we need is both freedom from prudery and the freedom to express our feelings.

What We Can Learn from Sex Education in Sweden

✥✖✖✥

Popularly, Sweden is regarded as the modern nation in which people have the greatest freedom—or license, if you take a different point of view—in their sexual lives. There has been much discussion of the liberality of Swedish laws and of the tolerant attitude of the Swedish people toward premarital sex. Many young women have hurriedly traveled to Sweden in the belief—mistaken, as it turns out—that there they could easily obtain an abortion. There is no longer censorship of publications or art, and avant-garde Swedish film makers have become internationally famous not only for imaginative use of their medium but also for their frank exploration of sex in human relations.

A small country—its population of about eight million could be set down with room to spare in any of the world's largest cities—Sweden historically has had a very rigorous Lutheran tradition. Today it is one of the nations toward which people turn in admiration for its success in meeting problems of contemporary society. Through United Nations agencies especially, Sweden has helped promote world-wide family planning and population control. At home, sex education for all school grades has been obligatory for more than ten years.

How has all this come about? Does Sweden provide us with a model for thinking about sex in the modern world? What kind of social legislation and what kind of sex education does Sweden have? Most important, is the Swedish way exportable to other, much larger and socially more complex countries?

The recent book *Sex and Society in Sweden* gives American readers an opportunity to look at the Swedish way of handling sex problems and teaching about sex in the schools. It was written by Birgitta Linnér, a Swedish lawyer, in collaboration with an American science writer, Richard J. Litell. As the daughter of a Lutheran pastor, Mrs. Linnér grew up in a religious home. Associated with the Stockholm Family Counseling Bureau (the first of its kind in Sweden) since its founding in 1951, she writes as a specialist and as a strong partisan of social change, but also as a woman deeply concerned with human relationships and adult responsibilities for children.

The surprising thing is that most Swedish legislation affecting family planning and sex is so recent. Until 1938, for example, it was illegal to provide information about contraception. Today, in the midst of the world-wide population explosion, Sweden takes pride in its low birth rate, but a generation ago drastic steps seemed called for to increase the number of children born and to provide every child, whatever the circumstances of his birth, with adequate care and a sense of being wanted and having an assured place in society.

Social reformers also had a more broadly philosophical goal: the democratization of family life and equality in the private and public relations of men and women. They believed that a new morality must be based on equal responsibility. It was on these grounds that new marriage and family regulations, enlightenment on contraception, more latitude in permitting abortion and great permissiveness in granting divorce were proposed and gradually enacted into law. Financial support, clinics for child development and family counseling, nursery schools, steps to increase women's autonomy and protect unmarried mothers and their children, and sex education for children and adults by many means, all are part of the program designed to bring about and stabilize change.

Government initiative has been very important in making the program effective. Today, for example, the government controls the sale of contraceptive devices and supports sex-information programs provided by various private organizations. This does not mean, however, that the goals or the means of arriving at them have been universally accepted, as foreigners tend to believe. On the contrary, in 1951 the bishops of the Church of Sweden reiterated the Church's traditional views on "marriage, divorce, extramarital relations, con-

traception, abortion, sterilization, artificial insemination and homo-
sexuality," and the nonconformist churches generally concurred.

There is, in fact, a continuing conflict in Sweden. In the past a
lusty, earthy attitude toward early sex and a sober acceptance of the
permanent responsibilities of marriage characterized rural Sweden,
while a strict, puritanical state-church code characterized the official,
urban position. What has happened today is that modern legislation
supports some parts of the older tradition (but with many sophisticated innovations), at the same time that it attempts to bring to bear
all the moral convictions inherent in the puritan ethic. Open discussion and mass education are part of the effort to provide a firm
foundation for the new morality.

The laws do not penalize premarital sex relations, but the age of
consent is high—eighteen years for heterosexual relations and twenty-
one years for homosexual relations. The laws give universal access to
contraceptive devices. They protect all children, including those born
out of wedlock (no longer called "illegitimate" in Sweden, where the
unmarried mother and her child form a recognized "two-person
family"). Women have parallel status with men in marriage. They
have reasonable access to abortion. (There are, however, many complicated regulations that must be complied with before an abortion is
permitted, and it is estimated that a large number of pregnant Swedish
women go abroad to places where the rules governing abortions are
less stringent.) The laws also make divorce accessible and equitable,
under some circumstances even obliging women to pay alimony or
contribute to the care of dependent children.

But success, in the long run, depends on the educational program.
Mrs. Linnér devotes half the book to this subject and to a presenta-
tion of examples of sex education intended for children, young people
and adults. American parents who aren't quite sure what sex education in the schools would be like can read these lessons with the sense
of distance that discussion of another society provides and make their
own judgments. This is the kind of sex education many propose for
inclusion in our school curriculum.

One thing these Swedish examples illustrate is the difficulty of
trying to introduce a set of ideas based on a new ethic. The difficulty
is vastly compounded when the subject is one on which any kind of
candid discussion always has been taboo among adults in the society.

For example, how are parents to accept the idea that masturbation is a harmless accompaniment of maturation when they themselves were taught that it might drive one insane? How are teachers who think that sex is smutty to teach children that it is a natural part of life? How are biology teachers who know little about human relations and are taught nothing about them in their official training to include the human implications of procreativeness in their teaching about life in all its forms? And how are teachers who have never uttered aloud the names of sex organs to describe them to children?

A comment made by a nineteen-year-old girl quoted by Mrs. Linnér is very much to the point: "Ever since I've been in school, I have had teachers whose faces turned from pale to violent red whenever they uttered a word having any sort of sexual implication. Can anyone refrain from laughing at a teacher who, instead of using the word 'copulate,' says that two rabbits 'got married'?"

In spite of the greater sexual candidness and freedom which Mrs. Linnér believes characterize modern Sweden, she comments that up to now "much of Sweden's success with sex education is only a veneer."

The evidence that teaching is not yet fully taking hold is plain. Nothing is more telling than the fact that in spite of sex education in the schools, strict laws and adequate, free and confidential medical care, venereal disease among teen-agers in Sweden is on the increase. Mrs. Linnér remarks that prostitution has "but slight influence on the prevalence of VD . . . so rare is prostitution in a society where sexual companionship for the unmarried has been accepted." She herself suggests that the use of an appropriate contraceptive device is undercut by continual warnings that such devices are not 100 per cent effective, since these warnings appear to be given in the interest of preserving conventional morality rather than of preventing pregnancy and protecting against infection. Her answer is more-effective education.

I would go further and suggest that what undercuts safe practice is the deeply ingrained, puritanical belief that the wages of sin is death or, stated more mildly, unwanted pregnancy or disease. Carelessness in casual sexual contacts as well as out-of-wedlock pregnancy can be seen as an acting out of an unrecognized sense of guilt. It is true that Swedish youngsters *say* they feel no guilt about premarital sex. But the most beautiful and insightful Swedish movies give the lie to this, and perhaps the statistics on venereal disease do also. It is hard to remodel a puritanical society within one generation, even with the best social legislation, the most articulate expression of a responsible ethic and a new curriculum to provide the framework for change.

Mrs. Linnér speaks also of the need for a better education for new teachers, retraining programs for older teachers and continuing education for parents. All these measures can help. But the problems remain: Who can do this ? And how can everyone be reached? The unmentionable often is harder to discuss honestly and precisely with adults than it is with children, who have fresh minds and fewer prejudices. There simply are not enough unself-conscious and well-informed instructors to teach the teachers and parents, let alone the children.

In the matter of appropriate instruction, we in America face these same problems, and we also face a problem that Sweden is spared. There *is* conflict in Sweden—between those whose attitudes are based on the different standards of rural and urban living, between the older and the younger generations, and especially between those who stand by the traditional ethic and those who are struggling to strengthen the newly emerging one. These, however, are essentially conflicts of viewpoint within a homogeneous society where people share a common past and differ only in certain respects in their expectations about a shared future.

By contrast, in the United States we have a pluralistic society. Americans come from many different ethnic backgrounds, and we have adapted to our common style of living in a great variety of ways. In our country, education, particularly in matters involving the individual's personal life and deepest beliefs, has to be directed toward bringing about a convergence of many points of view.

This has important implications for the ways in which we can successfully introduce changes in ideas and practices that are affected by strongly held traditional attitudes. As I see it, we must have the very best kinds of teaching for everyone. Teaching must be consistent in its aims, but we must expect to use many kinds of materials and a great variety of methods to convey new ideas. And as far as we can we must become aware of, so as to avoid, the kinds of statements that only set off the old, familiar arguments and that frighten away some and bore others who need and even wish to learn.

Fortunately, new media make possible new methods. In the past the printed book was the first medium that transcended the limitations of ideas and ways of teaching within a family, a school system, a community or a whole nation. People could turn to books in search of answers to questions they didn't dare to ask or didn't know how to ask. Anyone who could read and had access to books could enlarge his understanding. But each person had to read for himself. While you are reading, books do not help you to share with others the immediacy of your thoughts and feelings.

Today we have the choice of many media and can reach audiences wherever they are. Films and television programs can be shared by groups who are longing to be more realistic but who fumble for words, blush at the sound of their own voices or become strident out of confusion. They allow an audience to share the experience of learning things they did not know were there to be learned. Beautifully accurate still photographs and slides can be used to show us aspects of reality, details of development, for which few of us have an adequate vocabulary. We can design museum exhibits to which teachers can take their classes and which parents and children can visit together—for example, to look at the most exact models of a growing embryo. There are many things people never have talked about and still are unready to discuss because of old fears of saying words that seem too close to obscenity and blasphemy. But they can look at them together—not talking, perhaps, but able to look one another in the eye. There are many ways of building confidence, trust and shared concern. Not all of them begin with words.

A child analyst once told me that she had never known a parent who could tell a child about the facts of life and the joys of love at the same time. One or the other was always scanted. The new media allow us to make the best use of trained and talented people, certainly our scarcest resource. In making films we can draw on the very few people who can talk about sex as part of the body's functioning and in the same context speak about love and delight and tenderness.

However, even if we try to make full use of the best means at our disposal, I think we can only be cautiously optimistic. I would go further than Mrs. Linnér does in her appraisal of the difficulties we face. We have to contend with more than ignorance and poorly informed or misdirected teaching.

Puritanism is part of our heritage, as it is part of the Swedish heritage. No one of us is free from the scars of prudery, sentimentality and distortion that characterized Victorian culture in particular and in some measure have characterized all cultures. No people I know of have ever fully succeeded in integrating into one system the needs of the human body and of the human emotions, the needs of society and the visions of man transcending his own body and his society.

In planning and in making judgments we must realize, I think, that it is very hard to remodel a puritanical society within a single generation. Even with the best social legislation, the most articulate expression of a responsible ethic and a new curriculum to provide the framework for change, progress can be slow and uneven.

As far as sex education is concerned, I think we have no choice but to teach our basic knowledge about sex in the schools. This is the only situation in which we can be certain of reaching every child and young adolescent. In this rapidly moving and uncertain world, the risks involved in ignorance are much too serious for the individual and for our society. And because our state of preparedness for teaching is so deficient, we must make every use of the new media, especially films.

The transformation of the puritan ethic is very difficult, as the Swedish material shows. One of the dangers is that we may simply shift from one extreme to the other—from a disproportionate emphasis on chastity to an equally disproportionate and even less wholesome emphasis on lust. The swing in this direction today cannot be denied. Real change, which will help us face the problems we are trying to solve for our children's sake, must take place in the minds and beliefs of adults. It is in ourselves that ultimate responsibility rests. So far, the Swedish people have worked much harder than we have to find solutions, but much more is needed.

We can look to Sweden—and to other countries—for clarification, but not, I think, for answers. No one today knows many answers or the best answers for everyone. Whatever solutions have been found elsewhere we must be prepared to reinterpret, to fit our own style of living and our way of thinking.

On Aggression

❧❧❧❧❧

NOVEMBER, 1966

Konrad Lorenz is a great naturalist. A pioneer in modern experimental biology, he combines love of the natural world in all its manifestations with concern for the world man has made for himself. American readers—and readers in a dozen other languages—know him already through his delightful books *King Solomon's Ring* and *Man Meets Dog*. In his new book, *On Aggression*, Lorenz writes about that most enigmatic and complexly organized instinct that man, as a species, shares with other living creatures, some very distant from and others very close to him. It is natural history in which man is treated not as separate from but as part of the natural world.

Discussing the relationship between aggression and the ability of creatures to form deep attachments, Lorenz writes: "There are animals totally devoid of aggression which keep together for life in firmly united flocks. One would think that such animals would be predestined to develop permanent friendships and brotherly unions of individuals, and yet these characteristics are never found among such peaceable herd animals; their association is always entirely anonymous. A personal bond, an individual friendship, is found only in animals with highly developed intraspecific aggression; in fact, this bond is the firmer, the more aggressive the particular animal and species is. . . . Proverbially the most aggressive of all mammals, Dante's *bestia senza pace* [beast without peace], the wolf, is the most faithful of friends. Some animals are alternately territorial and aggressive, and nonaggressive and social, according to the season, and in these species every personal bond is limited to the period of aggressiveness."

Throughout human history, men have looked at the natural world as in a great mirror, in search of an understanding of man. What they found there was an image that reflected the human world as they conceived it. In Victorian England, for example, social philosophers seized upon Charles Darwin's theory of the evolution of species, and a favorite phrase for what he had called "the struggle for existence" was "Nature red in tooth and claw." But although they drew on Darwin's scientific theory, they used it allegorically rather than scientifically in their attempts to apply it to human life. The figure of speech "Nature red in tooth and claw" did not apply to competition in the natural world as Darwin described it, but to the nature of man as these philosophers perceived it.

In today's world we are more than ever before in need of an understanding of aggression. And now, for the first time, we know enough about the learned behavior of man, and also about the innate characteristics of living creatures, to draw on scientific knowledge to enlarge our understanding of man's inborn capacities. Today we *can* ask questions about the nature of aggression with the hope of working out at least partial answers. What are the functions of aggression? Is aggression in nature only ruthless and destructive, as the phrase "Nature red in tooth and claw" suggests? Or, in the struggle for existence, has aggression also a positive value, as Darwin himself thought?

Students come from all over the world to Konrad Lorenz' laboratories in Bavaria (especially the natural laboratory of lake and park and field) to find answers to questions like these through observation and experimental work. But whether they are following the unfolding life histories of geese and ducks and other animals in their natural environment or are working under special laboratory conditions, their focus is always this: *What is it for?* How does the brilliant coloring of the coral fish or the preening movement of a bird help the species survive and multiply? Are the myriad variations in color, form and behavior all beneficial, do all of them help in survival, or are some of them evolutionary blind alleys? What happens when living creatures are placed in situations to which they have no innate capacity to adapt themselves?

These questions and the search for answers also take Lorenz far afield. In the opening pages of the book, we meet him swimming in the warm, clear waters off one of the Florida keys. Here he takes us into the enchanting underwater world of the snorkel diver. We see the fish that come swimming in shoals, "the blue-striped, the white, and the yellow-striped grunts," the needlefish and the halfbeaks that swim by just below the surface "hunting the little silversides which frequent the water in millions, thick as snowflakes in a blizzard and gleaming like silver tinsel." And darting in and out of the coral crevices, attacking and fleeing, there are the brilliant, poster-colored coral fish. These are what Lorenz has come so far to study, and we see that "not only are male and female both brightly colored but even the tiny babies show brilliant colors which, strangely enough, are often quite different from those of the adults, and sometimes even more striking."

What purpose do these colors serve which mark out each species so brilliantly? Lorenz discovered that here, in their natural habitat, only one member of each species of coral fish, "*one* Beau Gregory, *one* small black angelfish and *one* butterfly fish," lived in peaceful association in one spot. As soon as another male of the same species swam into view, the owner of that bit of territory swam out in hot pursuit and the intruder departed "escaping in wild zigzags," until he reached his own territory. There he turned, ready to fight his pursuer, who then turned away.

Color in the coral fish serves as a signal. The interesting thing is that it elicits both an aggressive and an avoidance response. Lorenz tells us that in the sea, among fishes that defend a territory within which the individual may safely feed and breed, "the principle 'like avoids like' is upheld without bloodshed, owing to the fact that the conquered fish flees from the territory of his conqueror, who does not pursue him far." When coral fish are placed in an aquarium, however, something very different happens. Since neither fish has a place to escape to, fights to the death do occur. Each fish responds continually to the incitement of the other's color, so that only one can survive in the cramped and confined space.

Lorenz differentiates sharply between fighting between members of different species and fighting between members of the same species —"interspecific" and "intraspecific" fighting. In very large measure, members of *different* species can live side by side peacefully—as different species of birds can nest in and use the different possible feeding resources of the same tree. The three kinds of fighting *between* different species described by Lorenz are: the struggle between the eater and the eaten; the retaliatory fighting of the prey (for example, the "mobbing" behavior of blue jays or geese, which may chase a fox hunting in the woods); and, fiercest of all, the rat-in-a-corner fighting of a creature whose living space has been invaded and sees no escape. But even in interspecific fighting, destructiveness is modified as hunter and hunted have evolved patterns of attack and escape delicately adjusted to each other, so a fine balance results. If this were not so, Lorenz points out, the last lion would die of starvation before the last deer was killed.

But true aggression, in Lorenz' terms, is intraspecific—the competition for survival that takes place *within* each species. And it is mainly with intraspecific aggression that he is concerned in this book. What purposes does intraspecific aggression serve? Among animals that live in territories, the capacity to fight has the effect of spacing out the members of a species so that each individual that has acquired a territory has a better chance to feed and reproduce. In this way, of course, chances for the survival of that species are increased. Signaling among animals—for example, color in coral fish, the characteristic song of many species of birds, or scent in the case of many insects and hunting animals—serves both to threaten and to warn, to keep the animal alert and to alert others to danger.

Even more fascinating than the provision in nature of these signaling systems are all the devices that have developed in nature to "ritualize" conflict. In species in which males fight their rivals for the attention of females (where aggression has the obvious survival value of ensuring that the strongest and most able individuals reproduce and rear young), the fighters must literally live to fight another day. If this were not so, the mature and experienced among a species would destroy young, growing animals before these reached their full strength. Here ritualization of fighting behavior inhibits aggression so that, in one sense, what occurs is a sporting event instead of murder.

Among the fallow deer, for instance, Lorenz tells us that "the highly ritualized antler fight, in which the crowns are swung into collision, locked together and then swung to and fro in a special manner, is preceded by a broadside display in which both animals goose-step beside each other, at the same time nodding their heads to make the great antlers wave up and down. Suddenly, as if in obedience to an order, both stand still, swing at right angles toward each other, and lower their heads so that their antlers collide with a crash and entangle near the ground. A harmless wrestling match follows in which . . . the victor is the one with the longest endurance span.

"Among fallow deer, too, one of the fighters sometimes wants to proceed, in advance of the other, to the second stage of the fight and thus finds his weapon aimed at the unprotected flank of his rival. . . . But . . . the deer stops the movement, raises his head, and now, seeing his unwitting, still goose-stepping, enemy is already several yards ahead, breaks into a trot till he has caught up with him and walks calmly, antlers nodding, in goose-step beside him, till the next thrust of the antlers leads, in better synchronization, to the ring fight."

In certain species there is no rivalrous combat between males. Instead, females are automatically attracted by some special characteristic that varies among males. In a few species the display characteristics of the male have developed in such an exaggerated form that they interfere with survival. For example, Lorenz tells us that "the argus hen pheasant reacts to the large secondary wing feathers of the cock; they are decorated with beautiful eye spots and the cock spreads them before her during courtship. They are so huge that the cock can scarcely fly, and the bigger they are the more they stimulate the hen. The number of progeny produced by a cock in a certain period of time is in direct proportion to the length of these feathers, and, even if their extreme development is unfavorable in other ways . . . he will nevertheless leave more descendants than will a plainer cock. So the predisposition to huge wing feathers is preserved, quite against the interest of the species. . . . [Thus] the evolution of the argus pheasant has run itself into a blind alley."

Sometimes it is by studying related species that one can discover the function of certain innate behavior forms. The different ways in which creatures compete for space and food and mates have evolved through millenniums of small changes that occur spontaneously (that is, by mutation) and in response to conditions in the environment that favor one individual over another in reproduction (that is, by natural selection). By comparing, among related species, the colors of fishes, the calls of birds, the use of scent by mammals or the interlocking patterns of behavior involved in fighting, courtship and caring for the young, scientists can outline how rituals have developed that incorporate aggression and inhibit destructiveness. In some species, in fact, the ritual that has evolved appears to be far removed from its original function.

A very bizarre example of this kind of ritual is found in a group of fly-eating flies, among whom reproduction is placed under grave disadvantage because the female is likely to eat her mate. In several species of Empid flies, as Lorenz explains, a rite has developed in which "the male presents the female, immediately before copulation, with a slaughtered insect of suitable size. . . . In a North American species, the male spins a pretty white balloon that attracts the female visually; it contains a few insects which she eats during copulation. . . . But in . . . the tailor fly . . . the males no longer catch flies but spin a lovely little veil, spanned during flight between the middle and hind legs, to which optical stimulus the female reacts."

These rituals, like the bodily structures that evoke definite responses, are biological; that is, they are built into the species and recur generation after generation. But as we go up the evolutionary scale toward man, learning and the transmission of learned behavior—some of it useful and some of it fortuitous—become more and more important. In particular, the human species has developed, in its long history, a great number of cultural devices—each of which, in its special cultural setting, must be learned—for putting aggression at the service of a larger group, for mitigating aggression and for providing clues in mating as to which females may be courted, when, in what ways and by whom. This minimizing of built-in biological behavior and its replacement by behavior that is learned has given human societies much more flexibility. But this flexibility can become dangerous as men adopt habits of living too close together without recognizing the physical and psychological hazards of overcrowding and without altering their behavior to meet the difficulties of the situation. It can also endanger human survival as men drive themselves literally to death in competition for money, status and power, or as they invent more effectively lethal weapons of war.

There is still another aspect of aggression that must be considered. As we have seen, Lorenz discusses the importance of aggression in forming strong bonds among individuals in certain species. He contrasts the anonymous type of organization, such as the flock of sheep or the colony of night herons, where all huddle together without individual ties, with the social community built on complex interpersonal, long-lasting relationships, such as are found among graylag geese. Among these birds (as in human societies), infants and parents learn to recognize each other; members of families learn to recognize one another; mating involves recognition and choice. This Lorenz calls "the bond." In graylag geese the bond is formed by "a behavior pattern which not only in its prototype but even in its present form is partly motivated by aggression into a means of appeasement and further into a love ceremony which forms a strong tie between those that participate in it. This means neither more nor less than converting the mutually repelling effect of aggression into its opposite."

In the graylag goose the appropriate behavior patterns, putting aggression at the service of emotional, deeply meaningful relationships, are built in. In man, they must be learned. Given the tremendous importance of aggression throughout the living world, Lorenz does not think that man could better his state or his chances of survival, as a species, by any attempt biologically to "breed out" the aggressive instinct. It is too closely related to other crucial life-conserving capacities and needs in man, as in other species. Nor does he think that we can deal with aggression simply by inhibiting its expression. In man special behavior forms are not built in. But the capacity for aggression is part of man's nature, as it is of other species which survive through the formation of individual, personal bonds and the extension of these bonds to a larger social community.

Our hope, he thinks, lies in diverting aggression to "enthusiasm for causes which are commonly recognized as values of the highest order by all human beings, irrespective of their national, cultural, or political allegiances." It lies in recognizing the place of aggression in the formation of "the bond," and in extending the effectiveness of social bonds among men.

There is, however, a special difficulty in Lorenz' discussion of war. He considers that the problem of human survival today is primarily one of managing intraspecific aggression, because in war human beings, members of one species, attack and kill one another. What he fails to take into account is that warfare is a very complex cultural invention that relies on a cultural definition of the enemy as somehow less human than one's own group. The enemy may be defined as subhuman, and therefore as a suitable prey, or as an inhuman predator, against whom it is legitimate to fight in self-protection. Human beings have learned through warfare to practice a kind of "interspecific" fighting. The solution to the problem of warfare lies not in the control of individual aggression, but in the creation of a world climate of opinion within which men recognize all other men as members of the same species and develop institutions that implement this recognition.

Where human beings are concerned, Lorenz has only opened the door to discussion. As a great naturalist, however, he has laid the foundation for a way of thinking about human aggression within the whole natural world. And it is to the vivid details that the reader will turn with delight and fascination—and laughter. For Lorenz writes with an extraordinary appreciation of the humor, as well as the seriousness, of the living situation.

The Gypsies

❧❧❧❧

SEPTEMBER, 1967

On a late spring day in the 1930's Jan Yoors, a twelve-year-old boy, ran away to a Gypsy encampment on the outskirts of Antwerp, where he lived. The camp, different from anything he knew, delighted him: "Fifteen covered wagons were spread out in a wide half circle, partly hiding the Gypsies from the road. Around the campfires sat women draped in deep-colored dresses, their big, expressive eyes and strong white teeth standing out against their beautiful dark matte skin. The many gold pieces they wore as earrings, necklaces and bracelets sharpened their color even more. . . . Hordes of small barefoot children ran all over the campsite, a few dressed in rags but most nearly naked, rollicking like young animals. At the far end of the encampment a number of horses, tethered to long chains, were grazing; and of course there were the ever-present half-wild growling dogs. Several men lay in the shade of an oak tree."

For a long, magic afternoon, until darkness fell, Jan played with the ragged, exuberant Gypsy boys, looking at the horses, wrestling in the grass, learning the first words of their language, listening as the older men began to sing. "It was then," he says, "that I committed my one great semiconscious error; I stayed five more minutes. . . ."

These few minutes stretched out to ten years, a period of his life that Jan Yoors tells about in his book *The Gypsies*. They were years during which the boy, growing into young manhood, lived in two totally opposed worlds—now traveling to the farthest corners of Europe with the *kumpania*, the Gypsy band, which had taken him in and made him as one of them; and now, as if "waking up from a strange, wondrous dream," returning for a time to the home where he was a loved and happy son. Accepting his sudden restlessness, the Gypsies compared him to the wild goose of Romany legend; they knew he must go and they were certain he would come back, as he did again and again. Almost inexplicably his Belgian artist father also accepted this choice of a wandering life, even—when Jan himself hesitated in doubt—speeding him on his way.

After his first six months wandering, his reception at home astounded the boy: "I arrived there at dinnertime and as usual they had a number of guests, painters and writers. Nothing was said in front of them about my long absence, nor was my disheveled appearance explained. . . . In the morning, I confronted them with my long absence and emphasized the fact that I had run away with the Gypsies, possibly to make it even more provocative. With rare psychological insight and wisdom they replied that although of course this had caused them sorrow, since they loved me, they nevertheless wanted to respect my personal choice. . . . I was shocked. It was so unlike my anticipation of the event. My father added he had hoped I would become an artist like himself, but if I preferred to become a full-fledged member of a band of nomads, he wanted the choice to be entirely mine."

The next spring it was his father who alerted Jan to the presence of another Gypsy band near the town; somehow he understood how Jan was drawn to them "as by a magnet." And later he obtained a kind of pass for the boy so that he would not, as once happened, be arrested as a child carried away by Gypsy kidnapers.

It was certainly not that Jan was a rebel. His home, in his own eyes, was "sunny, comfortable, happy, permeated with the familiar smells of beeswax and freshly baked bread and cakes. There were books everywhere, paintings, Oriental rugs and classical music." But with the Romanies, in spite of hardship, he had found his "very own and secret domain." Each life enhanced the other.

This extraordinary accident of a boy who could move easily between two worlds, a permissive family which supported his freedom and a proud Gypsy leader who accepted within his own family the blond, blue-eyed young *Gaje* (outsider), a stranger from a world that despised his kind, has given us the first account written from within of the lives of these nomads. Other groups have been called

Gypsies, but the Rom, still living by ancient ways, are the people Yoors describes.

Who are the Gypsies? For more than five hundred years their wandering bands have crisscrossed the Western world, strangers in every land, wearing outlandish clothes, speaking a strange tongue, living always apart, even in the middle of great cities. Fortunetellers, horse traders, entertainers, tinkers, beggars, petty thieves, marauders, nomads who never have been tamed to the enclosed life of villages and towns or the occupations of settled men, a people of the high-roads and byways, the forests and plains, who appear and disappear, slipping by the tightest barriers and mocking the rules by which ordinary men are governed, the Gypsies are a living legend and the witnesses of a way of life that has been vanishing for five thousand years. The wildness of Gypsy life echoes through European balladry. And today, sitting in their limousines at the entrance to a great city hospital in which one of their number is a patient, they are still aloof, holding others at a distance by the very curiosity they excite. ✔

The true Gypsies, the Rom (which means, proudly, *man*), speak a language distantly derived from Sanskrit. A last remnant of the many peoples who have wandered into Europe, no one knows exactly where they came from or when. They also speak a smattering of many languages and are sophisticated in the customs of many lands, for they are not the people of a single area or country but of the whole world. The Rom recognize four major tribes (or, as they say, races), each with its distinctive ways—the Lowara, one group of which Jan Yoors traveled with, and the Tshurara, both mainly horse traders who lived in wagons; the Kalderasha, who worked as copper-smiths and lived in tents; and the Matchvaya. In each tribe there are many lineages, the descendants of great men by whose names they are known. The traveling group—the band, or *kumpania*—is made up of different family clusters, not all of them close relatives or even neces-sarily members of the same tribe. It is a composite group that grows and shrinks and changes its membership as one family breaks away or another whole band joins forces with it. Every journey holds the possibility of reunion, every meeting the possibility of change.

One thing that has held the Gypsies together is their fierce pride in the face of an inimical world, the world of peasants and townsmen, officials and judges and policemen, all those who threaten their existence and on whose existence they also depend, as hunters depend on dangerous prey. The Gypsies live, too, like those wild birds that have come to build their nests in human habitations—the storks that nest in chimney pots or the falcons that hunt from the cliffs of Wall Street. The naturalist Konrad Lorenz has pointed out that such birds, living very close to man, must have two characteristics—continual alertness, and a willingness to fly away quickly and to return intrepidly immediately when a threatened danger is past. Their day of grace over, the Gypsies pack up hurriedly, but they never leave; they only move on, keeping some other rendezvous, visiting friends, to return another year.

Surprisingly the Gypsy bands, living in the midst of complex civilizations, also remind one of the bands of hunters and gatherers who still lead a precarious existence in very faraway places—for example, the Pygmies of the Ituri Forest, in Africa, about whom Colin Turnbull has written in his book *Wayward Servants*. Superficially the differences are enormous. The Gypsies travel not afoot, but in carts (today, usually in cars); also unlike the Pygmies, they wear elaborate clothes, hoard gold in the form of ornaments, engage in trade. But closer attention to their life reveals an extraordinary likeness in their view of the world and their behavior and love of their way of living, even their sense of themselves as a people apart. For like these very primitive hunting bands of the forest, the Gypsies, turning to the outside world, create an image of themselves that allows them to make use of others and yet safely conceal who and what they are among themselves.

Yoors reports with gusto and honesty on both versions of Gypsy life. He describes how they traveled, harried and hounded by the police of every country, stealing their way across the Continent, changing their names to suit the occasion, carrying forged passports and falsified birth certificates, supplying one another with the documents necessary for safe passage and carrying on bits of paper scribbled addresses and telephone numbers that would connect them with their friends through the most-distant message posts. He tells how the Rom teased and attracted and fended off the curiosity of outsiders. The dirty, half-naked children, pressing up against the unwary stranger and begging loudly and furiously, both collected the stranger's pennies and drove him into hasty retreat. The women, dressed outlandishly, clutching at the wrists of passers-by, played on fears and hopes by telling fortunes, an occupation reserved for their relations with the superstitious *Gaje* and never practiced among themselves. Or sometimes they would feign a violent cough, frightening the too-bold stranger with vague fears of infection. And their outrageous tales, whose embroideries and exaggerations masked mockery and contempt of *Gaje* beliefs, contributed to their public's fear and fascination. Yoors describes also the Gypsy "kings," those individualistic, somewhat deviant men who liked to strut and boast of their power before outsiders when in fact they had none within the band, whose men of true worth and dignity stayed safely out of reach, protected by the antics of these men of little consequence.

But it was the other life of the Gypsies, their inner life as a group, which the boy discovered day by day and over the years as he came to feel himself one of them and those closest to him guided him to an understanding of what he saw and heard and experienced. There was the strict sense of privacy, maintained by rules of courtesy among families living in continual full view of one another. There were the rules separating men and women, the complicated etiquette arising from their conception of woman's "uncleanness" that not only prevented women from coming too close to men and tainting their manhood, but also protected all women from molestation. There were the rules of cleanliness, foremost in the different uses of water but extending also to matters of health, such as hiding an infectious disease that might threaten the well-being of the whole group. Fear of ritual uncleanness, *marhine*, was a central sanction of their lives.

Order within the group was maintained by the ancient device of the council of elders, the *Kris*, which functioned as the collective will of the Rom but had no means of direct coercion to enforce its solemn decisions. It was respect for the *Kris* as an idea and the dignity of those who sat in judgment, combined with the power of the judges, the *krisatora*, to curse the wrongdoer, known or unknown, that was the real source of power.

On his travels Yoors lived through days of death and mourning, feasts and quarrels, hasty retreats into the safe wilderness and rare occasions of mighty celebration at inns whose owners were lured into providing all manner of luxuries, for which the Gypsies paid with sweeping liberality. He writes of weddings and the meetings of bands at which the older men arranged for the marriages of their sons and daughters, before which they were children and after which men and women.

A child when he joined the Lowara band, Jan was a young man when Pulika, under whose protection he lived, selected a bride for his adopted son. But at this moment Jan drew back, recognizing his arrival at a turning point. He struggled how to tell Pulika of his final unwillingness, and "with a profound sense of life and with the simplicity of those close to the earth, Pulika sensed my agony. It was this subtle receptiveness that led me to blurt out . . . what was troubling me. I closed my eyes instinctively as he reached swiftly forward. I did not know what to expect but all the same I prepared for a blow. At the same instant, and instead of this, Pulika clasped me in a forceful, conciliatory embrace, dissipating my anguish." As long ago his father had let the twelve-year-old boy go to the Gypsies, now, on the verge of manhood, another man released him to live in a wider world, giving him the freedom of two ways of life, thousands of years apart and yet united in his unique experience.

"Everything I talk about in this book," Yoors tells us, "I saw, I heard, I was part of. . . ." Like his father he became an artist, and his narrative has all the vividness, the delight in the concrete and the feeling for the design of the whole that is characteristic of the person who "sees" with all his senses. Trusting and trusted, he carries the conviction of respect and love for the Rom in all he writes of them. Reliving their journeyings to a thousand crossroads, he creates a portrait of a whole people.

But one can see another level of significance as well in this re-creation of the Gypsies. In the past the imagination of generations of children was fed by the contrast—representing a rift centuries old—between the settled, enclosed lives of the peoples of Europe, safe in their well-built houses and ordered towns, and the roaming existence of the strange, wild Gypsies who treated civilized countries as their inherited hunting grounds. Children secure in their comfortable homes dreamed of running away to the Gypsies, and harassed adults, hoping to keep the children within bounds, threatened them with tales of Gypsy kidnapings and the dangers of the road.

At the turning point between childhood and adolescence the Gypsies represented romance—not romantic love for an individual, but the enchantment of an unknown way of life, the mystery of the strange. And adults, settled into the reality of daily life, vented their discontent upon the Gypsies—and yet at some moments captured the nostalgia of old dreams in the words of ballads, in the picture of the lady who deserted her lord not for a lover but to go off with a Gypsy band.

A romantic book about Gypsies, given to me when I was a small child, was one of the first things that made me think about people who were very different from any I knew, even from the Italian families my mother, a sociologist, was studying. But the first Gypsy encampment I saw was in Georgia during World War II. These Gypsies were traveling not in gay carts but in automobiles, and like everyone else, they were faced with the problems of gas rationing. The women were dressed in long satin dresses, but they were barefoot and were cooking a meal over open campfires. The chief, who styled himself a king, proudly showed us a letter from President Roosevelt, to whom he had written offering to have his people settle down for the duration while the men went off to war.

What most impressed me was the way in which these Gypsies, like Gypsies the world over, were able to meet the great of the world on an equal footing. Living their separate existence, they have been spared the experience of social stratification, as a result of which some men are regarded, and regard themselves, as less worthy of every kind of consideration. Among the Gypsies, men were respected in terms of their personal character and their experience, but each was unequivocally a man.

Today we are experiencing a strange kind of reversal as slowly, reluctantly, the nomadic Gypsies are settling down and young people the world over are stirring, setting out to discover for themselves ways of life far removed from the narrow confines of their too-comfortable, well-organized, perhaps overorganized, lives. They are going into the Peace Corps, into Vista, overseas with the Experiment in International Living, overseas on journeys to a thousand crossroads meetings with strangers, their other selves, who are recognizably speakers of the same language of questioning and discovery.

In the 1930's Jan Yoors was a precursor of today's young people as he lived out in reality the old dream of running away to find another life. Among the Gypsies, living in their bands, he touched on the most distant past of human nomadism. But his most-fortunate freedom to choose, his life in two worlds, also links him to the future that is the present of a new generation.

And for this generation too there is the romance of discovery of a whole world that is theirs both as wandering strangers and as the heritors of all the human tradition.

VI

THE
MEASURE
OF FREEDOM
New Guinea Revisited

Letter from Peri—Manus, I

FEBRUARY, 1965

A few minutes ago I stood at the edge of the sea, looking out toward the reef where twenty canoes, black silhouettes against the pale dawn sky, are out fishing. Very soon the canoes, with their crews of people of all ages, will begin to come in with a catch of fish for early-morning breakfast. Half a mile away, rising above the water of the salt lagoon, a cluster of trees marks the site where in the old days the people of Peri village lived in houses set high on stilts. Out on the water, away from the shore, they were safe from sudden attacks by the land people and were close to their all-important fishing grounds. That was where I also lived—in a Manus house with a high, thatched roof and a slatted floor through which small objects fell into the water—when I first studied the Manus people, in 1928.

This is my third field trip to Manus. On my first trip I studied the children; and now, thirty-six years later, these children are middle-aged. In 1928 I went to study the Manus because they had preserved their old, savage ways and had not yet taken on the ideas and the religion of the West. Twenty-five years later, in 1953, I returned to find out how much they had changed over the lifetime of a generation and what had become of them as they changed. And now, eleven years later, I have come back a third time to follow their racing course toward modernization.

Pokanau, the oldest and still one of the strongest men in Peri, stood beside me on the shore. He may be as old as seventy, but he does not know his exact age. Until 1946 nobody counted ages. As a boy, Pokanau had been reared by a wise old grandfather, and—in the days before the Australian government forbade warfare—he had been a special protégé of the last fierce old war leader. Today he is the best-informed man of all his village. In answer to every question about the distant past, people say: "Ask Pokanau!" And Pokanau himself is very anxious that all he knows be taken down on the tape recorder. He realizes that soon there will be no one who knows the old war songs and the tales of his people's wanderings as they spread out and built one village after another in the wide seas off the south coast of Great Admiralty Island. When I returned to Peri in 1953 he was already the senior man of any importance in the village. Now, on my third visit, he complained that his sight was failing, although he could still see and name the faint, distant stars. But when the old-age glasses came and he tried them, he found that instead of improving his sight, they made things look different. So he threw the glasses away—and stopped complaining that he was old. Recently he asked me for the present of an airplane trip to visit an island he has never seen, where one of his relatives is teaching school.

Formerly Manus men died young. In 1928 only one man in the village had lived long enough to witness the birth of his son's first child. Pokanau has lived to see his daughter's daughter give birth to twins—his great-grandchildren. However, he is alone; all his contemporaries among the men of Peri have died. He says they sat too much by the fire and dried out like the fish that are smoked for sale in the market. He himself has never flinched from going bare-skinned into the chilliest wind.

Old Pokanau was born a savage, knowing only the savage fighting world of the tiny archipelago of the Admiralty Islands, off the northeast coast of New Guinea. When he was a boy, before World War I, the Admiralty Islands were a German possession, but the Germans had not stopped intertribal fighting. People still went to market with obsidian-bladed daggers hidden in their elaborately dressed hair, alert to the ever-present danger of being ambushed by the land people with whom the Manus traded their fish for taros, yams, sago and coconuts. In his own lifetime Pokanau saw his people move from a world of small warring groups—a kind of world that would have been familiar to our own European ancestors thousands of years ago—into a present in which his people listen to the morning news broadcast over the radio much as we do, with accounts of the

Olympic games, foreign election campaigns, proceedings at the United Nations.

Immediately after World War II, in 1946, the Manus people took their fate into their own hands. Well ahead of the Australian government's plans for them, they overhauled their old customs and discarded everything they felt was out of key with the modern world. Basing their thinking on ideas they had gained by watching German missionaries, isolated Australian government officials, and the host of Americans—more than a million—who went through Manus when it was a World War II installation, they organized an entirely new way of life. They moved to the land and built new villages, neatly set out in streets, with modern houses all the same size. In keeping with their new understanding of the world, they also set up very simple versions of modern institutions—for example, a court and a bank.

Talking with Pokanau about the past, I think also about my own life. When I was a child in Pennsylvania, we made butter from big pans of milk set in a cold stone cellar, we studied by oil lamps and we drove to school in a horse and buggy. I remember the wild excitement when someone made a trip in a balloon that ascended from our local fairground. Americans as old as Pokanau have lived through vast changes, but Pokanau himself has spanned thousands of years of man's history.

When I returned to Peri in 1953 on my second visit, twenty-five years after the first trip, the young people who had been born in the intervening years eyed me appraisingly and the old women wept over the photographs I brought back of their friends and relatives who had died. Now, on my third visit, the old women wept over me because we were all old. Few of the women are more than sixty years old; but for these people, born savages, soaked by rains and buffeted by winds as they fish and travel in canoes, sixty is a great old age. Sitting and talking with these old women, I realize keenly how much our own picture of old age has changed—no sunken cheeks and toothless jaws, no squinting effort to see close work with aging eyes, no tired coughing through long, restless nights. This is the fate of people who have survived without medical care, with only magic and the guardian ghosts of their fathers to help them through a perilous childhood.

In 1928 these were the young married women. Their heads were shaved to indicate their married state; their ear lobes were distended and weighted down with ornaments made of dogs' teeth and shells; and they wore two small aprons, one in front and one in back, made of shredded grass. Like their mothers and grandmothers before them, they had learned to support their men's war dances, learned how to stand with a spear in each hand while their husbands and brothers danced.

In their lifetime they exchanged their grass skirts first for cloth wrap-around skirts and then for shapeless cloth garments. Now I see them walking through the village dressed in up-to-date, well-fitted cotton frocks. Their ear lobes are bare; ear ornaments of all kinds belong to the discarded, savage past. The old tattoo marks have faded; occasional old scarifications are almost obliterated. These old women are not merely witnesses to change. They have taken full part in their people's move from savagery into the modern world.

After World War II, when the Manus moved ashore and rebuilt their lagoon village on dry land, the oldest men and women as well as the youngest entered into the changing situation. And nowadays the very people who once quarreled about the sale of war prisoners to cannibal neighboring tribes argue about what shall be done with the sixteen dollars left over from the purchase of school uniforms for the village children.

Children in Peri village still leap and gambol at the edge of the sea and dive into the warm waters of the lagoon and run sure-footed up the bent trunk of a coconut palm. In the morning when they start off for school, carrying their school clothes, they are scantily clad, and they frolic in the water as they run along the beach. But once they have arrived in school they will learn about the whole wide world—how the Japanese cook on charcoal, what a lion looks like and an elephant—and their lesson on the meaning of time will end with a discussion of how a stop watch is used to time the races in the Olympic games that are taking place far away.

Eleven years ago there were no schools in the south-coast villages. But during World War II a young Manus villager had been given about two years' schooling by an itinerant chaplain. Somehow out of this experience he also came to understand the idea of a school. Then when the Peri people went to work to make their village modern, he set up a kind of shadow school in preparation for the "real" school that was to come. The children were sorted by size. They marched into the largest building in the village, where they sat down on benches; and their teacher, preparing the way for the real teacher who was to come, taught them to recognize letters and numbers. Today Dritakow, one of the boys who attended this first, preliminary school (but who, in fact, spent most of his time out fishing), has been trained to teach the kindergarten children. Ten years ago a real teacher was sent to the neighboring village, and the Peri children poured across the narrow shallows to the mainland to attend his school. Dritakow was one of the brightest of these children; given a real start, he skipped ahead. Now he teaches the six-year-olds about weights and measures and, during recess, how to play farmer in the dell. Just now the children are also practicing to sing "The Twelve Days of Christmas" for Carols by Candlelight. For last year Peri village got its own Australian teacher, a man who before he became a teacher had been an actor and a producer, and for a time the proto-col secretary of an Australian diplomat. He will tape-record his pupils' singing. If they do well enough, the program will be broadcast from a radio station to cheer Australian mainlanders over the progress that is being made in their Trust Territory and to encourage children in other parts of New Guinea to learn to sing European songs.

Thirty-three young people are away from Peri village. Some of them are already teachers; others are in training to become teachers or nurses in technical schools in Rabaul, Port Moresby and Lae. One is in a preparatory school in Australia. Several will soon be ready to take college entrance examinations. Parents who in their own child-hood never expected to sail out of sight of land and knew almost nothing about the world outside their archipelago now encourage their children to go away to school—a six-hour airplane trip—and are proud of their progress.

For they feel—and they are right—that they themselves prepared for this new world in which education, medical care and self-govern-ment are normal expectations. They organized the first school so that the children's minds would be clear—so that they would be ready to learn—when a real school came. They set aside a house as a hospital before the first midwife was trained. They began to tax themselves, and set the money aside as savings for community expenditures, at a time when there was no bank and before the government was ready to authorize elections for a local council. In the revolutionary period that began in 1946, the oldest grandmothers went along with the changes. They removed the dogs' teeth earrings from their ears and let their shaved hair grow. They learned, with everyone else, to sit in orderly meetings and to discuss differences of opinion about the next steps, instead of screaming at each other and threatening physical violence when they disagreed. In Manus the grandparents and the parents changed together; there was no real break between the living generations. And as the children went to school, older men also learned to write—in pidgin English, a lingua franca made up of English words set in their own Melanesian grammar.

And now old Pokanau has asked for an airplane trip as a present. Yet once, for him as for his ancestors, a canoe voyage of perhaps twenty miles was so dangerous that people wept when a canoe set out to sea across the reef and they wept again to see the returning canoe safely beached with all its crew alive.

But the Peri school children are learning English. For a knowledge of English will make it possible for the two million people of Papua—New Guinea, who speak more than five hundred different languages, to talk with one another (and with the people who come to the Territory) and work together toward the independence they have been promised.

When John Glenn flew over Australia and the people of Perth all turned on their lights as a greeting to him, the children in Peri village were listening to the broadcast—part of the same world Americans belong to. Because their parents and grandparents and all their neighbors in the village have taken part in the transformation of life in Manus, the children can say, "I would like to fly in a sputnik" (using "sputnik" to mean "satellite"), and describe the world that would be visible from an orbiting capsule, and at the same time realize and express their love for their village world.

Studying a people like the Manus gives me a sense of what we and our own children are capable of accomplishing. In our own lifetime—even in the lifetime of the youngest parents in America—the world we were born into has been transformed as fast and almost as unbelievably as the Manus world. Jet planes, hydrogen bombs, Telstar and other communications satellites, and new cures for ancient ills have created a new present and a new future. In this new world all children—whether they are growing up in the cities of America or in the villages of the Territory of Papua and New Guinea—are being drawn into a unique relationship to one another as they watch the satellites that flash in their orbits around the globe.

In Peri village, people are planning to build a special council house where the children can also go to do their homework undisturbed. Next year perhaps an experimental class will be formed to study the "new mathematics." Far away in the United States, parents by the thousands are attending school at night to learn the same "new mathematics" that their children are studying in the daytime and that Manus children may study very soon.

It is good to stand here at the door of my house in Peri village, talking with the men and women I have known so long. They say, as a matter of course, "But you remember *him!* He was one of the boat crew who took us from Balawan to Lou." They do not doubt that anyone can remember an event, such as this trip between two islands, that took place as long ago as 1928. In spite of all the changes that have taken place, these memories, sharp and clear, unite two worlds that are literally thirty-six years and figuratively thousands of years apart. Here in Peri, talking and listening, where a whole people have moved without losing their sense of continuity, I realize again how important it is to recognize both our common human capacity for change and for creating continuity in change.

Letter from Peri—Manus, II

I am writing in the little house made of rough wood and sago-palm thatch that was built for me by the people of Peri village. The wind brings the sound of waves breaking on the reef, but my house, its back to the sea, looks out on the great square where the public life of the village takes place. At the opposite end of the square is the meetinghouse, and ranged along the sides are the houses of eminent men. Everything is new and paint sparkles on the houses. The handsomest ones are built of corrugated iron; the others are built of traditional materials, with decorative patterns woven into the bamboo.

This is the fourth version of Peri that I have lived in over the last thirty-seven years. The first was the primitive village. When I first came to study the Manus, they were an almost landless sea people and all the houses of Peri were built on stilts in the shallow sea. When I returned twenty-five years later, in 1953, the Manus had moved ashore and the new Peri, located on a small strip of marshy land, was their first attempt to build a "modern" village, designed in accordance with their notions of an American town. By 1964, when I came back on a third field trip, this village had degenerated into a kind of slum, noisy, dilapidated, cramped and overcrowded, because the people of a neighboring village had moved in so that their children too could go to school. Now, a year later, an entirely new village has been built on a spacious tract of land bought with the people's own savings, and here Peri villagers, for so long accustomed only to sea and sand, are planting flowers and vegetables.

For two months everything went along quietly, but now the whole village is humming with activity. Last-minute preparations are in progress for a tremendous celebration at which Peri will entertain some two thousand members of the Paliau movement—all the people who, under the leadership of Paliau Moluat, have taken part in the strenuous and extraordinary effort to create a new way of life. It is the holiday season, and every day more of the adolescents who have been away at school and the young people who have become teachers in faraway parts of New Guinea are returning home to visit their families, see the new village and join in the festivities. Some families have built special rooms for the visitors. In one house there is a real room in which bed, chair and bench, all made by hand, are arranged to make a perfect setting for a schoolboy—the bed neatly made, pictures of the Beatles on the wall, schoolbooks on the table and a schoolbag hung in the window. In another house a few books piled on a suitcase in one corner of a barnlike room are all that signal the return of a school child. But whatever arrangements families have managed to make, the village is alive with delight in the visitors.

The children have come home from modern schools. But some of the young teachers have been working all alone in small bush schools among alien peoples only a few years removed from cannibalism and head-hunting. So the tales circulating in the village are extremely varied. There are descriptions of boarding-school life, stories of examinations and of prizes won in scholarship or sports. But there are also stories about the extraordinary customs of the people in the interior of New Guinea. Listening, I ask myself which is harder for the people of Peri to assimilate and understand—a savage way of life, which in many ways resembles that of their own great-grandfathers but which now has been so enthusiastically abandoned; or the new way of life the Manus have adopted, which belongs to the modern world of the planes that fly overhead and the daily news on the radio. Nowadays this may include news of the Manus themselves. Yesterday morning a newscaster announced: "At the first meeting of the new council in Manus, Mr. Paliau Moluat, member of the House of Assembly, was elected president."

I have come back to Peri on this, my fourth trip to Manus, to witness and record the end of an epoch. The new forms of local self-government, supported by an insistent and originally rebellious leadership, all are legalized. Paliau, the head of what the government once regarded as a subversive movement, now holds elective office and is immersed in work that will shape the future of the Territory of Papua—New Guinea. On a small scale this handful of people living on the coast of an isolated archipelago have enacted the whole drama of moving from the narrow independence of a little warring tribe to participation in the development of an emerging nation.

During the last two months I have been aware of all the different stages of change, as they can be seen simultaneously. On weekdays I see men and women passing by, stripped bare to the waist and holding pandanus hoods over their heads to keep off the rain. On holidays some of the younger women dress in fashionable shifts, bright with splashed flower designs. The oldest men and women, people I have known since 1928, were born into a completely primitive world, ruled over by ghosts, dominated by the fear of disease and death and endlessly preoccupied by the grinding work entailed in meeting their obligations and making the exchanges of shell money and dogs' teeth for oil and turtles, grass skirts and pots. The middle-aged grew up in the period when warfare was ending; as young men they still practiced throwing and dodging the spears they would never use as weapons of war. The next-younger group, in whose childhood the first Christian mission came, lived through the Japanese occupation and reached manhood when the people of the whole south coast were uniting in a small, decisive social revolution. And the youngest group, adolescents and children, are growing up in a world of school and clinic talk. Before them lies the prospect of career choice and the establishment of a new university, the University of Papua—New Guinea, in Port Moresby. These are the first-comers to a new epoch.

Yet, in spite of everything, the Manus have preserved their identity as a people and their integrity as individuals. The shy little boys I knew in the past have grown up into shy, quiet men. The boastfully brash still are brash. The alert-minded are keen and aware. It is as if the changes from savagery to civilization were new colors that had been laid on over the hard, clear outlines of their distinct personalities. At the same time, where once the Manus feared and plotted war, they now hear only echoes of distant battlefields in places of which formerly they were totally unaware. Where once they suffered hunger when storms kept the fishermen at home, they now can buy food for money in the village shops. Where once flight to live precariously among strangers was the outcome of a quarrel, now it is proud ambition that takes the Manus abroad.

One outcome of the chance that brought me to their village to do field work in 1928 is that their history has been chronicled. Unlike most simpler peoples of the world, the Manus can bridge past and present. Here in my house I hang up photographs of all the "big-fellow men belong before," who would otherwise be no more than half-remembered names. Seen from the vantage point of the present, pictures taken ten years ago and thirty-seven years ago have a continuity that overcomes strangeness. Instead of being ashamed of the life that has been abandoned, young people can be proud of an ancestral mode of life that is being preserved for others to know about and is mentioned in speeches made by visitors from the United Nations. Then old pride and new pride merge and the old men, nodding agreement, say: "After all, the Manus people started in Peri."

Each day I go about the ordinary business of field work. I accept the presents of fresh fish and accede to small requests for tobacco, matches, a postage stamp or perhaps four thumbtacks. Whatever I am working at, I listen to the sounds of the village, ready to go quickly to the scene of wailing or shouting or some child's uncharacteristic cry. As I type notes I also watch the passers-by to catch the one person who can answer a question, such as: "Is it really true that the same two women first married Talikat and then later married Ponowan?" Or word comes that two turtles, necessary for the coming feast, have been brought in, and I hurriedly take my camera out of its vacuum case and rush to record the event.

At the same time I think about field work itself. For an anthropologist's life is keyed to field work. Even at home, occupied with other activities, writing up field notes and preparing for the next field trip keeps your mind focused on this aspect of your life. In the past, actual field work has meant living with and studying a primitive people in some remote part of the world. The remoteness has been inevitable, for the peoples anthropologists have studied were primitive because they lived far from the centers of civilization—in the tropics or in the Arctic, in a mountain fastness or on an isolated atoll. Remoteness also has set the style of field work. Cut off from everything else, your attention is wholly concentrated on the lives of the people you are working with, and the effort draws on all your capacities, strength and experience. Now, as the most remote places become known, the conditions of field work are changing. But the need to see and respond as a whole does not change.

I am especially aware of the conditions of fieldwork on this trip because for the first time since my original field trip to Samoa forty years ago I am working alone, without any collaborators in the same or a nearby village. This and the fact that I am using only one camera, a notebook and a pencil—instead of all the complex paraphernalia of the modern field team—throws me back to the very core of field work: one person, all alone, face-to-face with a whole community. Equipped principally with a way of looking at things, the fieldworker is expected somehow to seize on all the essentials of a strange way of life and to bring back a record that will make this comprehensible as a whole to others who very likely never will see this people in their living reality. The role of the fieldworker and the recognition that every people has a culture, the smallest part of which is significant and indicative of the whole, go together. Once the two were matched, our field work helped us to learn more about culture and to train a new generation of anthropologists to make better field studies.

Nevertheless, as I sit here with the light of my pressure lamp casting long shadows on the dark, quiet square, wondering what may happen in the next few hours, I also reflect that field work is one of the most extraordinary tasks we set for young people. Even today it means a special kind of solitude among a people whose every word and gesture is, initially, unexpected and perhaps unintelligible. But beyond this, the fieldworker is required to do consciously something that the young child, filled with boundless energy and curiosity, does without conscious purpose—that is, learn about a whole world. But whereas the child learns as part of growing up and becomes what he learns, the anthropologist must learn the culture without embodying it, in order to become its accurate chronicler.

Whether one learns to receive a gift in both hands or with the right hand only, to touch the gift to one's forehead or to refuse it three times before accepting it, the task is always a double one. One must learn to do something correctly and not to become absorbed in the doing. One must learn what makes people angry but one must not feel insulted oneself. One must live all day in a maze of relationships without being caught in the maze. And above all, one must wait for events to reveal much that must be learned. A storm, an earthquake, a fire, a famine—these are extraordinary conditions that sharply reveal certain aspects of a people's conceptions of life and the universe. But the daily and the recurrent events that subtly shape people's lives are the ones on which the anthropologist must concentrate without being able to foresee what he can learn from them or when any particular event may occur. Equipped as well as possible with his growing knowledge of names and relationships, his experience of expectations and probable outcomes, the fieldworker records, learns—and waits. But it is always an active waiting, a readiness in which all his senses are alert to whatever may happen, expected or unexpected, in the next five minutes—or in an hour, a week, a month from now. The anthropological fieldworker must take a whole community, with all its transmitted tradition, into his mind and, to the extent that he is a whole person, see it whole.

And then my mind turns back to Manus. What is happening here is a kind of paradigm of something that is happening all over the world: grandparents and parents settle for the parts they themselves can play and what must be left to the comprehension of the children. The Manus have taken a direction no one could have foreseen thirty-seven years ago. Yet in the midst of change they are recognizably themselves. Field work provides us with a record of the experiments mankind has made in creating and handing on tradition. Over time it also provides a record of what men can do and become.

Filming Peri Village–Manus, III

NOVEMBER, 1968

More than a year has passed since the spring afternoon when I agreed to let a National Educational Television team come with me to Manus to make a film of the people of Peri village. I had no clear idea, then, how many long months of work lay ahead—months of planning and changing plans, tracing lost camera equipment, hoping for new film to arrive; days of impatient waiting and hours of harried activity, in the daytime under the torrid sun and at night under hot, brilliant lights; shifting moods of excitement and fatigue; and all the unexpected opportunities, dashed hopes and moments of triumph that are part of filming events as they happen in people's lives.

But now at last I can scrap the conditional phrase "barring accident. . . ." We have a film, which NET is calling "Margaret Mead's New Guinea Journal" and soon will telecast all across the United States. I have seen the film, but I wonder whether even now Craig Gilbert, whose idea it was and who produced and directed it, and Ellen Giffard, who became an expert on Manus in the course of editing it, believe that the transformation from idea to reality has been accomplished.

The original plan took shape quickly. Craig, an executive producer for NET, wanted to make a film with me in the field, working with a people I had studied. We decided on the Manus, who had been guided by a remarkable leader, Paliau, out of the Stone Age into the modern world.

There were many reasons for this choice. Our anthropological records on the Manus go back forty years, to 1928, when their traditional way of life was still virtually intact. I also had worked with them recently, so I knew which of my old friends were still living, what their state of mind was and how they were likely to respond to the exigencies of film making. Above all, I was sure that the people of Peri would be able to cope with the presence of the four-man team: Craig himself, two cameramen and a sound man. Over the years two generations of Peri villagers had learned to trust anthropologists and to co-operate delightedly in the kinds of enterprises that gave them access to some new aspect of modern living. The teen-aged boys who had washed our films in 1928, with one of them slapping mosquitoes so that the others would not drop the precious negatives, were now the established leaders of the community.

The plan was feasible. But I could not discount the risks for everyone. Anthropologists are used to certain kinds of risks—an earthquake, an epidemic, the loss of one's precious equipment, cannot be foreseen. Perhaps no major event will take place; one must be content with recording the daily round. There are risks also in taking anyone at all into a small native village with its precariously balanced well-being. So I have only rarely taken someone to the field with me to do a special piece of research or to take photographs, and then only someone I knew well.

This was to be an entirely different venture. I had to agree, here in New York City, to have the whole team come to New Guinea without knowing the men or how they themselves envisaged working in a native village.

At the same time, Craig Gilbert would be committing a year of his life to making the film. He had to trust that I would guide him to what he wanted to film, find the people, set up the arrangements and mediate between him and the village. He had to hope that I wouldn't fall ill or break an ankle. He had to believe I would stand by later during the long months of turning the raw footage into a finished film. How could he be certain I would accept his direction? How could he gauge my willingness to sit by while he and Ellen Giffard cut and edited scenes I valued most? Or my ability to narrate each new version "as if you were saying this for the first time"?

In those early days, Craig sat in my office trying to map out a program in terms of time and travel, equipment and funds and feet of film. In a film made by an anthropologist for the record, everything counts—the big events, the quiet sequences of a mother playing with her child or a group of men fashioning a new canoe. But a film designed for an audience, Craig pointed out, has to have a focus, a point of view, a sense of pace. I understood his dilemma. But I had to warn him against making specific plans for the actual film. There simply is no way of writing a script for ongoing life. One can move only with events.

Craig devoured all the books about Manus, my *Growing Up in New Guinea* and Reo Fortune's *Manus Religion*, which described life in Peri in 1928, when warfare had just been abolished and the Manus still lived in houses set on high posts in the lagoon. Then he read Theodore Schwartz's *The Paliau Movement in the Admiralty Islands, 1946–1954* and my *New Lives for Old*, accounts of the first re-study, in 1953–1954, when we learned how the Manus had made their tremendous leap into the modern world.

Craig also read my notes and letters about later visits in 1964 and 1965–66. As he read, his ideas expanded. He wanted to include the past as well as the present—today's young people enjoying their freedom contrasted with young girls of the past, dressed for their marriage feasts, weighted down with shell money and dogs'-teeth ornaments. He wanted to picture Pokanau, the oldest man in Peri, as we knew him in 1928 and now. He wanted to photograph Paliau in the House of Assembly. He wanted to film the fishermen, a birth, a death, the school children. . . .

All the old still photographs—and, from 1953 on, films—were there to draw upon. But I could promise nothing for the present. The House of Assembly might not be in session and Paliau might not be a candidate in the coming election. When I left Peri in 1953 Pokanau said in farewell, "You are like an old turtle going out to sea to die." John Kilepak comforted me: "He's really talking about himself." Now Pokanau was very old and might die before we reached Manus. Births and deaths cannot be arranged for, nor can one foresee who will take part in the events that do happen.

Finally the day came when I met the whole team in Port Moresby, on the southwest coast of New Guinea—cameraman Richard Leiterman, a dark giant of a man, bored with routine and nourished by the impossible, such as filming from a pitching outrigger canoe in the pouring rain; Christian Wangler, the sound man, blond, friendly and impulsive, the one who came to know the Peri children best; and Henri Fiks, the slight and lively French photographer. They had assembled from other assignments in different parts of the world, and now, shaking off official formalities, they were eager to get started. In Peri they would look like invaders from outer space, stripped bare except for the shortest shorts, Richard and Henri brown and Chris fiery red, weighted down by the great cameras, tape recorders and other equipment hanging from many straps around their necks.

Our first joint effort, in Port Moresby, was the filming of a lecture I gave to the students at the new University of Papua—New Guinea. In the audience was Niandros, a young girl who was the first Peri student at the university. The university holidays were beginning, and we invited Niandros to come with us to visit her family in the village.

The pattern of our work, however, was set in Lorengau, capital of the island of Manus, off the New Guinea coast. Craig wanted to film my arrival in Peri. Since I could arrive only once, talk with the people assembled to greet me only once and mourn only once with the old women as they told me who had died, everything had to go off perfectly. For the sun to be right, we would have to leave Lorengau soon after dawn. And, of course, it must not rain—the sun must shine on our arrival.

We assembled on time. Our gear already had been loaded onto a schooner. If it arrived safely, we would have food and something to sleep on that night; otherwise, not. Craig planned that I would cross in one outrigger canoe with Niandros, with Chris aboard to record our conversation. I hoped there would be wind enough to fill the sails, for the outboard motor would drown out our talk. Craig, Richard and Henri intended to sail alongside in the larger outrigger to photograph us. Wind enough, I hoped again—but not too much. I thought about the high winds that sometimes rise suddenly on the open sea. They could so easily swamp our heavily laden canoes.

Quickly we set sail. As it turned out, the sea was dangerously high, but we made the crossing and maneuvered the reef safely and arrived in Peri in sunshine, just twenty minutes ahead of a cloudburst that sent us rushing pell-mell to the safety of my waiting house. The first crisis had been met.

I settled into my house, which had been built for me by the people of Peri when I last visited, in 1965–66. The team members spread out their equipment in the large house the village turned over to them. As my assistant I had Lomot, a daughter of John Kilepak, whose family Craig had decided to focus on. Now for answers to questions.

How was old Pokanau? He was well but almost blind, and seldom ventured from his house. Were new babies expected? Several babies had been born the previous month; there was now just one pregnant woman. How pregnant? No one knew. What were our chances of filming a big catch of fish? The fish, which come in great numbers once a month, had just come—we'd have to trust to luck.

Then the news came that Lomot's grandmother was dying in Bunai, the next village. Crossing to Bunai by canoe, we found her, a very old woman, lying in her tiny house set on posts out over the lagoon. She was intermittently delirious. Her sons and grandchildren were gathered around, and now Lomot wept and pleaded with her grandmother to speak to her. The crew filmed the scene from the doorway. Finally the old woman rallied, joked mildly and began to fuss with the fire.

Her relatives looked on in awe, as if she had returned from the dead. They gave her food and tried to persuade her to sleep. They concluded that she wouldn't die that night, and everyone, exhausted by the emotions of a seven-hour vigil, wanted to rest. But when I suggested that we leave, Craig objected. Food and sleep meant nothing to him and his crew. I knew there was no telling when the old woman might die—the next day, or five days or five months hence. At midnight Craig gave in, but he left behind the lamp and the generator equipment.

When Lomot's grandmother did die, two days later, the people carefully moved our equipment at the same time that they carried her body to the big house arranged for the last rites. The crew filmed everything—the hours of mourning; people bringing gifts of food, money and clothing; her sons making the coffin; the funeral procession and the ceremony at the grave, where the children threw in flowers and said good-by as the Christian mission had taught the

Manus to do long ago. And the filming was not felt as an intrusion, for later one of the grandsons said to me, "Without the film no one could ever see my grandmother any more. Now she will live on for us."

We did not know when—if at all—we might expect a birth, but I decided that we had better inspect the birth house, out over the water. Although the village itself is now on land, the Manus have continued to build houses for the old, for the sick and for women in childbirth over the lagoon, where the shifting tides quickly carry away rubbish. As we made our way out over the precarious bridge, a rotting timber gave way; Craig might have broken a leg had he not jumped clear. We went on.

Fortunately the little house had two rooms, now uninhabited. I stipulated that the crew stay in one room while the birth, when it happened, went on in the other. I was not going to jeopardize the safety of the mother or the baby by bringing in strange men, brilliant lights and noisy machines at the moment of birth. Craig saw the point. Back on shore, when he suggested that the men repair the bridge, they said, "Tomorrow." It was Sunday, and this weekly day of rest is one of the modern things the Manus treasure. When they were pagans there were no holidays. So they insisted that no baby was ready to be born. Tomorrow would be time enough.

They were wrong. At ten o'clock that night Agnes, the acting midwife, came up on my veranda to tell me she had just taken a woman in labor to the birth house. Not the woman we knew about, but a different one, married in from another village, who hadn't been counted. The team was already in bed, worn out by the heat and the work of the day. When I routed out Craig, he called out, as he did in so many emergencies, "You're kidding!"

Hastily I collected the things I needed—tobacco and betel nut for the watching women, a lamp, a flashlight, matches, pencil and paper. Lomot came with me to the birth house, where we found the woman in labor placidly surveying the scene. I sat down, reflecting how lucky we were that Agnes was the midwife. In 1953 the anthropologist Theodore Schwartz had saved the lives of her newborn twins, whom he had filmed regularly for months afterward. So Agnes believed that films were good.

The team set up its equipment, bright lights and all, in the adjacent room. They took some pictures of the standing woman and the preparations laid out on the floor. I told them, "That is all for now." Time passed and their patience stretched thin. Couldn't they take just one more shot? I refused. The woman in labor moaned occasionally. Craig renewed his demand. Ought I be adamant? I asked Agnes and the other women for their opinion. Was it safe? They nodded.

The crew came in, looming incredibly tall above the seated women. The lights blazed and went out. They withdrew, only slightly mollified. Fortunately it was an easy birth. As soon as the baby was breathing well and the mother had relaxed, filming started again, and no one minded.

Now I began to feel more optimistic. I said, "We have two of the events you most wanted, either of which would make the film." But Craig's imagination was soaring. The more we had, the more he wanted. With every good sequence, his plans expanded. Now he wanted to film Paliau's return from the House of Assembly. He wanted to film an actual council meeting in Lorengau, a visit by Paliau to the village. Everything was to be filmed just as it happened, and each event had to happen with the right light at the right time. I could only hope. . . .

A crisis had been building up in the village. Day after day I had listened to the rising strains of anger as the conflict sharpened between a man named Peranis, the young elected head of the village, and the established leaders, the older men.

The explicit cause of the quarrel was the house Peranis was building on the village square. When the plots in the new village had been assigned in 1965 he was away, and he had returned to run for office with no house of his own. If he won, people said, he would build a big house, worthy of his fierce old grandfather, the biggest man in Peri two generations ago.

The established leaders had not expected this young man to be elected. When he was, they refused to assign him a dignified and appropriate place for his house. So Peranis, a proud and passionate man, defied them by beginning to build on the village square, which had been carefully designed as a symbol of the corporate strength of the community. When the village objected, Peranis in a rage would begin to dismantle the house. Then the village relented, and he would begin to build it up again. When we came, the skeleton of the house was standing there, an ugly blemish and a threat to village unity.

The underlying quarrel was not, of course, about this house but about the handing on of authority, a problem for which every society must have a solution so that each younger generation can move toward mature responsibility. Could the Establishment see this? One day while Peranis was away I sat down with the older men, who had been the carefree little boys of 1928, the courageous revolutionaries of the 1940's, and since the 1950's the secure leaders of the new way of life. I tried to help them find a way out of the impasse. Perhaps it would be a good idea to build a special house for the head of the village—like the White House or No. 10 Downing Street. They prophesied that Peranis would not agree.

When Peranis returned and heard the village gossip, he fell into a sudden, furious rage, as I had known he would. Standing in the square as the people came out of church, he harangued them and threatened to leave the village forever. This was the critical moment. The old leaders, again as I had thought they would, gave in and decided to help Peranis build his house on a good piece of land. Peranis, pacified, agreed to the plan. And I agreed to help with the housebuilding feast he would have to give. It would also mark my farewell to Peri.

This was a climax for the film that none of us could have planned. The team filmed the house moving and the feast, a piece of visual political behavior and a triumph for everyone. The elders were able to enforce, without rancor and almost with a feeling of benevolence, the will of the new kind of responsible community on someone whose anger and touchy pride recalled to them what a big man had been in the past. And Peranis, knowing he was winning the longer-term victory, could feast them for their present triumph. I too was re-assured. Now I could leave the village with a sense that the Manus were building a firm bridge from past to future.

The completion of the filming is, of course, only half the process of making a film, whose quality, like that of a painting or a poem, one knows only when the whole task is done. When I left the village ahead of the team, I knew that at no point had Craig or Richard or Chris or Henri injured the delicate fabric of my relationship to Peri or of the villagers' relationship to one another and to the modern world. And seeing the finished film now, I know that at no point was truth sacrificed to expediency or any sequence falsified. The true hazards of this kind of co-operative venture in portraying a way of life are not, in the end, the accidents or the physical and technical difficulties. These can be overcome. It is more deeply human flaws, failures of trust and integrity, empathy and insight, that cannot be remedied. For bound up with skill and experience, these are the qualities that give authenticity to a work of art.

Letter from Tambunam—Iatmul, I

✹✿✹

At last, on an early morning in June, 1967, I was on my way up the Sepik River, in New Guinea. More than four years had gone into the planning of this trip; and now, in a small speedboat, we raced up the seventy-mile stretch of river on the final stage of the trip, from the government station at Angoram to the village of Tambunam. The sun was just beginning to dissolve the banks of mist; on both shores the flat land stretched back, green and gold, as far as the eye could see. Now we looked upon a new garden, with spirals of yam leaves climbing slender poles; now on a long bank of elephant grass, silver plumes bending to the breeze; now on a white heron, floating down to a dark beach. And on the river itself floating islands of grass, torn loose upriver, moved swiftly downstream with the current. The speedboat swerved around them, leaving a wide wake in the smooth brown water. Once we startled a crocodile—or was it only a waterlogged tree?

This was my first trip up the Sepik since 1938, when I had spent eight months living in Tambunam. This time I would stay for only a month, but with me was another anthropologist, Rhoda Metraux, who would remain for nearly a year, to take up again the study of the village people. What had changed in Tambunam since I had seen it last, and what had remained the same?

Twenty-nine years is a long time, especially in the lives of a people who die young. Months earlier I had sent a list of the men and women I had known best, and from the report sent back I knew that very many of them were dead. I knew also that the Japanese had been on

the river during World War II, and that since the war, many men
were engaged in crocodile-hunting for the trade. There was a mission
church in Timbunke, upriver, in 1938; after the war a church and
then a school were established in Tambunam. That would mean that
the old, ceremonial life would be gone. But I knew little else now of
the village and its people.

I thought about Tambunam as it had been, the proudest and handsomest village on the river, with great houses sixty feet long and
thirty feet high ranged along the riverbank, deep in cool shade. Each
house was supported on tremendous carved posts and had a high-
pitched roof, the gables thatched in intricate patterns, with giant
woven faces peering down from the eaves at passers-by. Coconut
trees were planted on built-up mounds to protect them from being
washed away in the months when the river was in flood, and around
these mounds the women's road wound through the village. The men
had their own road, closer to the river and leading to the men's
houses—their clubs, in fact—where they sat at ease among their kin
and ate the bowls of boiled sago and fish brought there by their
submissive, hard-working wives.

Women's work began at gray dawn. Even before the west bank of
the river was visible through the morning mists, one small canoe after
another slipped out into the water. Each had the same hazy outline—
conical fish traps in the bow and the silhouette of a child's head, or
sometimes the heads of two children; in the stern, a seated woman
paddling swiftly and effortlessly. Later in the day I would meet the
same women working busily around the houses, clad in rich brown
and purple and crimson grass skirts, white shell coils swinging between their bare breasts.

While the women provided the daily fish and cooked it with sago,
the men of importance argued in the men's houses, stamping up and
down and beating the carved debating stools with bundles of leaves.
Occasionally a group of men built a big canoe or erected the posts for
a new house, or one man carved a mask or a new house post. And
they spent many hours making music. The older men played flutes
and trumpets or sounded out intricate rhythms on great wooden
drums. Nearby, the younger men, not yet ready for the solemnities of
the great men's house, gathered in their own house to amuse themselves by playing small instruments, whistles and little flutes.

The old tradition of the village was based on head-hunting. Heads had to be taken when a new house was built and when a boy became a man. In 1938 there still were men in Tambunam who wore the skin of the flying fox, permitted only to a man who had taken a head. A small boy who worked for us had lost his uncle in a head-hunting raid.

Still hurrying up the river, its waters burnished by the midmorning sun, I wondered what the fate of Tambunam was now, almost thirty years later. What would its people, almost twice as many as in 1938, have made of a world in which head-hunting was only a memory and from which the spirits had departed, spirits that had formerly possessed the "trancers," who stamped up and down, exhorting the men to hunt or fight? How was Tambunam making out in a world in which "business" had become an important word?

Twice before I had returned to the site of earlier field work, to find a new, exciting way of living. In 1953 I went back to the sea-dwelling Manus, who had skipped three thousand years of history in one generation to come into the modern world. In 1957 I had returned to Bali, to find that the new Indonesian nationalism, schooling, modern mathematics and a university all had become part of Balinese life. Traditionally the Manus had been interested in trade and in problems of ethics; and the Balinese had an ancient, intricate Hindu culture on which to build. But what would the Tambunams, whose pride had been based on head-hunting and war, find worthwhile in the modern world?

Already curio hunters had mined the river area, buying old masks and drums and carvings. And crocodiles were becoming scarce and very wary as hunters, responding to the requirements of "business," pursued them up branches of the river and through the canals connecting the river and inland waters. I had been told in Angoram that in the last two years river floods, the highest in living memory, had destroyed innumerable coconut trees and yam gardens, and that a devastating fire had swept the Tambunam sago patches. How, then, were the people feeding themselves and earning the money to buy food and pay their taxes? And the school children—were they now entirely cut off from the past, rootless as the grass islands floating by on the river? I felt rather as if I were hurrying to a deathbed, to record the death pangs of the Tambunams, once the fiercest, the proudest and most flamboyant people on the Sepik.

Though our speedboat moved swiftly against the current, I felt the trip was almost interminable, for we had been on our way from New York for a month. Our cargo, packed four months earlier (boxes for a first camp, boxes to be opened later, airtight boxes to keep cameras and tapes and films dry, crates of cooking gear, crates containing screen houses, beds and chairs), had been sent by freight through the Panama Canal, timed to meet us in Madang.

But we had reckoned without the vagaries of transport in New Guinea. One river boat had sunk; another was on the slips, being repaired. As a result we had had to spend two weeks at the government station at Angoram waiting. . . . And our only view of Tambunam people had been a meeting on the Angoram airstrip with the delegation that had come down the river to greet me—a dozen hearty, enthusiastic, possessive men who were prepared to sit a whole afternoon drinking beer and plotting how to carry us up to Tambunam the next morning with or without cargo. I had sent them back in their canoes, disappointed, and I sat waiting and wondering.

But I need not have been fearful. As the village swept into view I saw the big houses, old ones and new ones, still handsomely built and beautifully ornamented. The pride of the Tambunam people is not broken. In most of the other villages where their language is spoken, the men showed the women all the sacred, hidden things that had belonged to the men alone before they burned them and accepted the newly arrived Christian mission. By an accident of war Tambunam had been saved from this blow to pride. The village had been bombed and the great men's house, containing all its secret paraphernalia, burned to a heap of ashes. And after the war the men simply said, "It is finished." Nothing was *thrown* away, and school for the children and work away from the village have replaced the older initiation as a natural progression instead of a response to irreparable, angry loss.

Walking through the village, I discovered that the smaller men's houses still existed. They have simply been transformed into "carpenter shops." And here the older men still gather, as they always have, talking together and carving new objects, new designs and new forms, to sell abroad. The old excitement of fighting and head-hunting, celebrated by a little art, has been replaced by a tremendous outburst of imaginative carving. The men have found a way, based on an old tradition, of reaching out into the modern world.

It is impossible, of course, to know how long this activity can last. The destruction of the sago patches has weakened the village's self-sufficiency in food. And the men have responded with great enthusiasm to a whole series of the most modern inventions. They like outboard motors, preferably big, fifty-horsepower motors that allow them to race up and down the river on which, for long centuries, their ancestors laboriously paddled. They like transistor radios over which they can hear broadcast the music and songs of all the peoples of New Guinea who until now had been isolated for thousands of years, and they discover relationships between these different styles of singing and their own.

Although they still smoke their own home-grown tobacco, they like cigarette lighters that stay dry in the dampest weather on the river. They like watches to tell the exact time and flashlights to replace the uncertain light of palm-leaf torches. All these are expensive. Besides, children must have clothes to go to school and adults want to be dressed appropriately when they travel about. So even though they still build houses and canoes with the old materials, fish in the old way and prefer the older kinds of food, they need to earn money to live in a changing world and satisfy new ambitions.

But the bonds linking past and present are strong. This was reflected in the careful foresight with which the village prepared for my return. They had selected a house site for us within a cluster of old friends. Nginambun, my best informant, now a widow living peacefully with two co-wives of her husband, long since dead, is our next-door neighbor. On her first visit she brought the almost unrecognizable, smoke-blackened remains of the airline bag I had given her when I left all those years ago. Mbaan, who had been my linguistic informant and who is, now a gentle old man revered as the wisest in ancient lore, came to watch the housebuilding, and he daily sits by the screen house, answering our questions. Kami Asavi, who had been one of my houseboys, was now the recognized leader of his clan, and he took over the responsibility for organizing our new household, with Mbtenda, our other former houseboy, echoing his words. These are our neighbors, and they have brought their children to help in the household, to cook and carry water and chatter gaily about new things. We are picking up life just as it was laid down in 1938, when Kami Asavi and Mbtenda went downriver with me to Wewak to see the sights and bid me good-by.

On the first day in Tambunam I explained that I had come to see how much was different and how much the same; to learn who was still alive and who had died, and when; and to make the first contacts with the village for my younger colleague, who would stay longer and come to know them as once I had.

One of the first questions from the villagers was an unexpected one: Did we have a tape recorder? Yes, we did. This entranced them, for they want to have other people hear their songs. As once they came, eager and brimming with news of trouble and quarrels, to dictate the details of events into my typewriter, now they come every evening to sing, to chant, to play tunes on a jew's-harp, to shout totemic songs into bamboo trumpets, and then to listen to the recording and criticize the effects.

They have always been a theatrical people, carving to make a fine show and arranging elaborate dramatic performances for which their wives and mothers and uninitiated children were the only audience. And now, just as outboard motors have brought speed, flashlights a new brightness to the night and the carvers' market a new impetus to their imagination, so also radio and the anthropologist's tape recorder are providing a new setting for their gay sense of the dramatic. Without self-consciousness a man announces:

"I will now sing the song we used to sing when the heads of the slain were lined up in the men's house." And a few minutes later he tells me: "Yes, my youngest son is away at school. He is studying to be a doctor."

In the evening, their faces lighted by the warm glow of hurricane lanterns, the men sit on boxes in the front part of the house and talk about the past. Over and over again they tell about what happened when I was here before. They describe the night it rained on a crocodile hunt, when everyone rolled up the matting mosquito baskets and huddled in the wet darkness. They remember how Komankowi's baby was born with a "tail" (a bit of membrane hanging on his back, which I cut off) and tell me that he is now a married man with two children of his own. They recall the occasion when a baby refused to be born and the medium called in to help could do nothing because his possessing spirit had gone off to another man. Smilingly they speak of how I respected the taboos separating men and women and always sat properly on the periphery of sacred premises. And partly because they believe in reincarnation, they have accepted my explanation that another woman anthropologist will now take up my work here.

Kami Asavi, given a new opportunity to exercise his considerable executive ability, announces that he will boss this new Missis, as women without a man need to be bossed. And I discover that the harsh word "boss," which came into Pidgin English from the labor lines, now refers to the man who cares for women and children. So it is said, speaking of a widow, that her brother now "bosses" her; that is, he looks after her and her children and takes care of their food and shelter and welfare.

In this society women have followed in the footsteps of their father's father's sisters, and men have taken the names belonging to their father's father, telling tales of their exploits as if they were their own. So although it is good that I have come back, it is wholly comprehensible that another woman will take up the same work and sit among the women when in ceremonials the plumed serpent dances, as it will again when a Tambunam man who is now in prison returns to make a mourning feast for his dead brother.

I was surprised to find how detailed their memories were, for they are not a people with a deep interest in fact. Plots, counterplots, magnificent fabrications, retrospective falsifications, yes; accurate re-telling of some event, no. But as we went over all the old events (the records of which live on in my notebooks), the retelling took on a new significance.

What I realize now, more keenly than I ever have before, is how the experience of the anthropologist working on a culture, and the experience of a people for whom the passing events are the whole of life, meet in the intensity and significance of each detail as it happens. For a people whose lives are bounded within a few square miles and whose relationships are confined to a few hundred men and women and children, every birth, every death, every marriage and every quarrel carries a tremendous burden of meaning. Every event is described again and again. Only in this way will the children learn what life is and how it is to be lived. And the young men say: "I was not born when you were here, but the older people have told us . . ."

Meanwhile, on the other side of the world, I too had relived the same moments—felt the same horror at the idea of a baby born with a tail, recalled the wetness of the rainy night at Kangelme during the crocodile hunt. All these experiences came back to me again and again as I wrote and lectured and analyzed films and photographs, extracting from each intensely observed and recorded event some meaning for the wider understanding of human culture. Although the framework appears to be so different (a primitive village of recent headhunters and a lecture room at Columbia University), there is a matching of intensity in my observation and in the Tambunam attentiveness to each detail.

On this return to Tambunam it has become very clear to me that it is only through this kind of intense living in face-to-face relationships that life and the culture of a whole people can be fully experienced. It is through the records of such closely bound lives that we may hope to understand the human need for continuity, repetitive experience and intimacy. For intimacy has its source in just these familiar repetitions of laughter at old jokes, remembered anger at old quarrels, meals eaten together in the same twilight and children listening to accounts of things that happened before their parents were born, stories told and retold. And here in Tambunam, where change is still in the making, repetition binds the present to the past and to the future; repetition binds the events all of us recall to the events that now will be recorded.

Letter from Tambunam—Iatmul, II

by Rhoda Metraux

❧⳥❧⳥❧

AUGUST, 1968

When you come to a primitive community as an anthropologist, you enter a whole world in miniature whose significance to the people living in it you hope eventually to understand. This is what you have come to such a very distant place to do. But, inevitably, the process of moving into a strange world also has the effect of shaking you into startled awareness of much that you have always taken for granted. And so, slowly, as you stumble into the new language and begin to follow events more fully, and as the fragments of what you are learning merge into a more coherent picture, your own faraway world begins to appear in a new light. This, too, you hope for. Yet it is impossible to foresee how it will come about. Often it is only in retrospect, evoking certain moments, that you can see what the crucial steps were.

Though I came to Tambunam a stranger, it was not a place unknown to me. The many volumes of notes and vivid films made during research thirty years ago in the village had shaped my expectations about the Iatmul style of life. In this second study a generation later, my task has been to discover what has endured, what has been lost and what is new. Of course, most older men and women of that earlier time have died, and the children, so many of whose faces I had come to know through photographs, are parents with children of their own.

The circumstances of this study have given me an unusual time perspective. Thinking about the past, I am not wholly dependent on conjecture, but my own time sense continually shifts. Now time narrows down to the present as I record what is happening on paper or tape or through the camera's lens; now time expands as I reach out to the distant past through an old man's memory of events he heard about from men long dead.

"Then they sat down together and ate together like brothers," old Mbaan tells me, and this picture of a truce—after a quarrel that led to a fierce head-hunting raid just three generations ago—informs my imagination as I watch peaceful trading canoes traveling up and down the river today. Sometimes I also glimpse intentional change in the making, as when Kami Asavi, one of the older village leaders, describes how, fifteen years ago, he led a procession of 195 children, boys and girls, into the new mission school. "Then we decided," he comments, "that they would not learn about the past. That was finished."

But is the past really finished? How do people in Tambunam today really put together past and present and future? This is a question not only for the Iatmul village, but for every place in the world where rapid change is taking place—and that is virtually everywhere. Concretely, is there a way of seeing what adults in Tambunam (and perhaps elsewhere) make of time?

Often, taking a walk through Tambunam, I have a sense of moving within a world where time has stopped. In midafternoon the village is quiet and seems deserted. The women still are away, working in their gardens or tending their fish traps downriver. The men have gone off to look after their own affairs. I leave our pavilion at the bottom of the village and cross a little green that shimmers in the sun. On my right the brown water of the Sepik River flows, smooth and swift; and on the far bank, beyond the garden patches, marshes stretch to the horizon. Slender dugout canoes are moored close to the shore, and I watch how their carved crocodile prows dip and rise as a little wind stirs the water.

Entering the main part of the village, I am momentarily blinded by the extreme contrast between the brilliant sun outside and the dim, cool shade of the old palm groves through which the road winds. Here and there light flickers golden on the sewed thatch walls of the great houses set back from the road. I feel dwarfed by their size, for they rest on huge piles sunk deep into the clay and their steep gabled roofs rise thirty or more feet above my head. I stop to inspect progress on Wai's unfinished house, where yesterday a big crew of men worked from dawn to dusk binding the heavy floor beams a safe eight feet above the ground, so that even when the river is in flood Wai's family will live there high and dry. Farther on I pause again to admire the face carefully woven into the thatch of an old house—the round, staring eyes, enormous curving nose, entrance like an open mouth, and rattan earrings hanging from the eaves.

There are nine new houses planned for this year, and these houses, each an engineering feat and a work of art, are precisely like the ones that sixty years ago, when the first explorers came to Tambunam, gave this village its reputation as the handsomest one on the Sepik. The old skills have survived and young men are learning them. It is this proud preservation of style that gives me a sense not of continuity but of timelessness.

Suddenly the shrill sound of children's voices shatters my daydream. The village is not deserted after all, and I hurry to find out what is going on. First I come on two little boys perched high on the ladder leading up to a house door. They are coaching each other in a counting song—in English. Then in an open area I see a dozen shouting, swearing, laughing little boys chasing after a ball, practicing soccer, the favorite village sport. Three older boys who are strolling down the road stop beside me to look on and give advice to the soccer players. One boy is strumming a guitar, and they are practicing verses of a popular song heard on the transistor radio another of them swings from his wrist.

On the sidelines, a half-attentive audience to the boys, there is a group of big and little girls playing jacks with bottle caps. They too have a chattering audience—toddlers who press in so close that there is no room for the game. One girl lifts a crawling baby out of the way. The other girls wave their arms and shout threateningly. The toddlers scatter hurriedly into the middle of the ball game. But when the boys also threaten them, they scramble back to the sidelines, and the girls laughingly gather them in. The games continue.

Through these children I am caught up in the present, in a kaleidoscope of old and new fashions. None of the smallest ones, girls or boys, wear clothes. The baby has an old, polished shell ornament around her neck, and another little girl wears woven armbands and anklets, showing that she belongs to a family in mourning. Two other girls, a little older, wear diminutive grass skirts, just as so many of the women still do. The bigger girls have on loose blouses and dirndl skirts, current versions of the standard costume introduced everywhere by the missions. Two of them, however, are smoking pipes, and all of them are chewing betel nut, which stains their lips and tongues bright red.

The five- and six-year-olds are wearing shorts, and try as I may, I cannot tell the boys from the girls. All wear their hair cropped short, and nothing in their voices, their gestures or their laughter gives me a differentiating clue. At this age they look alike. The adolescent boys, however, are distinctively and fashionably dressed. One of them wears a new set of light-blue shorts and matching nylon shirt; he also has a wrist watch with a broad silver band. The long white feather tucked rakishly into his hair, setting off his dark eyes, is all that distinguishes him from teen-agers anywhere.

The older girls and all the boys know how to speak Neo-Melanesian, the language of communication up and down the river and with white men. Even now, while they are playing, their talk shifts effortlessly back and forth between this language and Iatmul. And proudly and shyly, the oldest boys try out some phrases of English, the language of school, when they speak to me. Many of the children have Western names—John and Francesca, Paulinus and Theresa, Peter and Clara. These are their church and school names, one more to add to the set given them by their fathers' and their mothers' families, often in pairs to a brother and a sister, Wiyenande-mali and Wiyenande-mange, the names that identify them as belonging to a family line and link them to ancestors who lived at the beginning of time.

The different cultures represented in the dress and speech and games of the children are so contrasting that I cannot help but see how past and present, the outer world and the village world, merge in their appearance and behavior. Are the contrasts greater here, I wonder, than among children in modern communities, or are they only less masked?

Certainly there is one real difference. For here in Tambunam, no one worries about leaving the whole village to the children. They can look out for themselves or one another, and nowadays, when there is no longer danger of raiding war parties, the village is very safe.

All day I hear their voices as they play on the riverbank or out on the water, tumbling in and out of their small canoes. Or I hear their voices out in the woods, where for days on end a gang of small boys and girls play together at ceremonials, drumming and shouting out the chants that go with the dances. They are teaching one another, just as their parents before them did. I have tried to record their versions of these traditional songs, but it is difficult, now as in the past, to come up close. As soon as an adult approaches, the game breaks up in helpless laughter and then silence falls. And sometimes, walking along the paths that thread the gardens and groves behind the village, I catch glimpses of boys practicing with slingshots or throwing darts at birds, training their eyes and hands, though nowadays they never will throw spears, except perhaps at game animals in sport.

As in the past, too, when the boys and girls approach adolescence their play groups split up. Sometimes I come on a cluster of girls sitting by themselves and weaving little baskets, or making pinwheels and bracelets to amuse their young charges. This kind of play is a prefiguration of women's work and their endless care of children. Boys at this age spend hours practicing singing, mostly the new popular songs, and the girls turn into a giggling audience. Off by themselves girls may sing a verse or two in endless repetition, but in public they no longer sing. Chanting and singing are men's activities.

The children's independence does not cut them off from the adult world. Wherever something is happening, that is where the children are. A strange canoe lands, bringing traders; the children are the first down at the shore. A man is slaughtering a pig for a ceremony; a crowd of children watch, fascinated with every detail of skinning and dismembering. A sobbing wail announces a death; the children gather by the roadside and stare up into the house. Taken to an all-night ceremony, the children will look on until, one by one, they doze off, wake and fall asleep again through the chilly hours before sunrise. Or hearing drums beating, children will gather around the group of men who are listening to chants sung to protect a sick person or to celebrate the naming of a new canoe. Only when the children crowd in and interfere too noisily will adults shout and threaten until they scatter. But five minutes later they are back again, as lively and curious as ever and entirely unabashed.

Once at midnight I was led up the dark road to witness a ceremony that was to take place outdoors, but secretly, while the village slept. At the spot, however, a huge crowd had gathered. The ceremony was one that had not taken place for many years and might never be given again, and almost every Tambunam mother had privately decided that her children should see it. My male escorts raged and fumed in vain. The women stood their ground. They did not want to penetrate the secret, but they were determined to watch as a bowl of food was snatched from a mourning woman by invisible hands and carried off to the great house where the sacred flutes are kept. Finally the men shrugged. What could they do?

A generation ago an invasion of this kind would not have been tolerated. Children might play at sacred ceremonies off by themselves in the woods, but women and children were banished from the scene of rites whose secrets were known only to men who had been disciplined by initiation into the adult male world. At most they were an admiring audience to public performances, which had one significance for them and another, a hidden one, for the male performers. Tambunam men even today preserve the most important of their secrets. These belong to the past about which they have decided school children will not learn. Yet, because these secrets belong to a part of life that will die with the men who were trained in its knowledge, it is also tempting to let the children draw near. The men protest, but they do not protest too much. And without knowing the secrets fully, the children will carry haunting memories of how their fathers felt.

At this juncture it became clear that Tambunam children themselves embody their parents' sense of how past, present and future fit together. In their dress and the languages they speak, in their games and play, in the skills they are learning in school and elsewhere, in their gay independence and their curiosity about events, in all these things they are the living expression of their parents' beliefs, explicit and implicit. And standing their ground against their fathers' protests, they provide the key to adult ambivalence.

This does not mean that Tambunam parents are re-creating themselves in their children. They hope their children's future will be different from their own. Men say of themselves, proudly and rue-fully, "I am a Tambunam-true," meaning by this that they have grown up in traditional ways, but also that they do not read or write and lack the skills for living in a larger world. Their children, who go to school, will have other opportunities. Kami Asavi, who led the first group to the village school, says of the children proudly, "Then all men, black men and white men, will walk along one road together, sit down together and eat together like brothers."

These are proud men looking out from the timeless security of their village toward another time and a wider world. Listening to them, I think about the future that other men elsewhere are building into their children's expectations.